OPTIMIZATION OVER LEONTIEF SUBSTITUTION SYSTEMS

OPTIMIZATION OVER LEONTIEF SUBSTITUTION SYSTEMS

Editors

Gary J. KOEHLER

Department of Management
University of Florida
Gainesville, Florida

and

Andrew B. WHINSTON and Gordon P. WRIGHT

The Krannert Graduate School of
Industrial Administration
Purdue University
West Lafayette, Indiana

1975

NORTH-HOLLAND PUBLISHING COMPANY – AMSTERDAM · OXFORD
AMERICAN ELSEVIER PUBLISHING CO., INC. – NEW YORK

North-Holland ISBN: 0 7204 2841 6
American Elsevier ISBN: 0 444 10956 0

PUBLISHERS:
NORTH-HOLLAND PUBLISHING COMPANY – AMSTERDAM
NORTH-HOLLAND PUBLISHING COMPANY, LTD. – LONDON

SOLE DISTRIBUTORS FOR THE U.S.A. AND CANADA:
AMERICAN ELSEVIER PUBLISHING COMPANY, INC.
52 VANDERBILT AVENUE, NEW YORK, N.Y. 10017

Library of Congress Cataloging in Publication Data

Koehler, Gary.
Optimization over Leontief substitution systems.

Bibliography: p.
Includes indexes.
1. Interindustry economics. 2. Linear programming.
I. Whinston, Andrew B., joint author. II. Wright, Gordon P., joint author. III. Title.
HB142.K63 330.1 74-28992
ISBN 0-444-10956-0

Printed in The Netherlands

TABLE OF CONTENTS

			Page
ACKNOWLEDGEMENTS			vii
PREFACE			ix
CHAPTER 1	Introduction		1
CHAPTER 2	Leontief Systems and Recursive Solution Procedures		5
	2.1	Notation	5
	2.2	Matrix Iterative Analysis	8
	2.3	Class Z and K Matrices	14
	2.4	Class K Matrices and Matrix Iterative Techniques	21
	2.5	Leontief Substitution Systems	30
	2.6	Optimization Over Totally Leontief Substitution Systems	37
	2.7	Some Totally Leontief Substitution Systems	48
		2.7.1 Discounted Discrete-Time and Action Markov Decision Processes	48
		2.7.2 Semi-Markov Decision Processes	49
		2.7.3 Totally Productive Input-Output Systems	50
		2.7.4 Transshipment Matrices and Shortest Path Problems	51
	2.8	Extensions of Algorithm 1	55
	2.9	Dynamic Leontief Models	71
		2.9.1 An Investment Selection Model	71
		2.9.2 Multi-Facility Economic-Lot-Size Model	74
	2.10	Optimization Over Leontief Substitution Systems	77
	2.11	Some Leontief Substitution Systems	80
		2.11.1 Single-Product Economic-Lot-Size Models	80
		2.11.2 Single-Product Warehousing Model	82
		2.11.3 General Comments	84
	2.12	Illustration of the Composite Algorithm	85
CHAPTER 3	Extensions of Leontief Models		94
	3.1	Hidden Leontief Substitution Systems	94
	3.2	An Application Exploiting Hidden Leontief Properties	99
	3.3	Integral Leontief Substitution Systems	106
	3.4	Some Integral Leontief Problems	109
		3.4.1 Transshipment Problems	109

			Page
		3.4.2 Equivalent Constrained Recursive Systems	110
	3.5	Concave Minimization over Leontief Substitution Systems	115
	3.6	Some Concave Minimization Problems	121
		3.6.1 Single-Product Economic-Lot-Size Model	121
		3.6.2 Fixed Cost Minimization over Leontief Substitution Systems	122
CHAPTER 4		Extended Discussion of Leontief Systems I	127
	4.1	Notation	127
	4.2	Matrix Iterative Analysis	131
	4.3	Class Z and K Matrices	136
	4.4	Class K Matrices and Matrix Iterative Techniques	158
	4.5	Leontief Substitution Systems	159
	4.6	Optimization Over Totally Leontief Substitution Systems	167
	4.7	Some Totally Leontief Substitution Systems	179
	4.8	Extensions of Algorithm 1	181
	4.9	Dynamic Leontief Models	184
	4.10	Optimization over Leontief Substitution Systems	185
	4.11	Some Leontief Substitution Systems	186
	4.12	Illustration of the Composite Algorithm	186
CHAPTER 5		Extended Discussion of Leontief Systems II	187
	5.1	Hidden Leontief Substitution Systems	187
	5.2	An Application Exploiting Hidden Leontief Properties	193
	5.3	Integral Leontief Substitution Systems	195
	5.4	Some Integral Leontief Problems	197
	5.5	Concave Minimization over Leontief Substitution Systems	204
	5.6	Some Concave Minimization Problems	207
REFERENCES			209
SUBJECT INDEX			217
AUTHOR INDEX			220

ACKNOWLEDGEMENTS

The authors wish to acknowledge the support received from the Krannert Graduate School of Industrial Administration and Dean John S. Day of Purdue University; the Department of Industrial Engineering and Management Sciences, Northwestern University; and the Department of Management, University of Florida.

We are indebted to many people for their suggestions and helpful discussions. We especially thank G. Zoutendijk for his encouragement in the writing of the book. Our appreciation is extended to Eric V. Denardo for his enlightening comments on our research in the area of solving linear programs over a Leontief Substitution System. We particularly acknowledge the help of Professor Christopher B. Barry and Charles H. Kauppauf, who read portions of the manuscript and made many valuable comments, along with Margaret James and Rony Adelsman, who read the preliminary chapters, suggested clarifications, and aided in organizational aspects.

The authors are particularly grateful to Mrs. Charlotte Gasker for the careful preparation and review of the manuscript.

This work was supported in part by the U.S. Army Research Office, DA-31-124-AROD-477.

PREFACE

The incentive to write such a book arose from a sequence of seminars on large scale mathematical programming with economic applications taught by the authors at Purdue University, Northwestern University, and the University of Florida. This book is addressed to anyone interested in the solution of large scale linear programming problems and who have some expertise in dynamic programming and stochastic control.

Stimulated by the need for efficient methods for solving large scale linear programs and by the many features of matrix iterative methods which, if exploited, could yield highly desirable advantages in solving large scale linear programs, the possibility of using matrix iterative techniques, or relaxation techniques as they are often termed, in solving large scale linear programs was investigated by the authors.

It was found that certain types of linear programs could be solved using iterative techniques and that many of the efficient techniques of matrix iterative analysis can be used in linear programming. The advantages of using iterative methods in solving linear programming problems are that supersparsity is maintained throughout the solution procedure (since no problem data need be changed in the computation), arithmetic rounding errors are easily controlled (since the actual solution is determined only to within a specified tolerance), no basis inverse is required (and, hence, storage and associated computational considerations are minimized), the knowledge of a good solution vector may be used to accelerate the speed of the iterative process, and, lastly, sub-optimal variables may be detected and eliminated as the solution procedure progresses (which results in a reduction in the problem size as the solution is carried out).

The organization of the book is as follows: In Chapter 2 the iterative method for solving large scale linear programs over Leontief Substitutions Systems is developed. Chapter 2 contains several applications and example calculations. Chapter 3 studies several extensions of programming problems with Leontief constraint sets. Specifically, hidden Leontief systems, recursive integral solutions of Leontief Substitution Systems, and concave minimization over Leontief Substitution Systems. To keep the exposition as smooth as possible, several of the more detailed proofs of the results in Chapter 2 and 3 are given in Chapter 4 and

Chapter 5, respectively. Chapters 4 and 5 also discuss further results of optimization of large scale linear programs over Leontief Substitution Systems and matrix iterative methods.

It should be emphasized that much of the material in this book is not new. Many writers have been responsible for the notions in this book. We particularly recognize Arthur F. Veinott, Jr.; his fundamental contributions to the literature in this area are the foundation of both our research and our book on solving mathematical programs over a Leontief Substitution System. We cannot fail to mention several others who have made major contributions to the literature in this area: E. V. Denardo, D. Blackwell, A. S. Manne, R. A. Howard, G. B. Dantzig, W. W. Leontief, M. Fielder, V. Ptak, J. MacQueen, R. Saigal, E. L. Porteus, and J. Totten.

CHAPTER 1

Introduction

"The development of efficient optimization techniques for large structured mathematical programs is of major significance in economic planning, engineering, and management science" [45, 46]. Real-world applications, for the most part, have been necessarily limited to the optimization of linear programs and their extensions which include some integer or non-linear components [120]. Hence the capability to solve large scale linear programs has significant importance in real-world applications.

Dantzig [15] noted that since the very inception of linear programming, very large linear programs were envisioned especially in modeling economic and military systems. Indeed, those visions are being realized. "Linear programming is widely used for economic planning in industry, particularly the process industry. It is also being used increasingly in other contexts, such as agriculture and defense, to throw light on the best allocations of scarce resources" [3]. Indeed, the very existence of Dantzig's System Optimization Laboratory represents the importance of large scale optimization. Dantzig [18] defines the function of such a laboratory:

> The purpose of such a laboratory would be to support the development of computational methods and associated computer routines for numerical analysis and optimization of large scale systems. The ultimate objective of the development would be to provide an integrated set of computer routines for systems optimization which:
>
> I. is freely and publicly available to users, government, science, and industry,
>
> II. is thoroughly practical and widely useful in applications to diverse kinds of large-scale systems optimization problems,
>
> III. embodies the most powerful techniques of mathematical programming and numerical analysis, and
>
> IV. has been thoroughly tested for efficiency and effectiveness on representative systems optimization problems arising in practice.

The solution of large scale linear programs having two to four thousand equations or more is limited by both cost and time [15]. Fortunately, most large scale problems are sparse [3] and usually have a density† not greater than 0.01. Due to this inherent sparsity we can consider solving large scale problems in a feasible time period and with an acceptable cost.

The most prominent solution strategies for large unstructured linear programs are the compact inversion methods. The focus of such procedures is the Revised Simplex method. The advocates of such methods realize that the total number of iterations are fixed and that savings in time and cost can come about by performing each operation efficiently [15]. "The objective is to find, for various classes of problems, ways of performing each Simplex iteration in less time or using less primary storage" [45]. The first such method involved the use of the product form of the inverse [19]. In this method, the inverse of the current basis is maintained as the product of elementary matrices which could be stored by one vector for each matrix. At each pivot of the Revised Simplex method a new vector is appended. At some point the series of vectors would have to be reduced so that computer storage, computational effort and arithmetic rounding errors would not become excessive. Markowitz [92] observed that the condensation, or reinversion as it is usually called, may produce non-zero elements in excess of the number in the original matrix. Hence maintaining sparsity of the number of non-zero elements had to be considered so that computer storage would not be a limiting factor in the solution of large scale problems. In summary, both efficient inverse compactions and efficient re-inversion techniques that maintain sparsity are required.

Recently, promising alternatives to the product form of the inverse have been suggested. Hellerman and Rarick [58, 59] presented a heuristic method that produces a faster inversion with a lower non-zero build-up than other methods. Furthermore, the arithmetic demands are lower and the resulting rounding errors smaller. Forrest and Tomlin [37] gave a product form method for updating a triangular factored basis at each iteration which reduced the rate of growth of the transformation files. The advantages, of course, are reduced computational effort and less frequent re-inversion.

Kalan [67] observed that the bottleneck in solving large scale linear programs was in peripheral activity. The continuous reading of structural elements and storage and retrieval of the elementary matrices used in the product

---

†If the constraint matrix is m by n, the density is defined as the ratio of the number of non-zero elements of the constraint matrix to mn.

form present the most important contribution to time required for solution when compared to any other factor in solving large scale linear programs. Such considerations impose upon a good linear programming solution procedure the consideration of handling the input and output of large volumes of data. These considerations are inherently linked with the hardware being used.

With this in mind, Kalan pointed out that "the number of distinct values is small compared with the number of non-zero coefficients." This property, termed supersparsity, can be taken advantage of by allowing the entire problem to be stored in the computer. Furthermore, "as it turns out, a major portion of the inverse matrix can be embedded within the constraint matrix, requiring, of course, no extra storage. With both the constraint and inverse matrices consuming little core, the prospect of in-core linear programming for large problems is as realistic as it is desirable" [67]. Using the methods of Kalan, in-core solutions of large scale linear programs are possible. It cannot be overemphasized, though, that the major consumer of computer storage is the inverse matrix. Major efforts have been made to limit the effect of re-inversion on solution costs, as noted above, and have led to the implementation of such procedures as generalized upper bounding [20] -(GUB)-which works with a smaller basis inverse implicitly representing a much larger basis inverse.

The purpose of the present work is to present computational methods for solving certain large scale linear programs. The method, referred to as relaxation or iterative programming, is similar in idealogy to the compact inversion techniques. The difference is that <u>no inverse matrix is maintained</u> either in compact or actual form. This results in a considerable reduction in computer storage requirements.

In the matrix iterative approach, the dual solution vector is determined by successive approximations. The final solution is accompanied by a basis identification so that the corresponding primal solution can be found. Since the optimal solution is found only to within a desired tolerance, rounding errors are not an important consideration unless the desired tolerance is very small. A further advantage inherent in an iterative procedure is that all numbers used in the computational process are given numbers contained in the objective coefficients and the constraint matrix. Hence, supersparsity is maintained and no additional storage space is required. Also, the prior knowledge of a good solution or advanced starting point provides a means to accelerate the convergence speed of the iterative algorithm. An additional property of iterative algorithms is that the problem size may be dramatically reduced as the solution procedure is carried out. So, in direct contrast to current linear programming solutions procedures, the storage requirements are actually reduced as the solution procedure is carried out.

The purpose of this book is to describe the iterative approach for solving a certain class of linear programs. The iterative solution procedure is applied to linear programs having a Leontief Substitution constraint set. Briefly, a constraint set of the form $X(b) = \{x: Ax = b, x \geqq 0\}$ is called a Leontief Substitution System if b is non-negative and A is Leontief. A Leontief matrix has exactly one positive element per column and gives a non-empty solution set for any positive b.

We devote a considerable amount of effort to discussions and characterizations of Leontief Substitution systems (and their extensions). This emphasis is due in large part to the fact that many practical problems can be modeled in whole or in part as an optimization over a Leontief Substitution System. (In fact, any linear constraint set is, in part, trivially equivalent to a Leontief Substitution System.) Among some of the many applications which can give rise to a Leontief Substitution constraint set are Markov decision problems, input-output problems with substitution, deterministic production-inventory problems, and shortest path and transshipment problems.

It is realized that the Leontief Substitution System is a special structure and that the iterative solution procedures given in this work are, for the most part, specialized to that structure. However, Geoffrion [45] has emphasized that "the principle focus of large-scale programming is the exploitation of various special structures for theoretical and computational purposes." The structures Geoffrion considered common are multidivisional, combinatorial, dynamic, and stochastic.

> Multidivisional problems consist of a collection of interrelated "subsystems" to be optimized. The subsystems can be, for example, modules of an engineering system, reservoirs in a water resources system, departments of divisions of an organization, production units of an industry, or sectors of an economy. Combinatorial problems typically have a large number of variables because of the numerous possibilities for selecting routes, machine setups, schedules, etc. Problems with dynamic aspects grow large because of the need to replicate constraints and variables to account for a number of time periods and problems with stochastic or uncertainty aspects are often larger than they would otherwise be in order to account for alternative possible realizations of imperfectly known entities [45].

The Leontief structure subsumes many practical linear programming problems having stochastic, dynamic,combinatorial, and multidivisional aspects. We discuss representative examples of each of these classes of problems.

CHAPTER 2

Leontief Systems and Recursive Solution Procedures

The purpose of this chapter is to show where matrix iterative methods can be used, with several computational advantages over the Simplex method, to solve linear programming problems having a Leontief constraint set. Leontief constrained linear programs are a general class of optimization problems, which include Markov decision problems, certain inventory, production, and network problems, to mention a few, which are amenable to solution by iterative procedures.

Many important linear programming models, some with a large number of constraints and variables, have what is termed a Leontief structure. Several applications and computational examples are presented in this chapter to illustrate various aspects of the iterative procedures proposed for use in the solution of Leontief constrained linear programs.

2.1 Notation

All matrices in this sequel are real matrices (i.e., $a_{ij} \in R$) and are represented by upper case letters. The letter I will be used to denote the identity matrix. Some typical matrix operations are given below. For an arbitrary matrix A, the standard operations are:

A'	is the transpose of A
A^{-1}	is the inverse of A where A is non-singular
$\det(A)$	is the determinant of A
$\|\|A\|\|$	is a norm of A
$\|A\|$	is a matrix formed from A by taking the absolute values of each element of A
$\rho(A)$	is the spectral radius of A
$\sigma(A)$	is the spectrum of A
$N(A)$	is the null space of A
$R(A)$	is the range of A

A(M) is the submatrix of A formed by the columns and rows listed in M

$A \geqq B$ means $a_{ij} \geq b_{ij}$ for all i,j

$A \geq B$ means $a_{ij} \geq b_{ij}$ with at least one $a_{ij} > b_{ij}$

$A > B$ means $a_{ij} > b_{ij}$ for all i and j.

(Note: see Chapter 4 for definitions of the above.)

Column vectors and scalars are real and are represented by lower case letters. Two special vectors are reserved for specific meanings. They are:

e is a vector of ones.

e_i is a vector of zeros with a one in position i.

When applicable, the matrix operations defined above are used for vectors. Hence, for an arbitrary vector v, v' is its transpose, $||v||$ is a norm, and so forth.

A subscript on a vector denotes an element of a vector. A superscript on a vector will imply a sequence identification. For example, v^3 is the third vector in a given sequence of vectors.

A superscript on a matrix denotes a power. That is,

$$A^N = \prod_{i=1}^{N} A.$$

A^0 will mean the identity matrix.

Convergence of either vector or matrix sequences is defined in terms of their respective elements. For example, for a vector of size n,

$$\lim_{N\to\infty} v^N \to 0$$

implies

$$\lim_{N\to\infty} v_i^N \to 0, \qquad i = 1, 2, \ldots n.$$

Also, for an n by n matrix A,

$$\lim_{N\to\infty} A^N \to 0$$

implies

$$\lim_{N\to\infty} a_{ij}^N \to 0, \quad i,j = 1,2,\ldots,n,$$

where a_{ij}^N is the ij^{th} element of the matrix A^N.

It will often be useful to consider a sub-matrix of a given m by n matrix A. Let N denote the set of natural numbers from 1 to n.

$$N = \{1,2,\ldots,n\}.$$

Let $J = (j_1, j_2, \ldots, j_k)$ be an ordered k-tuple where $j_i \in N$ for $i = 1,\ldots,k$. Then the matrix A_J will represent the m by k submatrix of A formed by the columns $j_1, j_2, \ldots, j_k$ of the matrix A. For example, consider

$$A = \begin{bmatrix} 1 & 1 & 3 & 2 \\ 3 & 4 & 6 & 1 \\ 2 & 1 & 2 & 5 \end{bmatrix}$$

and

$$J = (1,4).$$

Then

$$A_J = \begin{bmatrix} 1 & 2 \\ 3 & 1 \\ 2 & 5 \end{bmatrix}.$$

2.2 Matrix Iterative Analysis

Before considering the solution of linear programs by recursive or iterative methods, we first show how a system of equations can be solved by matrix iterative methods. In linear programming we are continuously asked to solve linear systems of the form

2.2.1 $$Ax = b$$

where A is an n by n non-singular matrix and x and b are n by 1 vectors. Methods used to solve the above system may involve a fixed number of arithmetic operations, such as Gaussian elimination, and are termed direct methods of solution. When indirect or iterative methods are used, a series of computational steps are repeatedly performed until a solution is found that satisfies a given tolerance.

When the order of A is large, the computational effort and resulting rounding errors become a limiting factor for finding the vector x by direct methods. Furthermore, if the matrix A is sparse, special efforts must be made to maintain sparsity, and hence, to keep computer storage and computational effort within reasonable bounds [115]. Lastly, if a vector y is known where $||x - y||$ is small, such information cannot be used to find x by direct methods.

Matrix iterative methods (i.e., indirect methods) present an alternative for finding the solution vector to the system of equations in (2.2.1). Furthermore, when A is sparse and large, matrix iterative techniques can be computationally superior to direct methods of solution. Also, such information as the knowledge of a close vector to the actual solution vector can be used to minimize computational effort.

In iterative methods, the matrix A is first split into two other matrices, say R and S, in the following manner.

2.2.2 $$A = R - S$$

where R is non-singular. Equation (2.2.1) can be rewritten as

2.2.3 $$Ax = (R - S)x = b.$$

Rearranging (2.2.3) gives

2.2.4 $$Rx = Sx + b.$$

Multiplying (2.2.4) by R^{-1} gives the following equivalent representation of equation (2.2.1)

2.2.5 $$x = R^{-1}Sx + R^{-1}b.$$

Using superscripts to denote the iteration count, a sequence of vectors can be generated by the following recursive relation.

2.2.6 $$x^{m+1} = R^{-1}Sx^{m} + R^{-1}b$$

where $R^{-1}S$ is called the iterative matrix. Equation (2.2.6) represents a typical iterative technique. At iteration m, vector x^m is refined to supply the $(m+1)^{st}$ approximation of x, x^{m+1}. Any vector x^0 may be used to initiate the process.

The error at the mth iteration is

2.2.7 $$\varepsilon^{m} = x^{m} - x.$$

Substituting the x from equation (2.2.5) into (2.2.7) above gives

$$\varepsilon^{m} = x^{m} - R^{-1}Sx - R^{-1}b.$$

By substitution of (2.2.6) and (2.2.7) the error ε^m can be written as

$$\varepsilon^{m} = (R^{-1}S)\varepsilon^{m-1}.$$

Thus,

2.2.8 $$\varepsilon^{m} = (R^{-1}S)^{m}\ \varepsilon^{0}.$$

We are interested in those problems where the sequence $\{\varepsilon^i\}_{i=0}^{\infty}$ converges to the zero vector as i approaches infinity. A sufficient condition for

$$\lim_{m\to\infty} \varepsilon^{m} \to 0$$

is (from (2.2.8))

$$\lim_{m\to\infty} (R^{-1}S)^{m} \to 0.$$

This occurs if and only if the spectral radius of $R^{-1}S$ is strictly less than one.

Theorem 2.2.1 (Infinite Power of a Matrix)

The infinite power of an n by n matrix A is zero if and only if $\rho(A) < 1$. That is, A is convergent if and only if its spectral radius is strictly less than one.

Proof.

See Chapter 4.

Therefore, by applying Theorem 2.2.1 to equation (2.2.8), it is seen that for an arbitrary non-zero initial error vector, the sequence of vectors $\{x^i\}_{i=1}^{\infty}$ will converge to the true solution vector x, if $\rho(R^{-1}S) < 1$.

Now equation (2.2.6) can be written in the form:

$$x^{m+1} = (R^{-1}S)^{m+1} x^0 + \sum_{\ell=0}^{m} (R^{-1}S)^{\ell} R^{-1}b.$$

If $\rho(R^{-1}S) < 1$, then

2.2.9 $$x = \lim_{m\to\infty} x^m = (R^{-1}S)^{\infty} x^0 + \sum_{\ell=0}^{\infty} (R^{-1}S)^{\ell} R^{-1}b$$

$$= \sum_{\ell=0}^{\infty} (R^{-1}S)^{\ell} R^{-1}b$$

where $(R^{-1}S)^{\infty} = \lim_{m\to\infty} (R^{-1}S)^m = 0$.

Theorem 2.2.2 (Neumann Series)

If $A^m \to 0$ as m approaches infinity, then I - A has an inverse, and

$$(I - A)^{-1} = \sum_{\ell=0}^{\infty} A^{\ell}.$$

Proof.

Consider $(I - A) \sum_{\ell=0}^{K} A^{\ell} = I - A^{K+1}, \qquad K = 0,1,\ldots .$

Then

$$(I - A) \sum_{\ell=0}^{\infty} A^{\ell} = I - A^{\infty} = I, \text{ since } A^{\infty} = 0.$$

Hence

$$\sum_{\ell=0}^{\infty} A^{\ell} = (I - A)^{-1}.$$

Q.E.D.

Hence the solution vector is given by

2.2.10 $$x = \sum_{\ell=0}^{\infty} (R^{-1}S)^{\ell} R^{-1} b = (I - R^{-1}S)^{-1} R^{-1} b.$$

With iterative methods, x is approximated using a finite number of terms in the above sum given in (2.2.10). The smaller the number of terms required, the faster x is found.

We now give two examples to illustrate Theorem 2.2.1 and Theorem 2.2.2.

Example 2.2.1

Consider the system

$$Ax = b$$

where

$$A = \begin{bmatrix} 1 & -1/2 & 0 \\ 2 & 3/2 & -3 \\ 0 & 0 & 1 \end{bmatrix}, \qquad x = \begin{bmatrix} x_1 \\ x_2 \\ x_3 \end{bmatrix},$$

and $b = \begin{bmatrix} 1 \\ 2 \\ 3 \end{bmatrix}$.

Then it is easily computed that

$$A^{-1} = \begin{bmatrix} 3/5 & 1/5 & 3/5 \\ -4/5 & 2/5 & 6/5 \\ 0 & 0 & 1 \end{bmatrix} \quad \text{and} \quad x = A^{-1}b = \begin{bmatrix} 14/5 \\ 18/5 \\ 3 \end{bmatrix}.$$

Next, consider the following split of the matrix $A = R - S$ with

$$R = \begin{bmatrix} 1 & 0 & 0 \\ 0 & 1 & 0 \\ 0 & 0 & 1 \end{bmatrix} \quad \text{and} \quad S = \begin{bmatrix} 0 & 1/2 & 0 \\ -2 & -1/2 & 3 \\ 0 & 0 & 0 \end{bmatrix}.$$

We have $R^{-1} = R$ and $R^{-1}S = S$.

Since $\sigma(R^{-1}S) = \sigma(S) = \{0, 1/4(-1 + i\sqrt{15}), 1/4(-1 - i\sqrt{15})\}$, we have

$$\rho(R^{-1}S) = \rho(S) = \text{Max } \{0,1,1\} = 1.$$

Therefore, by Theorem 2.2.1, the sequence $((R^{-1}S)^n)_{n=1}^{\infty}$ is not convergent.

<u>Example 2.2.2</u>

Consider $\tilde{A}x = \tilde{b}$ with $\tilde{A} = (1/m)A$ and $\tilde{b} = (1/m)b$ for A and b given in Example 2.2.1. We let m be the maximum positive element of A. That is, m = 2.

Any solution x of the system $\tilde{A}x = \tilde{b}$ is also a solution of $Ax = b$, and conversely. We have

$$\tilde{A} = \begin{bmatrix} 1/2 & -1/4 & 0 \\ 1 & 3/4 & -3/2 \\ 0 & 0 & 1/2 \end{bmatrix} \quad \text{and} \quad \tilde{b} = \begin{bmatrix} 1/2 \\ 1 \\ 3/2 \end{bmatrix}.$$

Consider the following split $\tilde{R} - \tilde{S}$ of $\tilde{A}$. Let

$$\tilde{R} = \begin{bmatrix} 1 & 0 & 0 \\ 0 & 1 & 0 \\ 0 & 0 & 1 \end{bmatrix} \quad \text{and} \quad \tilde{S} = \begin{bmatrix} 1/2 & 1/4 & 0 \\ -1 & 1/4 & 3/2 \\ 0 & 0 & 1/2 \end{bmatrix}.$$

Then

$$\tilde{R}^{-1} = \tilde{R}, \quad \tilde{R}^{-1}\tilde{S} = \tilde{S},$$

$\sigma(\tilde{R}^{-1}\tilde{S}) = \sigma(\tilde{S}) = \{1/2,\ 1/8(3 + i\sqrt{15}),\ 1/8(3 - i\sqrt{15})\}$, and

$\rho(\tilde{R}^{-1}\tilde{S}) = \rho(\tilde{S}) = \sqrt{24}/8 < 1.$

Thus the sequence $\{(\tilde{R}^{-1}\tilde{S})^n\}_{n=0}^{\infty}$ is convergent. To solve the system of equations $\tilde{A}x = \tilde{b}$ by iterative methods we choose, arbitrarily, x^0, say

$$x^0 = \begin{bmatrix} 0 \\ 0 \\ 0 \end{bmatrix}.$$

Then, by Equation (2.2.6),

$$x^1 = \tilde{R}^{-1}\tilde{S}\, x^0 + \tilde{b}$$

or

$$x^1 = \begin{bmatrix} 1/2 \\ 1 \\ 3/2 \end{bmatrix}.$$

Repeating,

$$x^2 = \begin{bmatrix} 1/2 & 1/4 & 0 \\ -1 & 1/4 & 3/2 \\ 0 & 0 & 1/2 \end{bmatrix} \begin{bmatrix} 1/2 \\ 1 \\ 3/2 \end{bmatrix} + \begin{bmatrix} 1/2 \\ 1 \\ 3/2 \end{bmatrix} = \begin{bmatrix} 1 \\ 3 \\ 9/4 \end{bmatrix} .$$

Continuing with Equation (2.2.6), we obtain

$$x^4 = \begin{bmatrix} 77/32 \\ 135/32 \\ 90/32 \end{bmatrix} .$$

Note that by Equation (2.2.7)

$$\varepsilon^0 = \begin{bmatrix} 0 \\ 0 \\ 0 \end{bmatrix} - \begin{bmatrix} 14/5 \\ 18/5 \\ 3 \end{bmatrix} = \begin{bmatrix} -14/5 \\ -18/5 \\ -3 \end{bmatrix} ,$$

$$||\varepsilon^0|| = 5.45,$$

$$\varepsilon^4 = \begin{bmatrix} 77/32 \\ 135/32 \\ 90/32 \end{bmatrix} - \begin{bmatrix} 14/5 \\ 18/5 \\ 3 \end{bmatrix} = \begin{bmatrix} -63/160 \\ 99/160 \\ -6/32 \end{bmatrix} ,$$

and

$$||\varepsilon^4|| = 0.76.$$

As seen above, matrix iterative techniques require a matrix to be split, as in Equation (2.2.2), in such a manner that R is non-singular and the spectral radius of $R^{-1}S$ is strictly less than one. In addition, R^{-1} should be easily computed.

2.3 Class Z and K Matrices

Much of the material presented in this section has been extensively studied and presented in the literature. We duplicate here a collection of results presented by Fiedler and Ptak [32] that summarize many of the basic properties of two classes of matrices, called class Z and K. The two classes of matrices, subsume, among others, the classical input-output matrices of Leontief [80]. Extensions of these results, given by Veinott [124], to rectangular matrices are discussed, which provide the setting for our discussion of linear programming problems with Leontief constraint sets.

Definition 2.3.1 (Class Z Matrices)

The set of all real square matrices whose off-diagonal elements are all non-positive forms class Z. [32]

For example, the identity matrix is a class Z matrix as well as any of the following:

$$\begin{bmatrix} 1 & -1 \\ -1 & 1 \end{bmatrix}, \quad \begin{bmatrix} -1 & -1 \\ -1 & -1 \end{bmatrix}, \quad \begin{bmatrix} 0 & 0 \\ 0 & -1 \end{bmatrix}.$$

Class Z matrices arise naturally in many applications. We now present a few standard problems that give rise to class Z matrices.

Example 2.3.1 Input-Output Problems [see 29, 42, 77, 80, 94]

Suppose we view an economy as consisting of n industries (which are aggregates of firms producing similar goods). Further assume that each industry produces exactly one good and that no two industries produce the same good.

Let

x_i = the total output, in dollars, of industry i where $x_i > 0$ and $i = 1,\ldots,n$

x_{ij} = the total transactions or sales, in dollars, between industry i and j for $i,j = 1,\ldots,n$

b_i = the final demand in dollars, required for industry i, $i = 1,\ldots,n$.

Assume non-substitutability of inputs, positive value of all inputs in each industry and the stationarity over a base time period x_{ij} in relation to x_i, i,j = 1,..,n. Then we can define an input-output coefficient as a_{ij} where a_{ij} is the input of good i required per unit output of good j. We have

$$a_{ij} = \frac{x_{ij}}{x_j} \geqq 0.$$

The model of the economy is

$$x_i = \sum_{j=1}^{n} a_{ij} x_j + b_i, \qquad i = 1,\ldots,n.$$

In matrix form, the above model can be expressed as

$$x = Ax + b$$

or

$$(I - A)x = b.$$

The matrix A is called a consumption matrix and (I - A) a net production matrix. We note that (I - A) has all non-positive off-diagonal elements. Hence, $(I - A) \varepsilon Z$.

<u>Example 2.3.2</u> <u>Markov Processes</u> [see 61, 71]

Assume we have an irreducible ergodic Markov chain with n states. Let $P = (p_{ij})$ denote the n by n one-stage transition probability matrix. Let π_i^m denote the unconditional probability that the process is in state $i(i = 1,\ldots,n)$ after m transitions (m time periods). The following recursion holds:

$$\pi_i^{m+1} = \sum_{j=1}^{n} \pi_j^m \, p_{ji} \, , \qquad i = 1,\ldots,n;\ m = 0, 1, \ldots .$$

It can be shown that $\lim_{m \to \infty} \pi_j^m$ exists. Furthermore,

$$\lim_{m \to \infty} \pi_j^m = \pi_j, \qquad j = 1, \ldots, n,$$

$$\pi_j > 0, \qquad j = 1, \ldots, n,$$

where

$$\pi_i = \sum_{i=1}^{n} \pi_j \, p_{ji} \quad \text{for} \quad i = 1, \ldots, n.$$

The π_i's are called the steady-state probabilities of the Markov chain. The last system of equations above can be put in the form

$$\pi = P'\pi$$

or

$$(I - P')\pi = 0$$

where $\pi = (\pi_1, \ldots, \pi_n)'$ and $(I - P') \in Z$.

In other applications of Markov chains, we may receive a known (expected) profit, say b_i, whenever the process visits state i. Assume a discount factor α, $0 \leqq \alpha < 1$, is specified, so that the present value of 1 unit of profit m periods in the future is α^m. α can be interpreted as equal to $1/(1+i)$ where i is the current interest rate. Let v_i be the expected total discounted profit of the process starting in state i (at the first observed time period) and evolving for an infinite number of periods. Let

$$v = (v_1, \ldots, v_n)' \text{ and } b = (b_1, \ldots, b_n)'.$$

Then it can be shown that

$$v = \alpha P v + b$$

or

$$(I - \alpha P)v = b.$$

We note that $(I - \alpha P) \in Z$.

Example 2.3.3 Finite Difference Approximations [see 122]

Consider the following general second-order differential equation used by Varga [122]:

$$-\frac{d}{dx}\left[p(x)\frac{dy(x)}{dx}\right] + q(x)\frac{dy(x)}{dx} + \sigma(x)y(x) = f(x), \quad a < x < b,$$

with boundary conditions

$$\alpha_1 y(a) - \beta_1 y'(a) = \gamma_1,$$

$$\alpha_2 y(b) - \beta_2 y'(b) = \gamma_2.$$

Assume that p, q, σ, and f are piecewise continuous with a finite number of discontinuities on $a \leq x \leq b$, and that $y(x)$ and $p(x)dy/dx$ are both continuous on $a \leqq x \leqq b$. Furthermore, assume

$$p(x) > 0, \quad \sigma(x) > 0, \quad \alpha_i \geqq 0,$$

$$\beta_i \geqq 0, \text{ and } \alpha_i + \beta_i \geqq 0 \quad \text{for } i = 1,2.$$

Choose N+2 distinct points (which include all the discontinuities of p, q, σ, and f) where $a = x_0 < x_1 \ldots < x_{N+1} = b$. These points are called the mesh points. Integrating the second order differential equation over

$$x_i \leqq x \leqq \frac{x_i + x_{i+1}}{2}$$

for each i ($i = 0, \ldots, N$) where x_i is not a boundary mesh point and using several approximating procedures [122], while assuming mesh spacings $(x_{i+1} - x_i)$ are sufficiently small, it is possible to represent a discrete approximation to $y(x)$ by

$$Ay = b + \tau(y)$$

where $y' = (y_0, y_1, \ldots, y_{N+1})$, b is a vector of constants, $\tau(y)$ is a vector of higher order effects (which tend to zero as the mesh spacings tend to zero), and $A \in Z$.

We now characterize several properties of class Z matrices which have non-negative inverses.

Theorem 2.3.3

Suppose $A \in Z$, $\sigma(A)$ contains at least one real eigenvalue, and each real eigenvalue of A is positive. Let $B \in Z$ satisfy the inequality $A \leqq B$. Then

1. both A^{-1} and B^{-1} exist and $A^{-1} \geqq B^{-1} \geq 0$.

2. each real eigenvalue of the matrix B is positive.

3. $\det(B) \geqq \det(A) > 0$.

Proof.

See Chapter 4.

Example 2.3.4 (Theorem 2.3.3)

Let

$$A = \begin{bmatrix} 1 & -1 \\ -1 & 1 \end{bmatrix}.$$

Then

$$A \in Z \quad \text{and} \quad \sigma(A) = \{0,2\}.$$

Note that 0 is a real eigenvalue of A but 0 is not positive. Hence A does not satisfy the conditions of Theorem 2.3.3.

Example 2.3.5 (Theorem 2.3.3)

Let

$$A = I - (.5)P, \qquad P = \begin{bmatrix} .5 & .5 \\ .6 & .4 \end{bmatrix},$$

and

$$B = I - \alpha P \quad \text{for } 0 \leqq \alpha \leqq .5.$$

That is,

$$A = \begin{bmatrix} .75 & -.25 \\ -.30 & .80 \end{bmatrix} \quad \text{and} \quad B = \begin{bmatrix} 1-(.5)\alpha & -(.5)\alpha \\ -(.6)\alpha & 1-(.4)\alpha \end{bmatrix}.$$

Note that $A \in Z$ and both of the real eigenvalues in $\sigma(A) = \{.775 + 1/2\sqrt{.3025}, .775 - 1/2\sqrt{.3025}\}$ are positive. Also, $B \geqq A$ for $0 \leqq \alpha \leqq .5$. Hence A and B, with $0 \leqq \alpha \leqq .5$, satisfy all of the conditions in Theorem 2.2.3. We have

$$A^{-1} = \frac{1}{.525}\begin{bmatrix} .8 & .25 \\ .3 & .75 \end{bmatrix} \geq 0, \quad \det(A) = .525 > 0, \quad A^{-1} \geqq B^{-1} \geq 0,$$

$\det(B) = 1 - (.9)\alpha - (.1)\alpha^2 \geqq 0.525 = \det(A)$ and each real $\lambda \in \sigma(B)$ satisfies the inequality $\lambda > 0$, for all $0 \leqq \alpha \leqq .5$.

Example 2.3.6 (Theorem 2.3.3)

Let

$$A = \begin{bmatrix} 1 & -2 \\ -2 & 1 \end{bmatrix}.$$

Then $A \in Z$ and $\sigma(A) = \{1 \pm \sqrt{2}\, i\}$.

A does not satisfy the conditions of Theorem 2.3.3 since $\sigma(A)$ has no real components. Note that A is non-singular but

$$0 \geq A^{-1} = -\frac{1}{3}\begin{bmatrix} 1 & 2 \\ 2 & 1 \end{bmatrix}.$$

We next consider matrices which belong to class Z and have non-negative inverses.

Definition 2.3.2 (Class K Matrices)

An n by n matrix A is a class K matrix if $A \in Z$ and $A^{-1} \geq 0$ where Z is the set of all class Z matrices (see Definition 2.3.1). (Class K matrices are also called type M matrices [122].)

The following theorem gives several equivalent definitions of a class K matrix.

Theorem 2.3.4

For $A \in Z$, the following are equivalent:

1. There exists a vector $x \geqq 0$ such that $Ax > 0$.
2. There exists a vector $x > 0$ such that $Ax > 0$.
3. There exists a diagonal matrix D with positive elements such that $ADe > 0$.
4. There exists a diagonal matrix D with positive elements such that AD is a matrix with dominant positive principal diagonal.
5. For each diagonal matrix R where $R \geqq A$, then R is non-singular and $\rho(R^{-1}(P - A)) < 1$ where P is the diagonal of A.

6. For $B \in Z$ and $B \geqq A$, then B is non-singular.

7. Each real $\lambda \in \sigma(A)$ is positive and there is at least one real $\lambda \in \sigma(A)$.

8. All principal minors of A are positive.

9. There exists a strictly increasing sequence $\emptyset \neq M_1 \subset M_2 \subset M_3 \ldots \subset M_n$ (where M_i means M_i contains i distinct elements from $\{1,2,\ldots,n\}$) and $\det A(M_i) > 0$.

10. There exists a permutation matrix P such that $PAP^{-1} = LU$ where L is lower triangular with positive diagonal elements and $L \in Z$ and U is upper triangular with positive diagonal elements such that $U \in Z$.

11. A is non-singular and $A^{-1} \geq 0$.

12. The real part of each $\lambda \in \sigma(A)$ is positive.

13. For each $x \neq 0$ there exists an index k such that $x_k y_k > 0$ for $y = Ax$.

Proof.

See Chapter 4.

Example 2.3.7 (Class K Matrices)

An input-output matrix I - A is called productive [42] if there exists an $x \geqq 0$ such that $(I - A)x > 0$. We note that $I - A \in Z$. Hence by condition (2) of Theorem 2.3.4 a productive input-output matrix is a class K matrix.

Example 2.3.8 (Class K Matrices)

Let

$$A = I - \alpha P$$

where $P \geqq 0$ and $Pe = e$ (i.e., P is a stochastic matrix). Then, $(I - \alpha P) \in Z$, and for $0 \leqq \alpha < 1$, $x = e$ satisfies condition (2) of Theorem 2.3.4. Hence $(I - \alpha P) \in K$ and conditions 1-13 of Theorem 2.3.4 hold.

2.4. Class K Matrices and Matrix Iterative Techniques

We now consider solving linear systems of the form

$$Ax = b \quad \text{for } A \in K$$

by matrix iterative techniques. To guarantee that the iterative procedure (2.2.6) converges to a solution of the above system we need to choose a split of the matrix A, say into R and S, $A = R - S$, such that R is non-singular and $\rho(R^{-1}S) < 1$ (see Theorem 2.2.1 and Theorem 2.2.2). In this section we give some useful splits of class K matrices, satisfying these two conditions, which have been proven successful in applications. However, we first consider the following theorem and lemma which give some key insights into the understanding and construction of splits of class K matrices.

Theorem 2.4.1

Let $A \in K$ and $A = R - S$ where $S \geqq 0$ and $R \in Z$. Then R is non-singular and $\rho(R^{-1}S) < 1$.

Before proving Theorem 2.4.1, we first show the following lemma given by Fiedler and Ptak [33].

Lemma 2.4.2

Let $A \in K$, $B \in Z$ and $B \geqq A$. Then $B \in K$ and B possesses the following properties:

1. $A^{-1} \geqq B^{-1} \geq 0$.
2. $\det B \geqq \det A > 0$.
3. $A^{-1}B \geqq I$ and $BA^{-1} \geqq I$.
4. $B^{-1}A \leqq I$ and $AB^{-1} \leqq I$.
5. $B^{-1}A \in K$ and $AB^{-1} \in K$.
6. $\rho(I - B^{-1}A) < 1$ and $\rho(I - AB^{-1}) < 1$.

Proof.

(1) By Theorem 2.3.4, part 7, each real eigenvalue of A is positive and there is at least one real eigenvalue. Hence, by Theorem 2.3.3,

$$A^{-1} \geqq B^{-1} \geq 0.$$

Note: $B \in Z$ and $B^{-1} \geqq 0$ imply $B \in K$, by part 11 of Theorem 2.3.4.

(2) $\det B \geqq \det A > 0$ follows from Theorem 2.3.3.

(3) Since $A^{-1} \geq 0$ and $B - A \geqq 0$ then $A^{-1}B - I \geqq 0$. Similarly, $BA^{-1} \geqq 0$.

(4) Since $B^{-1} \geq 0$ and $B - A \geqq 0$, then $I - B^{-1}A \geqq 0$. Similarly, $I - AB^{-1} \geqq 0$.

(5) Since $I \geqq B^{-1}A$, $B^{-1}A \in Z$. But $(B^{-1}A)^{-1} = A^{-1}B \geqq I \geq 0$. Hence, by part 11 of Theorem 2.3.4, $B^{-1}A \in K$. Similarly, $AB^{-1} \in K$.

(6) Since $I - B^{-1}A \geqq 0$ and $(I - I + B^{-1}A)^{-1} = A^{-1}B \geqq 0$, by Theorem 4.3.8 (see Chapter 4), $1 > \rho(I - B^{-1}A)$. Similarly, $1 > \rho(I - AB^{-1})$.

Q.E.D.

Proof of Theorem 2.4.1.

Since $R = A + S \geqq A$ and $A \in K$, $R \in Z$, by Lemma 2.4.2, part 6,

$$1 > \rho(I - R^{-1}A) = \rho(R^{-1}(R - A)) = \rho(R^{-1}S).$$

Q.E.D.

Let

$$A = D - L - U$$

where D is a diagonal matrix formed using the diagonal of A and L(U) is a strictly lower (upper) triangular matrix formed from the strict lower (upper) triangular portion of A. For example, consider

Example 2.4.1

$$A = \begin{bmatrix} 2 & -1 & -1 \\ -1 & 3 & 0 \\ -2 & -1 & 4 \end{bmatrix}.$$

Then

$$D = \begin{bmatrix} 2 & 0 & 0 \\ 0 & 3 & 0 \\ 0 & 0 & 4 \end{bmatrix}, \quad L = \begin{bmatrix} 0 & 0 & 0 \\ 1 & 0 & 0 \\ 2 & 1 & 0 \end{bmatrix}, \quad \text{and} \quad U = \begin{bmatrix} 0 & 1 & 1 \\ 0 & 0 & 0 \\ 0 & 0 & 0 \end{bmatrix}.$$

Below the form of a few elementary splits R and S of a matrix $A \in K$ are given where R and S satisfy Theorem 2.4.1. We include with each split the component form of Equation (2.2.6), the iterative equation, which was

2.2.6 $$x^{m+1} = R^{-1}S\, x^m + R^{-1}b.$$

1. Jacobi Split [see 122]

$$R = D,$$
$$S = L + U,$$

and

$$x_i^{m+1} = \frac{1}{a_{ii}} \{ b_i - \sum_{\substack{j=1 \\ j\neq i}}^{n} a_{ij}\, x_j^m \} \quad \text{for } i = 1,\ldots,n.$$

2. Gauss-Seidel Split [see 122]

$$R = D - L,$$
$$S = U,$$

and

$$x_i^{m+1} = \frac{1}{a_{ii}} \{ b_i - \sum_{j=1}^{i-1} a_{ij}\, x_j^{m+1} - \sum_{j=i+1}^{n} a_{ij} x_j^m \}$$

for $i = 1,\ldots,n$.

(In the above $\sum_{j=1}^{i-1}$ for $i = 1$ and $\sum_{j=i+1}^{n}$ for $i = n$ are taken to mean there is no summation.)

3. Let $c > 0$ such that $cI - A \geqq 0$. Then

$$R = cI,$$
$$S = cI - A,$$

and

$$x_i^{m+1} = x_i^m + \frac{1}{c} \{ b_i - \sum_{j=1}^{n} a_{ij}\, x_j^m \} \quad \text{for } i = 1,\ldots,n.$$

To illustrate the preceding three splits, consider the following system using matrix A of Example 2.4.1.

$$\underset{(A)}{\begin{bmatrix} 2 & -1 & -1 \\ -1 & 3 & 0 \\ -2 & -1 & 4 \end{bmatrix}} \underset{(x)}{\begin{bmatrix} x_1 \\ x_2 \\ x_3 \end{bmatrix}} = \underset{(b)}{\begin{bmatrix} 2 \\ -1 \\ 4 \end{bmatrix}}.$$

The solution to this system is

$$x = \frac{1}{13} \begin{bmatrix} 31 \\ 6 \\ 30 \end{bmatrix}.$$

Let

$$x^0 = \begin{bmatrix} 1 \\ 1 \\ 1 \end{bmatrix},$$

and $A = D - L - U$, as in Example 2.4.1.

Example 2.4.2 (Jacobi Split: $R = D$ and $S = L + U$)

$$x_1^1 = \frac{1}{2}\{2 + 1(1) + 1(1)\} = 2,$$

$$x_2^1 = \frac{1}{3}\{-1 + 1(1) + 0(1)\} = 0,$$

$$x_3^1 = \frac{1}{4}\{4 + 2(1) + 1(1)\} = 7/4.$$

That is,

$$x^1 = \begin{bmatrix} 2 \\ 0 \\ 7/4 \end{bmatrix}.$$

Example 2.4.3 (Gauss-Seidel Split: $R = D - L$ and $S = U$)

$$x_1^1 = \frac{1}{2}\{2 + 1(1) + 1(1)\} = 2,$$

$$x_2^1 = \frac{1}{3}\{-1 + 1(2) + 0(1)\} = 1/3,$$

$$x_3^1 = \frac{1}{4}\{4 + 2(2) + 1(1/3)\} = 25/12.$$

That is,

$$x^1 = \begin{bmatrix} 2 \\ 1/3 \\ 25/12 \end{bmatrix} .$$

Example 2.4.4

Let c = 4, R = cI, and S = cI - A. Then

$$x_1^1 = 1 + \frac{1}{4}\{2 - 2(1) + 1(1) + 1(1)\} = 3/2,$$

$$x_2^1 = 1 + \frac{1}{4}\{-1 + 1(1) - 3(1) + 0(1)\} = 1/2,$$

and

$$x_3^1 = 1 + \frac{1}{4}\{4 + 2(1) + 1(1) - 4(1)\} = 7/4.$$

Some splits arise naturally in various applications. Consider the following.

Example 2.4.5 (Cornfield-Leontief Multiplier Process [29])

Suppose we accept the static input-output representation of an economy given in Example 2.3.1 and consider the series expansion

2.4.1 $$x = b + Ab + A^2b + \cdots = \sum_{\ell=0}^{\infty} A^{\ell}b$$

where $A = (a_{ij})$, as in Example 2.3.1, is the n by n matrix of input-output coefficients. The above equation has an interesting interpretation. First, the gross demand must consist of the final bill of goods, b. To turn out b, each industry i in the system must produce an additional quantity $\sum_{j=1}^{n} a_{ij}b_j$ to be used in the production of b by industry i and other industries. That is, Ab must be made in addition to b. However, to produce the amount Ab, an additional quantity $A(Ab) = A^2b$ must be produced. To produce A^2b requires an additional output A^3b, and so forth. Hence, the total required production for each industry i (i = 1,...,n) is given by (2.4.1). The solution for all of the n activity levels in this production process, called the Cornfield-Leontief Multiplier Process, can be obtained by iterative methods applied to the system $(I - A)x = b$ by using the split R = I and S = A, and setting $x^0 = 0$.

Example 2.4.6 (Markov Process with Rewards)

Again, consider Example 2.3.2. Let v_i^m be the expected total discounted profit of a process starting in state i (at the first observed time period) and evolving for m time periods. Let $v^m = (v_1^m, v_2^m, \ldots, v_n^m)'$. Let b_i be the (expected) profit whenever the process visits state i. Let $b = (b_1, b_2, \ldots, b_n)'$. Thus v^m consists of two components, namely (1), b, the vector of profits received at the first observed time period and (2), Pv^{m-1}, the vector consisting of total expected profits of the system evolving over the remaining m-1 time periods. Thus the recursive equation

$$v^m = b + Pv^{m-1}$$

where $v^1 = b$ and P is the probability transition matrix. Suppose that future profits are discounted by α, $0 \leqq \alpha < 1$. Then

$$v^m = b + \alpha Pb + \alpha^2 P^2 b + \cdots + \alpha^m P^m b.$$

For an infinite horizon, the total expected profit v is given by

$$v = \sum_{\ell=0}^{\infty} (\alpha P)^{\ell} b = b + \alpha P v.$$

To solve for v we need only solve the linear system $(I - \alpha P)v = b$ by use of the split $R = I$ and $S = \alpha P$ with $v^0 = 0$.

As shown in Examples 2.4.1, 2.4.2 and 2.4.3, there are many many ways to choose a split of a class K matrix A, say into R and S, $A = R - S$, such that $\rho(R^{-1}S) < 1$ and R is non-singular. In the following sections we limit our discussion to such splits satisfying the inequality $R^{-1}S \geqq 0$. Splits given by Theorem 2.4.1 always satisfy this condition since $S \geqq 0$ and $R \in K$. Since $R \in K$, by Theorem 2.3.4, part 11, $R^{-1} \geqq 0$. Hence $R^{-1}S \geqq 0$. It is important to note that Theorem 2.4.1 provides only sufficient conditions for generating such splits. A split that provides R non-singular, $\rho(R^{-1}S) < 1$, and $R^{-1}S \geqq 0$ can be formed from conditions other than those given in Theorem 2.4.1. For example consider the following generalization of a split by Totten [121].

Theorem 2.4.3

Let $A \in K$ and $A = \tilde{R} - \tilde{S}$ where $\tilde{R} \in Z$ and $\tilde{S} \geqq 0$. Choose Q to satisfy

$$\tilde{R}^{-1}\tilde{S} \geqq Q \geqq 0$$

and $I - Q \in K$. Then $R = \tilde{R} - \tilde{R}Q$ and $S = \tilde{S} - \tilde{R}Q$ are such that

$$R \text{ is non-singular}, \quad \rho(R^{-1}S) < 1, \text{ and } R^{-1}S \geqq 0.$$

Proof.

We have $R = \tilde{R}(I - Q)$. We note that $R \in K$ and $(I - Q) \in K$, therefore R is non-singular. Now,

$$\begin{aligned} R^{-1}S &= (I - Q)^{-1}\tilde{R}^{-1}(\tilde{S} - \tilde{R}Q) \\ &= (I - Q)^{-1}(\tilde{R}^{-1}\tilde{S} - Q). \end{aligned}$$

Since $I - Q \in K$, $(I - Q)^{-1} \geqq 0$. Also, we are given that $\tilde{R}^{-1}\tilde{S} \geqq Q$. Hence $R^{-1}S \geqq 0$.

Finally,

$$A = \tilde{R} - \tilde{S}$$

and

$$\tilde{R}^{-1}A = I - \tilde{R}^{-1}\tilde{S}$$

implies

$$I - \tilde{R}^{-1}\tilde{S} \in Z.$$

But $A \in K$ implies there exists an $x \geqq 0$ such that $Ax > 0$. Now $\tilde{R}^{-1} \geqq 0$ which implies $\tilde{R}^{-1}Ax > 0$. Hence, since $I - \tilde{R}^{-1}\tilde{S} = \tilde{R}^{-1}A$, $I - \tilde{R}^{-1}\tilde{S} \in K$ by Theorem 2.3.4 part 1.

Now given $\tilde{R}^{-1}\tilde{S} \geqq Q$, then $I - Q \geqq I - \tilde{R}^{-1}\tilde{S}$. Hence, by Lemma 2.4.2 part 6,

$$\begin{aligned} 1 > \rho(I - (I - Q)^{-1}(I - \tilde{R}^{-1}\tilde{S})) &= \rho((I - Q)^{-1}(I - Q - I + \tilde{R}^{-1}\tilde{S})) \\ &= \rho((I - Q)^{-1}(\tilde{R}^{-1}\tilde{S} - Q)) = \rho(R^{-1}S). \end{aligned}$$

Q.E.D.

<u>Definition 2.4.1</u> (Asymptotic Isotone Contraction)

A matrix C is called an <u>asymptotic isotone contraction</u> if $C \geqq 0$ and $\rho(C) < 1$.

As we have shown, there are many ways to split a given matrix A by matrices R and S such that $A = R - S$, $R^{-1}S \geqq 0$, and $\rho(R^{-1}S) < 1$. Thus, there are many splits which give isotone contractions, $R^{-1}S$. A critical problem is how to determine which split is "best."

Since there are many ways to split a given matrix to yield asymptotic isotone contractions, it is appropriate to decide which split is the "best." Several factors to consider in choosing a best split of a given n by n matrix A are:

1. The computational effort in computing $x^{m+1} = R^{-1}S\,x^m + R^{-1}b$ (required by the recursive solution procedure given in Section 2.2).

2. The amount of computer storage required for an iteration.

3. The number of iterations required for $||x^m - x|| < \varepsilon e$ (where here ε is a desired non-negative tolerance).

For example, the number of calculations per iteration (multiplications and divisions) for the Jacobi split is the same as the Gauss-Seidel split but the Gauss-Seidel split requires only one computational vector (which is equal in size to the order of A). The Jacobi procedure requires two vectors--one for x^m and one for x^{m+1}. This consideration may be critical if the order of A is large.

The split of Theorem 2.4.3 requires more data than the predecessor split of Theorem 2.4.1 and may result in a loss of problem sparsity. Note that the Jacobi split, Gauss-Seidel split, and others do not require the use of any data other than those given in A, b, x^m and x^{m+1}. The split of Theorem 2.4.3 may require the calculation of $(I - Q)^{-1}$. In this case we may realize a loss of problem sparsity. Typically, large scale problems are sparse (that is, the ratio of the number of non-zero entries of A to n^2 is small). In solving large problems it is of utmost importance to preserve the problem sparsity. See [2, 3, 11, 19, 48, 49, 54, 55, 58, 59, 67, 92, 115, 117, 118, 119] for related discussions.

Finally, we would like our iterative procedure to provide good approximations to the solution vector in as small a number of iterations as possible.

In summary, the best split is dependent on several considerations and on the particular system of equations. We do not conclude that any particular split is best but do give a basic comparison theorem that pertains only to the asymptotic domination of iterates. (See Varga [122].)

Theorem 2.4.4 (Split Comparison Theorem)

Let $A \in K$ and $A = R_1 - S_1 = R_2 - S_2$ where $R_1 \in Z$, $R_2 \in Z$, and $S_1 \geqq S_2 \geqq 0$. Then

$$0 \leqq \rho(R_2^{-1}S_2) \leqq \rho(R_1^{-1}S_1) < 1.$$

Proof.

Since $A \in K$, $A^{-1} \geqq 0$, and $S_1 \geqq S_2 \geqq 0$, we have $A^{-1}S_1 \geqq A^{-1}S_2$ and, from Theorem 4.3.3 (see Chapter 4),

$$\rho(A^{-1}S_1) \geqq \rho(A^{-1}S_2).$$

Now

$$R_1^{-1}S_1 = (I + A^{-1}S_1)^{-1}A^{-1}S_1.$$

Thus

$$\rho(R_1^{-1}S_1) = \frac{\rho(A^{-1}S_1)}{1+\rho(A^{-1}S_1)} \geqq \frac{\rho(A^{-1}S_2)}{1+\rho(A^{-1}S_2)} = \rho(R_2^{-1}S_2) \geqq 0.$$

Finally, from Theorem 2.4.1, $\rho(R_1^{-1}S_1) < 1$.

Q.E.D.

Theorem 2.4.4 implies that, asymptotically, split $R_2^{-1}S_2$ gives closer estimates to x than $R_1^{-1}S_1$. That is $||(R_1^{-1}S_1)^m \varepsilon^0|| \geqq ||(R_2^{-1}S_2)^m \varepsilon^0||$ for all $m \geqq k$ and k appropriately large (again, the reader is referred to Varga [122]).

We note that Theorem 2.4.4 gives an immediate result that, asymptotically, the Gauss-Seidel split yields a sequence $\{x^i\}_{i=0}$ which converges to x faster than a sequence generated by a Jacobi split.

2.5 Leontief Substitution Systems

In this section the concepts of class Z and K matrices are extended to rectangular systems where we specifically characterize the extreme points of the set of non-negative solutions of such systems. The results of this section, for the most part, were either derived or generalized by Veinott [124]. Consider the following two definitions.

Definition 2.5.1 (Pre-Leontief Matrix)

A matrix is called pre-Leontief if each column has at most one positive element.

Definition 2.5.2 (Leontief Matrix)

A pre-Leontief matrix A is Leontief if each column has exactly one positive element and there exists an $x \geqq 0$ such that $Ax > 0$.

Consider the system

2.5.1
$$Ax = b \geqq 0$$
$$x \geqq 0.$$

Equation 2.5.1 is called a (pre)Leontief Substitution System if A is (pre)Leontief. Let $X(b) = \{x\colon Ax = b,\ x \geqq 0\}$. We are interested in characterizing the extreme points of $X(b)$ for non-negative b. We show in this section that extreme points of $X(b)$ are associated with basis matrices belonging to class K.

Example 2.5.1 (pre-Leontief Matrix)

Let

$$A = \begin{bmatrix} 2 & 0 & 0 & 3 \\ 0 & 1 & -1 & -1 \\ -1 & 0 & -2 & -1 \end{bmatrix}.$$

A is pre-Leontief but not Leontief since there is no $x \geqq 0$ that gives

$$(Ax)_3 > 0$$

since row 3 of A contains no positive elements.

Example 2.5.2 (pre-Leontief Matrix)

Let

$$A = \begin{bmatrix} 1 & 0 & 0 & 0 \\ 0 & 1 & -1 & 0 \\ -1 & -1 & 1 & -2 \end{bmatrix}.$$

A is pre-Leontief but A is not Leontief since there is no $x \geqq 0$ giving $(Ax)_2 > 0$ and $(Ax)_3 > 0$, simultaneously.

Example 2.5.3 (Leontief Matrix)

Let

$$A = \begin{bmatrix} 1 & 0 & -1 & 0 \\ 0 & 1 & 0 & 1 \\ 0 & -1 & 1 & -2 \end{bmatrix}.$$

A is Leontief since $x' = (3, 1, 2, 0)$ satisfies Definition 2.5.2.

Example 2.5.4 (pre-Leontief Matrix)

In Example 2.3.1 we considered a simple input-output model. We assumed that one and only one industry produces each good. Suppose we allow several firms within the same industry to produce the same good. We call such a model a general Leontief model [42]. Let N_i be the set of firms producing good i. Let a_{ij} be the production column associated with the jth firm of N_i. Let $A = (a_{ij})$, $j \in N_i$, $i = 1,\ldots,m$. Then $Ax = b$, $x \geqq 0$, is a pre-Leontief Substitution System.

We next show, in the following theorems, the relationship between extreme points of pre-Leontief and Leontief Substitution Systems.

Definition 2.5.3 (sub-Leontief Matrix)

A pre-Leontief matrix is called sub-Leontief if the only $x \geqq 0$ giving $Ax \geqq 0$ is $x = 0$.

Theorem 2.5.1

If A is pre-Leontief, then one can partition A, after suitably permuting its rows and columns, so that

$$A = \begin{bmatrix} A_1 & A_3 \\ 0 & A_2 \end{bmatrix}$$

where A_1 is Leontief, A_2 is sub-Leontief, and each positive element of A_3 appears above a column of A_2 (call it A_{2i}) where $x_2 \geqq 0$ and $A_2x_2 \geqq 0$ implies $x_{2i} = 0$. Some of the submatrices may be vacuous.

Proof.

See Chapter 4.

Theorem 2.5.2

Consider the system

$$Ax = b$$
$$x \geqq 0, \quad b \geqq 0,$$

where A is pre-Leontief and partitioned as in Theorem 2.5.1:

$$\begin{bmatrix} A_1 & A_3 \\ 0 & A_2 \end{bmatrix} \begin{bmatrix} x_1 \\ x_2 \end{bmatrix} = \begin{bmatrix} b_1 \\ b_2 \end{bmatrix}$$

with $b_2 = 0$ and $b_1 \geqq 0$. Then the following are equivalent:

1. $x = (x_1, x_2)'$ is an extreme point of $Ax = b$, $x \geqq 0$, $b \geqq 0$.

2. $x_2 = 0$ and x_1 is an extreme point of $A_1x_1 = b_1$, $x_1 \geqq 0$.

Proof.

See Chapter 4.

Jointly, Theorems 2.5.1 and 2.5.2 imply that we may consider a non-empty pre-Leontief Substitution System by considering an equivalent Leontief Substitution System. Consider the following examples.

Example 2.5.5 (Theorem 2.5.1)

Let

$$A = \begin{array}{c} \begin{array}{cccc} (1) & (2) & (3) & (4) \end{array} \\ \left[\begin{array}{cccc} 2 & 0 & 0 & 3 \\ 0 & 1 & -1 & -1 \\ -1 & 0 & -2 & -1 \end{array}\right] \begin{array}{c} (1) \\ (2) \\ (3) \end{array} \end{array} .$$

Then

$$\begin{bmatrix} 0 & 1 & 0 \\ 1 & 0 & 0 \\ 0 & 0 & 1 \end{bmatrix} A \begin{bmatrix} 0 & 1 & 0 & 0 \\ 1 & 0 & 0 & 0 \\ 0 & 0 & 1 & 0 \\ 0 & 0 & 0 & 1 \end{bmatrix} = \begin{array}{c} \begin{array}{cccc} (2) & (1) & (3) & (4) \end{array} \\ \left[\begin{array}{c|ccc} 1 & 0 & -1 & -1 \\ \hline 0 & 2 & 0 & 3 \\ 0 & -1 & -2 & -1 \end{array}\right] \begin{array}{c} (2) \\ (1) \\ (3) \end{array} \end{array} .$$

Example 2.5.6 (Theorem 2.5.2)

For A given in Example 2.5.5 above, it is easily shown that X(b) has a feasible solution, for $b \geqq 0$, if and only if

$$b \in \left\{ \begin{bmatrix} 0 \\ 1 \\ 0 \end{bmatrix} \lambda : \lambda \geqq 0 \right\} .$$

The corresponding extreme point is $x' = (0, \lambda, 0, 0)$.

Example 2.5.7 (Theorem 2.5.1)

The partitioning given in Theorem 2.5.1 has an economic interpretation when A is an input-output matrix formed from a general input-output problem (see Example 2.3.1).

The activities associated with A_1 are called productive activities and the goods associated with A_1 are called producible goods. Activities associated with A_3 are non-productive where goods associated with A_2 are non-producible [42]. Hence, in Example 2.5.5, activity 2 is productive, good 2 is producible, activities 1, 3, and 4 are non-productive, and goods 1 and 3 are non-producible.

In the following it is shown that every extreme point of a Leontief Substitution System is determined by a square Leontief matrix (and hence a class K matrix).

Theorem 2.5.3

If A is an m by n Leontief matrix, then x is an extreme point of $X(b) = \{x: Ax = b, x \geqq 0\}$ for $b \geqq 0$ if and only if x is determined by an m by m Leontief matrix.

Proof.

See Chapter 4.

Example 2.5.8 (Theorem 2.5.3)

Let

$$A = \begin{bmatrix} 1 & -1 & 1 \\ -1 & 1 & 0 \end{bmatrix}, \qquad b = \begin{bmatrix} 2 \\ 1 \end{bmatrix}.$$

The only extreme point of $Ax = b$, $x \geqq 0$ is

$$x = \begin{bmatrix} 0 \\ 1 \\ 3 \end{bmatrix}$$

and is determined by $J = (3,2)$ with

$$A_J x_J = b$$

and the remaining x_i set to zero.

Note that

$$A_{(3,2)} = \begin{bmatrix} 1 & -1 \\ 0 & 1 \end{bmatrix}$$

is the only Leontief basis in A.

Recall, Definition 2.3.1, a real matrix B is a member of class Z if B is square and has non-positive off-diagonal elements. Also, by Definition 2.3.2 and Theorem 2.3.4, a matrix B is a member of class K if $B \in Z$ and $B^{-1} \geq 0$. We now characterize the set of all class Z sub-matrices of a given Leontief matrix A.

Let $A = (a_{ij})$ be an m by n Leontief matrix. Let

$$N_i = \{j: a_{ij} > 0\}, \; i = 1, \ldots, m.$$

Let

$$N = \mathop{X}_{i=1}^{m} N_i .$$

Then $A_J \in Z$ for all $J \in N$. Let $M \subseteq N$ be the set of all class K matrices of A. That is, $A_J \in K$ for $J \in M$.

Example 2.5.9

Let

$$A = \begin{bmatrix} 1 & -1 & 1 \\ -1 & 1 & 0 \end{bmatrix}.$$

Then

$$N_1 = \{1,3\},\ N_2 = \{2\},\ N = \{(1,2),\ (3,2)\} = \{J_1,\ J_2\}.$$

Note:

$$A_{J_1} = \begin{bmatrix} 1 & -1 \\ -1 & 1 \end{bmatrix} \in Z \text{ but is not in class K since } A_{J_1}^{-1} \text{ does not exist.}$$

$$A_{J_2} = \begin{bmatrix} 1 & -1 \\ 0 & 1 \end{bmatrix} \in K \text{ since } A_{J_2} \in Z \text{ and } A_{J_2}^{-1} = \begin{bmatrix} 1 & 1 \\ 0 & 1 \end{bmatrix} \geq 0.$$

In this example $M \subset N$ and $M = \{J_2\} = \{(3,2)\}$.

Definition 2.5.4 (Totally Leontief Matrix)

If A is Leontief and there exists a $y \geqq 0$ such that $y'A > 0$, then A is totally Leontief.

Theorem 2.5.4

The following are equivalent:

1. A is totally Leontief.
2. $M = N$.
3. $X(b) = \{x: Ax = b,\ x \geqq 0\}$ is bounded for all $b \geqq 0$.

Proof.

See Chapter 4.

We note that by using Theorem 2.5.1 we can extend the results of Theorem 2.5.4 to pre-Leontief matrices.

Example 2.5.10 (Theorem 2.5.4)

Let

$$A = \begin{bmatrix} 1 & -1 & 1 \\ -1 & 1 & 0 \end{bmatrix}$$

and

$$b = \begin{bmatrix} 1 \\ 1 \end{bmatrix}.$$

Note that A is a pre-Leontief matrix and

$$x = \begin{bmatrix} 0 \\ 1 \\ 2 \end{bmatrix} + \lambda \begin{bmatrix} 1 \\ 1 \\ 0 \end{bmatrix}$$

is a solution of $Ax = b$, $x \geqq 0$, for any $\lambda \geqq 0$. In this example $X(b)$ is not bounded and $M \neq N$. Also, A is not totally Leontief.

Example 2.5.11 (Theorem 2.5.4)

Let

$$A = \begin{bmatrix} 1 & 0 & 1 \\ -1 & 1 & 0 \end{bmatrix}.$$

Choose

$$x' = (1, 2, 1)$$

and

$$y' = (2, 1).$$

Then $Ax > 0$ and $y'A > 0$. Hence, A is a totally Leontief matrix, $M = N$, and $X(b)$ is bounded for all $b \geqq 0$.

2.6 Optimization Over Totally Leontief Substitution Systems

In this section we consider solving the problem

2.6.1
$$\begin{aligned} &\text{Max } c'x \\ &\text{subject to} \\ &Ax = b \\ &x \geqq 0 \end{aligned}$$

where A is an m by n totally Leontief matrix and $b \geqq 0$. We note that, according to Theorems 2.5.3 and 2.5.4, one (or more) optimal solution(s) are associated with some A_J, $J \varepsilon M$ (i.e., $A_J \varepsilon K$). We will focus on solving the dual to Problem 2.6.1. The dual problem is

2.6.2
$$\begin{aligned} &\text{Min } b'v \\ &\text{subject to} \\ &A'v \geqq c. \end{aligned}$$

We show in the following that Problem 2.6.2 can be solved by iterative procedures. Of course, once Problem 2.6.2 is solved, we know the optimal basis to Problem 2.6.1 and can solve Problem 2.6.1 by solving the linear system

2.6.3
$$A_{J^*} x_{J^*} = b$$

for x_{J^*} with J^* being the optimal basis and all non-basic variables set to zero. We note that $A_{J^*} \varepsilon K$ and x_{J^*} can be found by matrix iterative techniques as given in Section 2.2 using splits such as those given in Section 2.4.

By Theorem 2.5.4 and Theorem 2.5.3, we can limit the search of dual bases to those formed from A_J, $J \varepsilon M$. Recall from Section 2.5 (see the definition of N, Definition 2.5.4 and Theorem 2.5.4) that M denotes the set of indices of all class K matrices formed from the matrix A in Problem 2.6.1 to within column and row permutations. Specifically, we call A_J' a "dual basis" and the v determined by A_J':

2.6.4
$$A_J' v = c_J \qquad \text{for } J \varepsilon M,$$

a dual basic solution. First, consider the following theorem due to Fielder and Ptak [33].

Theorem 2.6.1

$A \in K$ if and only if A can be written as $A = \lambda I - P$ where $\lambda > \rho(P)$ and $P \geqq 0$.

Proof.

($\Rightarrow$) Given $A \in K$ then, as noted in split 3 of Example 2.4.1 given in Section 2.4, $A = \lambda I - P$ with $P \geqq 0$ for some $\lambda > 0$. Then $P = \lambda I - A$ and $\lambda - \rho(P)$ is a real eigenvalue of A. According to Theorem 2.3.4, part 7, $\lambda - \rho(P) > 0$.

($\Leftarrow$) Suppose we have the matrix $\lambda I - P$ where $P \geqq 0$ and $\lambda > \rho(P) \geqq 0$. Then $\lambda I - P \in Z$ and $\rho(\frac{1}{\lambda} P) < 1$. Thus

$$(I - \frac{1}{\lambda} P)^{-1} = \sum_{\ell=0}^{\infty} (\frac{1}{\lambda} P)^{\ell} \geqq 0$$

or

$$(\lambda I - P)^{-1} = \frac{1}{\lambda} (I - \frac{1}{\lambda} P)^{-1} \geqq 0.$$

Hence, $A = \lambda I - P \in K$.

Q.E.D.

Using Theorem 2.6.1 we can always write Equation (2.6.4) as

2.6.5 $$v = R^{-1} S_J \, v + R^{-1} c_J$$

with $R = \lambda I$, $S_J = R - A_J' \geqq 0$, $\lambda \geqq 0$, $\lambda \geqq \lambda_J$ for all $J \in M$ (for example, $\lambda = \underset{J}{\text{Max}} \{\lambda_J\}$), where λ_J is as defined in Theorem 2.6.1, that is, $\lambda_J > \rho(S_J)$.

Suppose v is feasible to the dual Problem (2.6.2). Then

$$A_J' \, v \geqq c_J \qquad \text{for all } J \in M$$

or

$$R \, v \geqq S_J \, v + c_J \qquad \text{for all } J \in M.$$

Hence

2.6.6 $$v \geqq R^{-1} S_J \, v + R^{-1} c_J \qquad \text{for all } J \in M.$$

Similarly, if v satisfies Equation (2.6.4) and (2.6.6) then it is feasible to Problem (2.6.2).

Consider the problem of finding the fixed point (if one exists) of the function $\mathscr{L}(\cdot)$ where

2.6.7 $$\mathcal{L}(v) = \underset{J\varepsilon M}{\text{Max}}\ [R^{-1}S_J v + R^{-1}c_J].$$

We will show that the fixed point of $\mathcal{L}(\cdot)$ solves the dual problem given in (2.6.2) and that (2.6.7) gives the optimal basis of Problem (2.6.1). Note that since $Ax = b$, $x \geqq 0$, is a totally Leontief system, $\rho(R^{-1}S_J) < 1$ for all $J \varepsilon M$.

Theorem 2.6.2

If $\rho(R^{-1}S_J) < 1$ and $R^{-1}S_J \geqq 0$ for $J \varepsilon M$, then

1. $\mathcal{L}(\cdot)$ has a unique fixed point v^*.
2. There exists a $J^* \varepsilon M$ such that $v^* = R^{-1}S_{J^*}v^* + R^{-1}c_{J^*}$.
3. v^* is the limit point of

$$v^{n+1} = \mathcal{L}(v^n) = \underset{J\varepsilon M}{\text{Max}}\ [R^{-1}S_J v^n + R^{-1}c_J],$$

that is, $\lim_{n\to\infty} v^n = v^*$.

4. v^* solves Problem (2.6.2).

Proof.

See Chapter 4.

Theorem 2.6.2 suggests the following algorithm for solving Problem (2.6.2) with $R = \lambda I$ and $S_J = R - A_J'$ for $J \varepsilon M$.

Algorithm 1

Step 0

Specify an arbitrary vector v^0 and a solution tolerance $\varepsilon > 0$. Construct the set M and let $n = 0$.

Step 1

Solve

$$v^{n+1} = \underset{J\varepsilon M}{\text{Max}}\ [R^{-1}S_J v^n + R^{-1}c_J].$$

Step 2

If

$$|v^{n+1} - v^n| < \varepsilon e,$$

stop. Otherwise increment n by 1 and go to Step 1.

Algorithm 1 does not determine, necessarily, the exact solution to Problem 2.6.2 unless $\varepsilon = 0$, and then only asymptotic convergence to v^* is assured. We will consider refinements to this basic algorithm. We note that since $R = \lambda I$ ($R^{-1} = \frac{1}{\lambda} I$), we can perform Step 1 as:

$$v_i^{n+1} = \underset{j \varepsilon M_i}{\text{Max}} \left[\frac{1}{\lambda} (a_j + (\lambda-1)e_i)' v^n + \frac{1}{\lambda} c_j \right], \qquad i = 1,\ldots,m$$

where a_j is column j of A and c_j is component j of c. That is, we can perform iterations using activities instead of bases.

As an illustration of Algorithm 1, consider the linear program (Howard's taxicab problem [61]) given in Table 2.6.1.

Table 2.6.1

	x_{11}	x_{12}	x_{13}	x_{21}	x_{22}	x_{31}	x_{32}	x_{33}		
Max	8.0000	2.7500	4.2500	16.0000	15.0000	7.0000	4.0000	4.5000		
s.t.	.5500	.94375	.7750	-.4500	-.05625	-.2250	-.1125	-.67500	=	.33
	-.2250	-.67500	-.1125	1.0000	.21250	-.2250	-.6750	-.05625	=	.33
	-.2250	-.16875	-.5625	-.4500	-.05625	.5500	.8875	.83125	=	.34

with $x_{ij} \geqq 0$.

Let

$$M_1 = \{x_{11}, x_{12}, x_{13}\},$$

$$M_2 = \{x_{21}, x_{22}\},$$

$$M_3 = \{x_{31}, x_{32}, x_{33}\},$$

and

$$M = M_1 \times M_2 \times M_3$$

be the set of all feasible bases. It is readily shown that for all $J \varepsilon M$, $A_J' \varepsilon K$, and that we can let $\lambda = 1$.

<u>Step 0</u>

Let $v^{0'} = (0, 0, 0)$ and $\varepsilon = 10^{-5}$. Let $n = 0$.

Step 1

$$v^1 = \max_{J \varepsilon M} R^{-1} c_J = \max_{J \varepsilon M} c_J$$

or

$$v^1 = \begin{bmatrix} 8.0000 \\ 16.0000 \\ 7.0000 \end{bmatrix} \quad \text{with} \quad J = (x_{11}, x_{21}, x_{31}).$$

Step 2

$|v^1 - v^0| > \varepsilon e.$ Set n = 1 and return to Step 1.

Step 1

$$v^2 = \max_{J \varepsilon M} \left[R^{-1} S_J v^1 + R^{-1} c_J \right] = \max_{J \varepsilon M} \left[S_J v^1 + c_J \right].$$

That is,

$$v_1^2 = \text{Max} \begin{cases} 8.0000 + (0.45)(8.0000) + (0.225)(16.0000) \\ + (0.225)(7.0000) = 16.7750 \\ \\ 2.7500 + (0.05625)(8.0000) + (0.675)(16.0000) \\ + (0.16875)(7.0000) = 15.18125 \\ \\ 4.2500 + (0.225)(8.0000) + (0.1125)(16.0000) \\ + (0.5625)(7.0000) = 11.78750 \end{cases}$$

$$v_2^2 = \text{Max} \begin{cases} 16.0000 + (0.45)(8.0000) + (0.45)(7.0000) = 22.7500 \\ \\ 15.0000 + (0.05625)(8.0000) + (0.7875)(16.0000) \\ + (0.05625)(7.0000) = 28.44375 \end{cases}$$

$$v_3^2 = \text{Max} \begin{cases} 7.0000 + (0.225)(8.0000) + (0.225)(16.0000) \\ + (0.45)(7.0000) = 15.5500 \\ \\ 4.0000 + (0.1125)(8.0000) + (0.675)(16.0000) \\ + (0.1125)(7.0000) = 16.48750 \\ \\ 4.5000 + (0.675)(8.0000) + (0.05625)(16.0000) \\ + (0.16875)(7.0000) = 11.98125 \end{cases}$$

or

$$v^2 = \begin{bmatrix} 16.77500 \\ 28.44375 \\ 16.48750 \end{bmatrix} \quad \text{with } J = (x_{11}, x_{22}, x_{32}).$$

A summary of the solution sequence is given in Table 2.6.2.

Table 2.6.2

Summary of Algorithm 1--Example

Iteration	v_1	v_2	v_3	J
1	8.00000	16.00000	7.00000	x_{11}, x_{21}, x_{31}
2	16.77500	28.44375	16.48750	x_{11}, x_{22}, x_{32}
5	43.87727	57.52882	45.06097	x_{12}, x_{22}, x_{32}
10	75.72678	89.37959	76.91021	x_{12}, x_{22}, x_{32}
25	112.19757	125.85038	113.38101	x_{12}, x_{22}, x_{32}
136	121.65339	135.30620	122.83682	x_{12}, x_{22}, x_{32}
-STOP-				

In solving systems of equations (Section 2.4) we allowed different types of splits such as the Jacobi Split or the Gauss-Seidel Split. We can also solve the dual problem (2.6.2) using splits other than $R_J = R = \lambda I$ and $S_J = R - A_J'$. For example, the Gauss-Seidel split in Algorithm 1 changes Step 1 to:

$$v_i^{n+1} = \underset{j \in M_i}{\text{Max}} \left[(c_j - \sum_{\ell=1}^{i-1} a_{\ell j} v_\ell^{n+1} - \sum_{\ell=i+1}^{n} a_{\ell j} v_\ell^n)/(1 - a_{ij}) \right], \quad i = 1,\dots,m.$$

(See [78] for a proof of convergence for this and the related Jacobi iterative procedure.)

Consider the linear program in Table 2.6.1 and its solution using Algorithm 1 with a Gauss-Seidel Split.

Step 0

Let $v^{0'} = (0, 0, 0)$ and $\varepsilon = 10^{-5}$. Set $n = 0$.

Step 1

$$v_1^1 = \text{Max} \begin{cases} \frac{1}{0.5500}(8.0000) & = 14.54545 \\ \frac{1}{0.94375}(2.7500) & = 2.91391 \\ \frac{1}{0.7750}(4.25) & = 5.48387 \end{cases}$$

$$v_2^1 = \text{Max} \begin{cases} \frac{1}{1.0000}[16.0000 + (0.45)(14.54545)] & = 22.54546 \\ \frac{1}{0.2125}[15.0000 + (0.05625)(14.54545)] & = 74.43850 \end{cases}$$

$$v_3^1 = \text{Max} \begin{cases} \frac{1}{0.5500}[7.0000 + (0.2250)(14.54545) + (0.2250)(74.43850)] \\ \quad = 49.12980 \\ \frac{1}{0.8875}[4.0000 + (0.1125)(14.54545) + (0.675)(74.43850)] \\ \quad = 62.96603 \\ \frac{1}{0.83125}[4.5000 + (0.675)(14.54545) + (0.05625)(74.43850)] \\ \quad = 22.26207 \end{cases}$$

or

$$v^1 = \begin{bmatrix} 14.54545 \\ 74.43850 \\ 62.96603 \end{bmatrix} \quad \text{with } J = (x_{11}, x_{22}, x_{32}).$$

The salient feature of the Gauss-Seidel iteration is that once a component of v_i^n is computed it replaces v_i^{n-1} in storage and is used in subsequent computations. A summary of the Gauss-Seidel solution sequence is given in Table 2.6.3.

Table 2.6.3

Algorithm 1 with Gauss-Seidel Iterations

Iteration	v_1	v_2	v_3	J
1	14.54545	74.43850	62.96603	x_{11}, x_{22}, x_{32}
2	70.75640	105.98535	94.08474	x_{11}, x_{22}, x_{32}
5	115.32155	131.77333	119.34723	x_{12}, x_{22}, x_{32}
10	121.46037	135.19855	122.73049	x_{12}, x_{22}, x_{32}
25	121.65346	135.30627	122.83690	x_{12}, x_{22}, x_{32}
-STOP-				

Note from Tables 2.6.2 and 2.6.3 the difference in convergence rate of Algorithm 1 using two different splits. We next generalize an earlier result (Theorem 2.4.4) to Algorithm 1.

Theorem 2.6.3

In using Algorithm 1, where $A'_J = R_{J_1} - S_{J_1} = R_{J_2} - S_{J_2}$ are asymptotic isotone splits of A'_J for $J \varepsilon M$ with

$$S_{J_1} \geqq S_{J_2} \geqq 0,$$

and the subscripts on J denote the split type (Jacobi, Gauss-Seidel, and so forth),

$$v_2^{n+1} = \underset{J \varepsilon M}{\text{Max}} \left[R_{J_2}^{-1} S_{J_2} v_2^n + R_{J_2}^{-1} c_{J_2} \right]$$

converges to v^* faster from below and above than

$$v_1^{n+1} = \underset{J \varepsilon M}{\mathrm{Max}} \left[R_{J_1}^{-1} S_{J_1} v_1^n + R_{J_1}^{-1} c_{J_1} \right].$$

(In the above, the subscript of v is used to distinguish v's for different split processes.)

Proof.

(1) Assume $v^i \to v^*$ from below, then

(i) let n = 1 and $v^0 \leq v^*$ be the initial guess.

The first iteration gives

$$v_1^1 = \left[\underset{J \varepsilon M}{\mathrm{Max}} \; R_{J_1}^{-1} S_{J_1} v^0 + R_{J_1}^{-1} c_{J_1} \right] = R_{J_{1*}}^{-1} S_{J_{1*}} v^0 + R_{J_{1*}}^{-1} c_{J_{1*}}$$

and

$$v_2^1 = \left[\underset{J \varepsilon M}{\mathrm{Max}} \; R_{J_2}^{-1} S_{J_2} v^0 + R_{J_2}^{-1} c_{J_2} \right] = R_{J_{2*}}^{-1} S_{J_{2*}} v^0 + R_{J_{2*}}^{-1} c_{J_{2*}}.$$

Since $R_{J_{1*}} = R_{J_2} - S_{J_2} + S_{J_{1*}}$ for $J_2 = J_1^*$,

$$v_1^1 = \left[I - R_{J_2}^{-1} S_{J_2} + R_{J_2}^{-1} S_{J_{1*}} \right]^{-1} R_{J_2}^{-1} \left[S_{J_{1*}} v^0 + c_{J_2} \right]$$

or

$$\left[I - R_{J_2}^{-1} S_{J_2} + R_{J_2}^{-1} S_{J_{1*}} \right] v_1^1 = R_{J_2}^{-1} S_{J_{1*}} v^0 + R_{J_2}^{-1} c_{J_2}$$

$$= \left[R_{J_2}^{-1} S_{J_{1*}} - R_{J_2}^{-1} S_{J_2} \right] v^0 + R_{J_2}^{-1} c_{J_2}$$

$$+ R_{J_2}^{-1} S_{J_2} v^0.$$

But

$$v_2^1 \geqq R_{J_2}^{-1} S_{J_2} v^0 + R_{J_2}^{-1} c_{J_2}.$$

Thus

$$v_2^1 + \left[R_{J_2}^{-1} S_{J_{1*}} - R_{J_2}^{-1} S_{J_2}\right] v^0 \geqq \left[I - R_{J_2}^{-1} S_{J_2} + R_{J_2}^{-1} S_{J_{1*}}\right] v_1^1.$$

It is readily verified that $R_{J_2}^{-1} S_{J_{1*}} \geqq R_{J_2}^{-1} S_{J_2}$ and, with $v_1^1 \geqq v^0$ we have

$$v_2^1 \geqq v_1^1.$$

(ii) Assume $v_2^K \geqq v_1^K$ and consider

$$v_1^{K+1} = \underset{J \varepsilon M}{\text{Max}} \left[R_{J_1}^{-1} S_{J_1} v_1^K + R_{J_1}^{-1} c_{J_1}\right]$$

and

$$v_2^{K+1} = \underset{J \varepsilon M}{\text{Max}} \left[R_{J_2}^{-1} S_{J_2} v_2^K + R_{J_2}^{-1} c_{J_2}\right].$$

As above

$$v_1^{K+1} = \left[I - R_{J_2}^{-1} S_{J_2} + R_{J_2}^{-1} S_{J_{1*}}\right]^{-1} R_{J_2}^{-1} \left[S_{J_{1*}} v_1^K + c_{J_2}\right]$$

which gives

$$\left[I - R_{J_2}^{-1} S_{J_2} + R_{J_2}^{-1} S_{J_{1*}}\right] v_1^{K+1} = R_{J_2}^{-1} S_{J_{1*}} v_1^K + R_{J_2}^{-1} c_{J_2}$$

$$= \left[R_{J_2}^{-1} S_{J_{1*}} - R_{J_2}^{-1} S_{J_2}\right] v_1^K + R_{J_2}^{-1} S_{J_2} v_1^K + R_{J_2}^{-1} c_{J_2}\ .$$

Since $v_2^{K+1} \geqq R_{J_2}^{-1} S_{J_2} v_2^K + R_{J_2}^{-1} c_{J_2}$, then

$$v_2^{K+1} + \left[R_{J_2}^{-1} S_{J_{1*}} - R_{J_2}^{-1} S_{J_2}\right] v_1^K \geqq R_{J_2}^{-1} S_{J_2} v_2^K + R_{J_2}^{-1} c_{J_2} + \left[R_{J_2}^{-1} S_{J_{1*}} - R_{J_2}^{-1} S_{J_2}\right] v_1^K.$$

Since $v_2^K \geqq v_1^K$, it follows that

$$v_2^{K+1} + \left[R_{J_2}^{-1} S_{J_{1*}} - R_{J_2}^{-1} S_{J_2}\right] v_1^K \geqq \left[I - R_{J_2}^{-1} S_{J_2} + R_{J_2}^{-1} S_{J_{1*}}\right] v_1^{K+1}$$

or

$$v_2^{K+1} + \left[R_{J_2}^{-1} S_{J_{1*}} - R_{J_2}^{-1} S_{J_2}\right] \left(v_1^K - v_1^{K+1}\right) \geqq v_1^{K+1} .$$

As above, $R_{J_2}^{-1} S_{J_{1*}} \geqq R_{J_2}^{-1} S_{J_2}$ and $v_1^{K+1} \geqq v_1^K$.

Hence

$$v_2^{K+1} \geqq v_1^{K+1}.$$

(2) The proof for convergence from above is similar.

Q.E.D.

Veinott [123] defines the spectral radius of the process given in Step 1 of Algorithm 1 as ρ where

$$\rho = \max_{J \varepsilon M} \rho(R_J^{-1} S_J)$$

As shown in Chapter 4, ρ is an important factor in the rate of convergence of Step 1 of Algorithm 1. In Theorem 2.6.3 we are choosing splits that yield smaller spectral radii (see Theorem 2.4.4) and therefore expect a better asymptotic rate of convergence. Porteus [101, 102] pursues this notion and several others to give faster convergence of the sequence $\{v^i\}$ to v^*.

2.7 Some Totally Leontief Substitution Systems

In earlier sections we have discussed to a limited degree, Markov Decision Processes and input-output problems. Under certain conditions, these problems can be formulated as totally Leontief Substitution problems. We now discuss these and other totally Leontief problems.

2.7.1 Discounted Discrete-Time and Action Markov Decision Processes

"Markovian decision processes are stochastic processes that describe the evolution of dynamic systems contolled by sequences of decisions or actions" [26]. Suppose a system is observed at equally spaced points of time t (= 0, 1, 2, ...). At each point in time the system is observed to be in one of a finite set of states S. For any state $i \in S$ observed at time t (= 0, 1, 2, ...), a decision $a \in A_i$ is made. Each set A_i is finite. The outcome of the decision at state $i \in S$ is an immediate expected profit $c_i(a)$ and the probability of observing state $j \in S$ next period is $P_{ij}(a)$. A policy, π, is a decision procedure that specifies, for each time period, a method for choosing actions for each $i \in S$. In the problem we are to address, it has been shown [8, 27, 70] that we can restrict ourselves to considering only nonrandomized stationary policies. A nonrandomized stationary policy $\pi = (J,J,J,\ldots)$ specifies an action for each state. That is, $J_i \in A_i$, $i \in S$ and J is independent of the period. Let M be the set of all nonrandomized stationary policies and denote each such nonrandomized stationary policy as J when, in fact, we mean $\pi = (J, J,J,\ldots)$. Associate with each $J \in M$ an m by 1 vector of expected profits c_J and an m by m matrix of transition probabilities P_J where m is the cardinality of S. (Other references for this problem are [26, 61, 108].)

In choosing the "optimal" policy we assume that we are trying to maximize the expected total discounted profits. Let α be the discount factor where $0 \leqq \alpha < 1$. We assume that all $c_i(a)$ for $i \in S$ and $a \in A_i$ are bounded. For a given policy, the total expected discounted profit is

$$v(J) = \sum_{\ell=0}^{\infty} (\alpha P_J)^{\ell} c_J$$

By Corollary 4.3.2.1 (see Chapter 4) and Theorems 2.2.1 and 2.2.2, we have:

$$v(J) = (I - \alpha P_J)^{-1} c_J$$

and that $I - \alpha P_J \in K$ for all $J \in M$.

D'Epenoux [25] gave the following linear programming formulation for finding an optimal policy.

2.7.1 $$\text{Max} \sum_{i \varepsilon S} \sum_{a \varepsilon A_i} x_{ia}\, c_i(a)$$

subject to

$$\sum_{i \varepsilon S} \sum_{a \varepsilon A_i} (\delta_{ij} - \alpha P_{ij}(a)) x_{ia} = d_j \quad \text{for all } j \varepsilon S \text{ and } d_j > 0$$

$$x_{ia} \geqq 0 \quad \text{for } \; i \varepsilon S, \, a \varepsilon A_i$$

with each d_j chosen such that

$$\sum_{j=1}^{m} d_j = 1$$

and

$$\delta_{ij} = \begin{cases} 0 & \text{if } i \neq j \\ 1 & \text{if } i = j. \end{cases}$$

Let $A_J = I - \alpha P_J'$ for $J \varepsilon M$. We note that Problem 2.7.1 has a constraint set of one positive element per column and that the set of stationary policies, M, corresponds to the column identifications of each feasible basis. Furthermore $A_J = I - \alpha P_J' \varepsilon K$ for each $J \varepsilon M$. Hence the above linear program is a totally Leontief linear program. The optimal bases correspond to optimal policies in the Markov Decision process.

2.7.2 Semi-Markov Decision Processes

A more general setting for considering stochastic control problems is the semi-Markov decision process [62, 65, 66, 108]. Here the times between transitions are random variables.

At time 0 the system is observed to be in state $i \varepsilon S$ and action $a \varepsilon A_i$ is chosen. The probability of observing state j as the next state is $P_{ij}(a)$, but the time until the transition from i to j is a random variable with a probability distribution of $F_{ij}(\cdot|a)$. After the transition occurs, another action is chosen and the above is repeated. For a given state i and action a let $c_i(a)$ be a (bounded) immediate expected profit and $r_i(a)$ a (bounded) profit rate effective until the next transition occurs. Suppose that profits are continuously discounted. That is, a profit c at time t is equal to a reward $ce^{-\alpha t}$ at time 0. Again we assume $0 \leqq \alpha < 1$. We also assume that an infinite number of transitions does not occur in a finite time interval [108]. Define the discounted probabilities $q_{ij}(a)$ as

$$q_{ij}(a) = P_{ij}(a) \int_0^\infty e^{-\alpha t} dF_{ij}(t|a) \qquad i,j \in S$$

and the expected one period discounted profit for action $a \in A_i$ as

$$\overline{c}_i(a) = c_i(a) + \sum_{j=0}^{\infty} \{ P_{ij}(a) r_i(a) \int_0^\infty \int_0^t e^{-\alpha s} ds dF_{ij}(t|a)\} .$$

Let Q_J be the m by m discounted transition matrix formed by elements $q_{ij}(a)$ where $J_i = a$. As in the case of discounted discrete-time Markov decisions, let M be the set of all policies, c_J the vector containing the present values of the expected profits, and v(J) the limiting present values produced under policy J. That is

$$v(J) = \sum_{\ell=0}^{\infty} Q_J^\ell c_J.$$

By construction $I - Q_J \in K$ for each $J \in M$ and Equation 2.7.1 can be used to find the optimal policy. Furthermore, the corresponding linear program is totally Leontief.

We note that a further generalization is the transient Markov decision process of Veinott [123].

2.7.3 Totally Productive Input-Output Systems

We say an Input-Output System with substitute activities is totally productive if, for every combination of m activities which each produce a different good, the resulting simple Leontief input-output model is productive. More formally, let M_i contain the set of all activities (or alternative ways) of producing good i. Then $M = \overset{m}{\underset{i=1}{X}} M_i$ is the set (to within permutations) of all ways of selecting m activities each of which produces a different good. We have already shown (see Section 2.3) that a productive square input-output matrix is a class K matrix.

Suppose we were given a Leontief economy having possible substitute activities. Let c_{ij} be the cost per unit of production of good i using process j. The following linear program gives the minimum cost production schedule for the above Leontief economy.

2.7.2 $$\text{Min} \sum_{i=1}^{m} \sum_{j \varepsilon M_i} c_{ij} x_{ij}$$

subject to

$$\sum_{i=1}^{m} \sum_{j \varepsilon M_i} a_{ij} x_{ij} = b$$

$$x_{ij} \geqq 0 \qquad i = 1, \ldots, m \text{ and } j \varepsilon M_i.$$

In the above, a_{ij} is the net production vector for good i using process j. Let $A_J = (a_{1J_1}, a_{2J_2}, \ldots, a_{mJ_m})$. Then, for a totally productive system, $A_J \varepsilon K$ for each $J \varepsilon M$. Hence Problem 2.7.2 is a totally Leontief Substitution System.

2.7.4 Transshipment Matrices and Shortest Path Problems

Consider a directed graph G = (N, A) where N is a non-empty set of nodes (vertices, points) and A is a set of ordered pairs of nodes (n_1, n_2) which correspond to an arc connecting nodes n_1 and n_2. We assume N and A are finite sets. Let c_{ij} be the length (cost per unit flow, etc.) of arc (i, j). G, together with a scalar function defined on A, is a network. We may wish to minimize the distance in tranversing from a given node k to some node ℓ. This can be formulated as a linear program of the form:

2.7.3 $$\text{Min} \sum_{(i,j)\varepsilon A} c_{ij} x_{ij}$$

subject to

2.7.4 $$\sum_{(i_1,j)\varepsilon A} x_{i_1 j} - \sum_{(j,i_1)\varepsilon A} x_{j i_1} = 0, \quad i_1 \varepsilon N, i_1 \neq k, \ell$$

2.7.5
$$\sum_{(\ell,j)\varepsilon A} x_{\ell j} - \sum_{(j,\ell)\varepsilon A} x_{j\ell} = 1$$

$$x_{ij} \geqq 0, \qquad (i,j) \varepsilon A.$$

Equations 2.7.4 and 2.7.5 give a pre-Leontief matrix. For example, consider the simple graph:

2.7.6

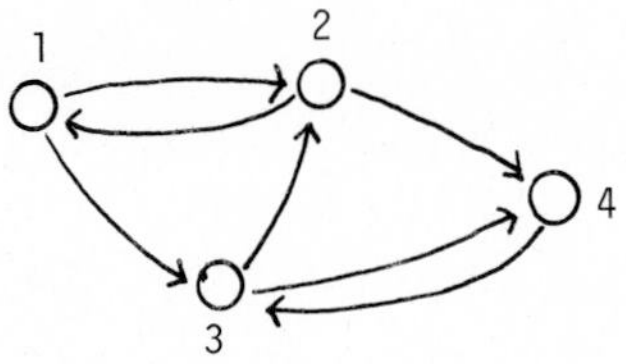

Letting $\ell = 1$ and $k = 4$ we have for Equation 2.7.4 and 2.7.5 the following:

2.7.7
$$Ax = \begin{bmatrix} 1 & 1 & -1 & 0 & 0 & 0 & 0 \\ -1 & 0 & 1 & 1 & -1 & 0 & 0 \\ 0 & -1 & 0 & 0 & 1 & 1 & -1 \end{bmatrix} \begin{bmatrix} x_{12} \\ x_{13} \\ x_{21} \\ x_{24} \\ x_{32} \\ x_{34} \\ x_{43} \end{bmatrix} = \begin{bmatrix} 1 \\ 0 \\ 0 \end{bmatrix}.$$

Notice that A is pre-Leontief.

Theorem 2.7.1

The constraint matrix arising from Equations 2.7.4 and 2.7.5 is Leontief if and only if there is no arc leading out of node k and there is a chain to node k from every other node. [124]

Proof.

See Chapter 4.

In the above theorem, a chain is a set of arcs such that the ending node of the first arc is the beginning point of the second and, the ending node of the second arc is the beginning node of the third arc, and so forth.

In the example given in 2.7.6 we note that arc (4,3) leads out of node 4 and, according to Theorem 2.7.1, the A matrix of 2.7.7 is not Leontief (notice that the last column does not have a positive element).

A cycle is defined to be a chain having distinct nodes and where the ending node is coincident with the initial node. We can now state the conditions under which 2.7.3 is totally Leontief.

Theorem 2.7.2

Call the matrix associated with 2.7.4 and 2.7.5 A. A is totally Leontief if and only if there is no arc leading out of node k, there is a chain to node k from every other node, and there are no cycles.

Proof.

See Chapter 4.

From the graph in 2.7.6, remove arc (4.3) to get:

2.7.8

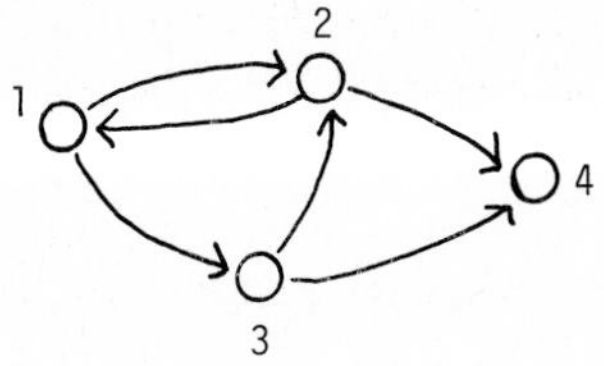

The corresponding constraint matrix is:

$$A = \begin{bmatrix} 1 & 1 & -1 & 0 & 0 & 0 \\ -1 & 0 & 1 & 1 & -1 & 0 \\ 0 & -1 & 0 & 0 & 1 & 1 \end{bmatrix}.$$

Let $x' = (0, 4, 0, 5, 0, 5)$. Then $Ax > 0$ and A is Leontief. Note though that in the graph of 2.7.8 there is a cycle {(1,3), (3,2), (2,1)} and, according to Theorem 2.7.2, A is not totally Leontief. (Note that {(1,2), (2,1)} is also a cycle.)

From graph 2.7.8 construct the following graph by removing arc (2,1). We get:

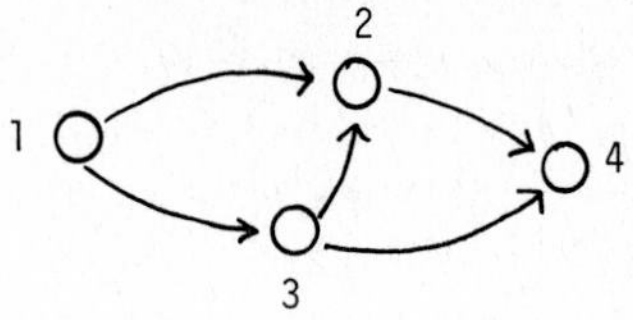

The corresponding constraint matrix is:

$$A = \begin{bmatrix} 1 & 1 & 0 & 0 & 0 \\ -1 & 0 & 1 & -1 & 0 \\ 0 & -1 & 0 & 1 & 1 \end{bmatrix}.$$

Let $x' = (0, 4, 5, 0, 5)$ and $y' = (3, 1, 2)$. Then $Ax > 0$ and $y'A > 0$ which implies that A is totally Leontief.

Veinott [124] goes the other way and constructs a graph from a transshipment matrix. A transshipment matrix, A, is a matrix having, at most, two non-zero elements per column, a + 1 and a - 1. These matrices are pre-Leontief. To associate A with a graph, append to A the row $-e'A$ and associate nodes with rows and arcs with columns. Let the appended row correspond to node k as in the above.

The interested reader is referred to [28, 47] for a detailed discussion of algorithms for the shortest path problem and other related network flow problems.

2.8 Extensions of Algorithm 1

Algorithm 1 has several advantages over the Revised Simplex procedure. The main advantage is that no basis inverse is required. Of course R_J^{-1} is required, but if R_J is chosen diagonal or triangular, then inversion is trivial. For large problems (i.e., problems having many rows) the (re)-inversion of the basis matrix and its maintenance (i.e., updating the current basis inverse to give the next basis inverse) are, perhaps, the most time consuming and expensive parts of the Revised Simplex procedure. Also, to maintain a basis inverse it is necessary to have storage available that is not required in Algorithm 1 (storage is required to maintain a basis inverse).

Another advantage of Algorithm 1 is that if a good guess of v* is available, then convergence is accelerated. The knowledge of a close dual solution vector does little to aid the solution progress of a linear program using the Revised Simplex procedure.

An apparent disadvantage of Algorithm 1 is that the procedure appears not to be finite. v* is a limit point of an infinite sequence. Nevertheless, Shapiro [111] and Grinold [51] give a turnpike theorem which demonstrates a particular type of finiteness for Algorithm 1. Let M^n be the set of all $J \varepsilon M$ that are candidates for the optimal basis at stage n of the iterative procedure in Step 1 of Algorithm 1.

Theorem 2.8.1

There exists an n* such that $M^n \subseteq M^\infty$ for all $n \geqq n^*$.

Proof.

Suppose the theorem is false. This implies that there is some $\bar{J} \varepsilon M^\infty$ and an infinite sequence $\{n_i\}_{i=1}^{\infty}$ such that

$$v^{n_i+1} = \underset{J \varepsilon M^{n_i}}{\text{Max}} \left[R_J^{-1} c_J + R_J^{-1} S_J v^{n_i} \right] = R_{\bar{J}}^{-1} c_{\bar{J}} + R_{\bar{J}}^{-1} S_{\bar{J}} v^{n_i}.$$

Taking the limit as $i \to \infty$ gives

$$v(\bar{J}^\infty) = v^*$$

or $\bar{J} \varepsilon M^\infty$, a contradiction.

Q.E.D.

The above theorem states that for an appropriate ε (i.e., an ε terminating Algorithm 1 with an $n \geqq n^*$), Algorithm 1 is finite. That is, we will terminate with an optimal basis J.

Let us now consider improving Algorithm 1. Step 1 of Algorithm 1 has an "expensive" step since it involves the search over all columns of A for a new $J = (j_1, j_2, \ldots, j_m)$. Denardo [24] and Porteus [103] suggested several modifications for improving Algorithm 1. Since the J solving Step 1 may be repeated for several iterations, it may be computationally "cheaper" to maintain a constant J for several iterations of the form given in Equation 2.2.6. Let $I+1 \geqq 0$ be the number of such iterations. Consider a new algorithm, Algorithm 2, incorporating this idea.

Algorithm 2

Step 0

Specify a starting vector v^0, a stopping solution tolerance $\varepsilon > 0$ and a cheap iteration count I. Let $n = 0$. Go to Step 2.

Step 1 (Cheap Iterations)

If $I + 1 = 0$, go to Step 2. Otherwise

$$v^{n+I+1} = (R_J^{-1} S_J)^{I+1} v^n + \sum_{\ell=0}^{I} (R_J^{-1} S_J)^{\ell} R_J^{-1} c_J.$$

Set n to n+I+1. Go to Step 2.

Step 2 (Basis Selection)

Solve

$$v^{n+1} = \underset{J \varepsilon M}{\text{Max}}\ R_J^{-1} S_J v^n + R_J^{-1} c_J .$$

Go to Step 3.

Step 3

If

$$|v^{n+1} - v^n| < \varepsilon e \quad \text{stop.}$$

Otherwise, increment n by 1 and to to Step 1.

At this point, it is worthwhile to compare the procedure of Algorithm 2 with the traditional Simplex method.

In Step 1, the system of equations

$$A_J'v = c_J$$

is partially solved using matrix iterative methods. Let the initial starting vector be v^n. Then

$$v^{n+1} = R_J^{-1}S_Jv^n + R_J^{-1}c_J$$

and, by repeated substitutions

$$v^{n+I+1} = (R_J^{-1}S_J)^{I+1}\ v^n + \sum_{\ell=0}^{I} (R_J^{-1}S_J)^{\ell}\ R_J^{-1}c_J.$$

When using the Simplex method, v is computed directly by finding $v = (A_J')^{-1}c_J$ using a fixed number of arithmetic operations. In the iterative framework, the extreme point is never computed exactly (at least not intentionally).

In Step 2 a search is undertaken to find an improved basis. There are two basic differences between the search in Step 2 of the iterative procedure and a traditional Phase 2 search in the Simplex method. The first difference is that the search is not necessarily initiated at an extreme point of the constraint set. This is true since v is only an approximation to the value $(A_J')^{-1}c_J$. The second difference is that the new basis is not necessarily associated with an extreme point which would be adjacent to the vertex associated with the current basis. In other words, the new and old J may differ by more than one component, which is equivalent to a block pivot.

To illustrate Algorithm 2, we again use the linear program given in Table 2.6.1. We will also use the Gauss-Seidel iterative procedure in Step 2.

Step 0

$v^{o'} = (0, 0, 0)$

$\varepsilon = 10^{-5}$

$I = 1$

$n = 0.$

Step 2

As before (see Table 2.6.3)

$$v^1 = \begin{bmatrix} 14.54545 \\ 74.43850 \\ 62.96603 \end{bmatrix}, \qquad J = (X_{11}, X_{22}, X_{32}),$$

n = 1.

Step 3

Go to Step 1.

Step 1

$$v_1^2 = \frac{1}{0.5500}\left[8.0000 + 0.2250(74.43850) + 0.2250(62.96603)\right] = 70.75640$$

$$v_2^2 = \frac{1}{0.2125}\left[15.0000 + 0.05625(70.75640) + 0.05625(62.96603)\right]$$

$$= 105.98535$$

$$v_3^2 = \frac{1}{0.8875}\left[4.0000 + 0.1125(70.75640) + 0.6750(105.98535)\right]$$

$$= 94.08474$$

and

$$v_1^3 = \frac{1}{0.5500}\left[8.0000 + 0.2250(105.98535) + 0.2250(94.08474)\right]$$

$$= 96.39231$$

$$v_2^3 = \frac{1}{0.2125}\left[15.0000 + 0.05625(96.39231) + 0.05625(94.08474)\right]$$

$$= 121.00863$$

$$v_3^3 = \frac{1}{0.8875}\left[4.0000 + 0.1125(96.39231) + 0.6750(121.00863)\right]$$

$$= 108.76052.$$

n = 3. Go to Step 2.

A summary of the Gauss-Seidel solution sequence for both I = 0 and I = 1 is given in Table 2.8.1.

Table 2.8.1

Algorithm 2 with Gauss-Seidel Iterations

I = 0

Iteration	v_1	v_2	v_3	J
1	14.54545	74.43850	62.96603	X_{11}, X_{22}, X_{32}
2	96.39231	121.00863	108.76052	X_{11}, X_{22}, X_{32}
5	121.25928	135.08636	122.61967	X_{12}, X_{22}, X_{32}
10	121.65310	135.30607	122.83670	X_{12}, X_{22}, X_{32}
13	121.65346	135.30627	122.83690	X_{12}, X_{22}, X_{32}

-STOP-

I = 1

Iteration	v_1	v_2	v_3	J
1	14.54545	74.43850	62.96603	X_{11}, X_{22}, X_{32}
2	108.91037	128.20700	115.82213	X_{12}, X_{22}, X_{32}
5	121.62969	135.29967	122.83038	X_{12}, X_{22}, X_{32}
9	121.65346	135.30627	122.83690	X_{12}, X_{22}, X_{32}

-STOP-

We now turn to another aspect of the iterative approach for solving totally Leontief Substitution Systems. The following theorem due to Hastings and Mello [56 , 57] is a generalization and improvement of a result initially given by MacQueen [87]. We give the result first in basis elimination form and then in column elimination form.

Suppose we can form vectors v^n and ℓ^n such that

$$u^n \geqq v^* \geqq \ell^n$$

with

$$u^n = v^n + b_1$$

$$\ell^n = v^n + b_2$$

Theorem 2.8.2

The basis $J \varepsilon M$ is sub-optimal if:

$$R_J^{-1}S_J\, v^n + R_J^{-1}c_J \leq v^n + b_2 - R_J^{-1}S_J b_1$$

Proof:

By the statement of the Theorem

$$R_J^{-1}S_J(v^n + b_1) + R_J^{-1}c_J \leq v^n + b_2$$

But

$$u^n = v^n + b_1$$

$$\ell^n = v^n + b_2$$

Hence:

$$R_J^{-1}S_J\, v^* + R_J^{-1}c_J \leq v^* .$$

Thus J is sub-optimal.

Q.E.D.

Corollary 2.8.2.1

Suppose each A_J' is split so that the dimensionality of $R_J^{-1}S_J$ and $R_J^{-1}c_J$ remains the same as A_J' and c_J†. If for $\bar{J} = (j_1, \ldots, j_m)$

$$e_i'(R_{\bar{J}}^{-1}S_{\bar{J}}\, v^n + R_{\bar{J}}^{-1}c_{\bar{J}}) < e_i'(v^n + b_2 - R_{\bar{J}}^{-1}S_{\bar{J}}\, b_1),$$

then $j_i \varepsilon M_i$ is a sub-optimal column. Here $\bar{J}$ is formed from J by replacing the ith component of J by some $j_i \varepsilon M_i$.

†Loosely speaking, Porteus [101] describes a process as preserving dimensionality if row i of $R_J^{-1}S_J$ and element i of $R_J^{-1}c_J$ depend only on j_i (for example, the split may be a Jacobi split) or if R_J is triangular and the multiplication by R_J^{-1} is carried out implicity as in the Gauss-Seidel iterative procedure.

The advantage of using sub-optimal column detection is the reduction in the problem size as the computational procedure progresses. With this reduction a decrease in the total computational effort per iteration is realized. Furthermore, the use of column elimination procedures allows one to solve a portion of a totally Leontief linear program (the largest portion that can be core-resident with at least one column from each M_i, $i = 1, \ldots, m$) reduce that portion, and then augment the reduced portion with more of the original problem. This approach permits the solution of very large problems. (See [38, 39] for a somewhat related issue of approximating larger problems by a sequence of smaller ones.)

Of course to use Theorem 2.3.2 or its corollary, we need to develop bounds on v^* at each iteration. Porteus [103] and Denardo [24] have developed bounds on v^* for certain cases. We give the results of Porteus [103]:

Lemma 2.8.3

If J satisfies

1. $0 \leqq \underline{\alpha}\, e \leqq R_J^{-1} S_J e \leqq \overline{\alpha} e$ and

2. $ae \leqq u - v \leqq be$, letting

$$\alpha \equiv \alpha(a) \equiv \begin{cases} \underline{\alpha} & \text{if } a \geqq 0 \\ \overline{\alpha} & \text{otherwise} \end{cases}$$

$$\beta \equiv \beta(b) \equiv \begin{cases} \overline{\alpha} & \text{if } b \geqq 0 \\ \underline{\alpha} & \text{otherwise,} \end{cases}$$

then

3. $a\alpha e \leqq R_J^{-1} S_J\, u - R_J^{-1} S_J\, v \leqq b\beta e.$

If (1) holds for all $J \in M$, then

4. $a\alpha e \leqq \mathscr{L}(u) - \mathscr{L}(v) \leqq b\beta e\,.$

Proof.

(1,2) $\Longrightarrow$ (3)

$$u - v \leqq be$$

then

$$R_J^{-1}S_J(u - v) \leqq bR_J^{-1}S_Je \leqq e\ \mathrm{Max}(b\underline{\alpha},\ b\overline{\alpha}) = b\beta e.$$

Similarly

$$v - u \leqq -ae$$

$$R_J^{-1}S_J(v - u) \leqq -aR_J^{-1}S_Je \leqq e\ \mathrm{Max}\ (-a\overline{\alpha},\ -a\underline{\alpha}) = -a\alpha e.$$

(1,2 for all $J \in M$) $\Rightarrow$ (4)

Let J_u be the $J \in M$ giving $\mathcal{L}(u) = R_{J_u}^{-1}S_{J_u}u + R_{J_u}^{-1}c_{J_u}$.

Then

$$u - v \leqq be$$

and

$$\mathcal{L}(u) - R_{J_u}^{-1}S_{J_u}v - R_{J_u}^{-1}c_{J_u} \leqq b\beta e$$

gives

$$\mathcal{L}(u) \leqq R_{J_u}^{-1}S_{J_u}v + R_{J_u}^{-1}c_{J_u} + b\beta e \leqq \mathcal{L}(v) + b\beta e$$

or

$$\mathcal{L}(u) - \mathcal{L}(v) \leqq b\beta e\ .$$

Similarly, let J_v be the $J \in M$ giving $\mathcal{L}(v) = R_{J_v}^{-1}S_{J_v}v + R_{J_v}^{-1}c_{J_v}$.

Then

$$a\alpha e \leqq R_{J_v}^{-1}S_{J_v}u + R_{J_v}^{-1}c_{J_v} - \mathcal{L}(v) \leqq \mathcal{L}(u) - \mathcal{L}(v)$$

Q.E.D.

Using the above lemma, we give bounds developed by Porteus [103] for a restrictive class of splits.

Theorem 2.8.3

If, given v^n,

1. $0 \leqq \underline{\alpha}e \leqq R_J^{-1}S_J e \leqq \overline{\alpha}e < e$ for all $J \varepsilon M$

2. $v^{n+1} = R_{\overline{J}}^{-1}S_{\overline{J}}\, v^n + R_{\overline{J}}^{-1}c_{\overline{J}} = \mathcal{L}(v^n)$

3. $\underline{\alpha}_{\overline{J}}\, e \leqq R_{\overline{J}}^{-1}S_{\overline{J}}\, e \leqq \overline{\alpha}_{\overline{J}}\, e$ and

4. $ae \leqq v^{n+1} - v^n \leqq be$, then, letting

$$\alpha \equiv \alpha(a, \overline{J}) \equiv \begin{cases} \underline{\alpha}_{\overline{J}} & \text{if } a \geqq 0 \\ \overline{\alpha}_{\overline{J}} & \text{otherwise} \end{cases}$$

$$\beta \equiv \beta(b, \overline{J}) \equiv \begin{cases} \overline{\alpha}_{\overline{J}} & \text{if } b \geqq 0 \\ \underline{\alpha}_{\overline{J}} & \text{otherwise} \end{cases}$$

we have

5. $v^n + \frac{a}{(1-\alpha)}\, e \leqq v^* \leqq v^n + \frac{b}{(1-\beta)}\, e$

6. $v^{n+1} + \frac{\alpha a}{(1-\alpha)}\, e \leqq v^* \leqq v^{n+1} + \frac{\beta b}{(1-\beta)}\, e.$

Proof.
(1-4) $\Rightarrow$ (5)

Given

$$ae \leqq \mathcal{L}(v^n) - v^n \leqq be$$

then, by Lemma 2.8.3, we have

$$\alpha ae \leqq \mathcal{L}^2(v^n) - \mathcal{L}(v^n) \leqq \beta be$$

or adding the above two inequalities

$$a(1 + \alpha)e \leqq \mathcal{L}^2(v^n) - v^n \leqq b(1 + \beta)e$$

Repeating gives for $\ell \geqq 1$

$$a\left(\sum_{j=1}^{\ell+1} \alpha^{j-1}\right)e \leqq \mathcal{L}^{\ell+1}(v^n) - v^n \leqq b\left(\sum_{j=1}^{\ell+1} \beta^{j-1}\right)e$$

or

$$\frac{a(1-\alpha^{\ell+1})}{(1-\alpha)} e \leqq \mathscr{L}^{\ell+1}(v^n) - v^n \leqq \frac{b(1-\beta^{\ell+1})e}{(1-\beta)} .$$

Taking the limit as $\ell \to \infty$ gives (note α, $\beta < 1$)

$$\frac{a}{(1-\alpha)} e \leqq v^* - v^n \leqq \frac{b}{(1-\beta)} e$$

(1-4) $\Longrightarrow$ (6)

Using the above results and Lemma 2.8.2, we have

$$\frac{\alpha a}{1-\alpha} e \leqq \mathscr{L}(v^*) - \mathscr{L}(v^n) \leqq \frac{\beta b}{1-\beta} e$$

Q.E.D.

Theorem 2.8.3 provides a method for computing bounds on v^* when $R_J^{-1}S_Je < e$ for all $J \varepsilon M$. To illustrate Corollary 2.8.2.1 and Theorem 2.8.3 consider solving the linear program given in Table 2.6.1 where $A_J' = I - S_J = R_J - S_J$. It is easily verified that $R_J^{-1}S_Je = 0.9e < e$ for all $J \varepsilon M$. (As a matter of fact, when $\alpha e = R_J^{-1}S_Je$ for all $J \varepsilon M$, then the results of Porteus [103] reduce to those given by MacQueen [86, 87].)

Example 2.8.1

From Table 2.6.2, we have

$$v^1 = \begin{bmatrix} 8.0000 \\ 16.0000 \\ 7.0000 \end{bmatrix}, \qquad \bar{J} = (X_{11}, X_{21}, X_{31}).$$

Thus $v^1 - v^0 = v^1 - 0 = v^1$ and

$$a = 7,$$
$$b = 16,$$

$$R_{\bar{J}}^{-1}S_{\bar{J}} = \begin{bmatrix} .450 & .225 & .225 \\ .450 & 0 & .450 \\ .225 & .225 & .450 \end{bmatrix},$$

$$R_{\bar{J}}^{-1}S_{\bar{J}}\, e = .9e = \underline{\alpha}e = \bar{\alpha}e.$$

Thus

$$\alpha = .9 \quad \text{and} \quad \beta = .9.$$

Using part (5) of Theorem 2.8.3, we have

$$u^o = v^o + \frac{b}{(1-\beta)} e = 0 + \frac{16}{(1-.9)} e = 160e$$

$$\ell^o = v^o + \frac{a}{(1-\alpha)} e = 0 + \frac{7}{(1-.9)} e = 70e.$$

From part (6) of Theorem 2.8.3, we have

$$u^1 = v^1 + \frac{\beta b}{1-\beta} e = \begin{bmatrix} 8.0000 \\ 16.0000 \\ 7.0000 \end{bmatrix} + \frac{.9}{0.1} 16e$$

$$= \begin{bmatrix} 152.0000 \\ 160.0000 \\ 151.0000 \end{bmatrix}$$

and

$$\ell^1 = v^1 + \frac{\alpha a}{1-\alpha} e = v^1 + .9 \begin{bmatrix} 70 \\ 70 \\ 70 \end{bmatrix} = \begin{bmatrix} 71.0000 \\ 79.0000 \\ 70.0000 \end{bmatrix}.$$

Using u^o and ℓ^o with Corollary 2.8.2.1, we have

X_{11}: .45(8.0000) + .2250(16.0000) + .2250(7.0000) + 8.0000
= 16.575,

8.0000 + 62.0000 - .450000(152.0000) - 0.2250(144.0000)
- 0.2250(153.0000)
= -65.225.

16.575 > -65.225. Hence X_{11} can not be said to be sub-optimal at this step.

Had the reverse inequality been realized, then we would replace M_1 by $\{X_{12}, X_{13}\}$ and $M^1 = M_1 \times M_2 \times M_3$. That is, X_{11} would have been removed from further consideration.

At this point we have both bases and column elimination procedures limited to the case where $R_J^{-1}S_Je < e$ for $J \varepsilon M$. Porteus [101] has recently given a procedure for transforming one iterative process into another so that the norm of the new process (i.e., the maximum norm of $R_J^{-1}S_J$ for all $J \varepsilon M$) is less than one. In addition he shows that a process having norm less than one can be transformed into one having equal row sums (i.e., $\overline{\alpha}_J = \underline{\alpha}_J < 1$ for all $J \varepsilon M$). Finally, Porteus has given a new method for computing bounds when all the row sums are equal and strictly less than one. This method requires more computational effort than those in Theorem 2.8.3, but gives tighter bounds, which, of course, is desirable.

We state now what we refer to as the composite algorithm. Let M^n be the set of bases that are still available for consideration at stage n of the iterative procedure.

Algorithm 3

Step 0 (Pre-Processing)

Transform the process, if desired, into an equivalent one having desired properties such as equal row sums, and so forth. Specify a starting vector, v^0, a solution tolerance $\varepsilon > 0$ and cheap iteration count I. Let $n = 0$ and $M^0 = M$. Go to Step 2.

Step 1 (Refinement - Cheap Iterations)

If $I + 1 \leqq 0$ go to Step 2. Otherwise

$$v^{n+I+1} = (R_J^{-1}S_J)^{I+1}\, v^n + \sum_{\ell=0}^{I} (R_J^{-1}S_J)^{\ell}\, R_J^{-1}c_J.$$

Set $M^{n+I+1} = M^n$, n to n+I+1, and go to Step 2.

Step 2 (Basis Selection)

Solve

$$v^{n+1} = \max_{J \varepsilon M^n} R_J^{-1}S_J\, v^n + R_J^{-1}c_J.$$

Go to Step 3.

Step 3 (Basis Elimination)

Form M^{n+1} using basis elimination procedures. If the cardinality of M^{n+1} is 1, go to Step 5. Otherwise, go to Step 4.

Step 4 (Termination)

If $|v^{n+1} - v^n| < \varepsilon e$ or $|u^n - \ell^n| < \varepsilon e$, go to Step 5. Otherwise, increment n by 1 and go to Step 1.

Step 5

Perform any post-optimal computations such as solving for v^* and the optimal primal values.

Remark:

Note that termination at Step 5 resulting from the test at Step 3 always gives the optimal solution basis while termination at Step 5 resulting from one of the tests at Step 4 only guarantees optimality if $n \geqq n^*$ (n^* is in reference to Theorem 2.8.1).

We give a comprehensive example of Algorithm 3 in Section 2.12. We note that there are still several extensions of Algorithm 3 that can be made. One suggestion is the extrapolation [101, 103] of bounds or v^n values. Also, one could use the bounds to form the v^0 vector and begin the iterative procedure over with a better initial guess.

Another consideration is the following. If the linear programming problem has a reducible structure determined by a method similar in nature to [131], then the problem can be solved by a sequence of smaller problems [17].

Consider the linear program

2.8.1
$$\begin{aligned} &\text{Max } c'x \\ &\text{Subject to} \\ &\quad Ax = b \\ &\quad x \geqq 0 \\ &\quad b \geqq 0 \end{aligned}$$

where A is totally Leontief but reducible. Using Definition 4.3.1, after possibly permuting rows and columns, Equation 2.8.1 may be rewritten as

2.8.2

$$\text{Max} \sum_{i=1}^{N} c_i' x_i$$

subject to

$$\begin{bmatrix} A_{11} & \cdots & A_{1N} \\ \vdots & & \vdots \\ A_{N1} & \cdots & A_{NN} \end{bmatrix} \begin{bmatrix} x_1 \\ \vdots \\ x_N \end{bmatrix} = \begin{bmatrix} b_1 \\ \vdots \\ b_N \end{bmatrix}$$

$$\begin{bmatrix} x_1 \\ \vdots \\ x_N \end{bmatrix} \geqq 0, \qquad \begin{bmatrix} b_1 \\ \vdots \\ b_N \end{bmatrix} \geqq 0,$$

where

$$A_{ij} = 0 \qquad \text{for } i > j,$$

and

$$A_{ij} \leqq 0 \qquad \text{for } j > i.$$

The above structure is referred to as a block upper triangular structure. The following theorem characterizes the matrix A.

Theorem 2.8.4

A, as given in Equation 2.8.2, is totally Leontief if and only if each diagonal block is totally Leontief.

Proof.

See Chapter 4.

Dantzig [16, 17] noted that Leontief models with substitution having the reducible or dynamic structure given in Equation 2.8.2 can be solved as a sequence of smaller Leontief linear programs.

Theorem 2.8.5

Consider the dual problem to that given in Equation 2.8.2. Then

$$\bar{v} = \begin{bmatrix} \bar{v}_1 \\ \cdot \\ \cdot \\ \cdot \\ \bar{v}_N \end{bmatrix}$$

solves (2.8.2) if and only if $\bar{v}_N$ solves

$$\text{Min } b_N' v_N \qquad \text{(subproblem N)}$$

subject to

$$A_{NN}' \; v_N \geqq c_N$$

and $\bar{v}_i$ for i = 1, ..., N-1 solves

$$\text{Min } b_i' \; v_i \qquad \text{(subproblem i)}$$

subject to

$$A_{ii}' \; v_i \geqq c_i - \sum_{j=i+1}^{N} A_{ij}' \; \bar{v}_j .$$

Proof.

See Chapter 4.

Theorem 2.8.5 states that one can first solve

$$\text{Min } b_N' \; v_N$$

subject to

$$A_{NN}' v_N \geqq c_N$$

and then solve

$$\text{Min } b_{N-1}' v_{N-1}$$

subject to

$$A_{N-1,N-1}' v_{N-1} \geqq c_{N-1} - A_{N-1,N}' \bar{v}_N .$$

This process would be continued until all blocks have been solved. That is, the results of solving the first linear program are used to price-out the variables in that block. The net effect is that a series of smaller problems may be solved. Hence, for each solution a savings is experienced in computational effort and storage requirements when compared to the requirements of the original problem.

We note that reducible Leontief structures are usually called dynamic (or recursive) Leontief Structures. Such structures arise when time is considered in a model or (in a non-dynamic sense) when processes are divided into stages. In the following section we elaborate on dynamic Leontief structures.

2.9 Dynamic Leontief Models

We now present some applications which give rise to dynamic Leontief Substitution Systems. Veinott [125] summarized many such applications. We will present a representative sample of such applications.

2.9.1 An Investment Selection Model [90]

Let K_t be the number of alternative investment projects available in period t (t = 1, ..., T). Assume that each investment opportunity available to the firm is deterministic and of the type known as "point input-stream output." That is, for each dollar invested in project type i during period t there is a cash throwoff of $a^i_{t\tau}$ dollars during period τ where $\tau > t$ and $a^i_{t\tau} \geqq 0$. This assumption implies for each investment opportunity j, that all investment expenditures are incurred at a single point in time t and that no costs or benefits occur prior to t, and finally, benefits are nonnegative during each period τ subsequent to t. The assumption excludes arbitrary time streams of costs, but allows for arbitrary time streams of net cash benefits. The following examples due to Manne [90] illustrate this assumption.

Example 2.9.1

For an investment opportunity of storing one dollar for one period in a bank that pays no interest, the stream of net cash benefits is:

$$a^j_{t,t+1} = 1.00, \text{ and } a^j_{t,t+2} = a^j_{t,t+3} = \ldots = a^j_{t,T} = 0.$$

Example 2.9.2

For an investment opportunity in an oil well being depleted at a constant factor α $(0 < \alpha < 1)$, the time stream of benefits is:

$$a^j_{t,\tau+1} = \alpha a^j_{t,\tau} \qquad \text{for } \tau = t, \ldots, T.$$

Example 2.9.3

For an investment opportunity in a "one-hoss shay" with an n-period service life, the benefit stream is:

$$a^j_{\tau,t+1} = a^j_{\tau,t+2} = \cdots = a^j_{\tau,t+n} > 0, \text{ and } a^j_{\tau,t+n+1} = \cdots = a^j_{\tau,T} = 0.$$

Let b_t denote the funds available from external sources (exogenous cash inflows) during period $t(t = 1,\ldots, T)$. We allow the possibility of cash withdrawals in any period t. For this purpose let w_t denote the number of dollars withdrawn in the form of dividends in period $t(t = 1, \ldots, T)$. Let x_{jt} denote the number of dollars invested in project j in period t, $j = 1, \ldots, k_t$ and $t = 1, \ldots, T$. Let u_t denote the marginal utility (as of time zero) per dollar of dividends to be withdrawn in period t where $u_t > 0$ for $t = 1, \ldots, T$.

The objective function is linear in the dividends to be withdrawn and is given by:†

$$\text{Maximize} \sum_{t=1}^{T} u_t w_t .$$

The firm is assumed to be self-financing with dividend and investment policies subject to the following cash balance identities:

number of dollars invested in new projects in period τ	+	number of dollars withdrawn in the form of dividends in period τ	=	exogenous cash inflows to be available during period τ	+	endogenous cash inflows to be available from investment to period τ
$\sum_{j=1}^{k_\tau} x_{j\tau}$	+	w_τ	=	b_τ	+	$\sum_{t=1}^{\tau-1} \sum_{j=1}^{k_\tau} a^j_{t\tau} x_{j\tau}$

$$(\tau = 1, \ldots, T)$$

with the following nonnegativity restrictions on the decision variables

$$x_{jt}, w_t \geqq 0.$$

†For a detailed discussion of this maximand see the footnote to page 121 of [90].

To show that the investment selection model is Leontief, let

$$w_t = x_{jt} \quad \text{for some } j, \text{ say } j = k_t+1 \text{ with}$$

$$a_{tt}^{k_t+1} = 1 \text{ for } t = 1, \ldots, T \text{ and}$$

$$a_{t\tau}^{k_t+1} = 0 \text{ for } t = 1, \ldots, T-1 \text{ and}$$

$$\tau = t+1, \ldots, T.$$

Let

x_t = (k_t+1)-vector of the amounts invested in the k_t securities and the amount $w_t = x_{k_t+1}$ withdrawn in period t for $t = 1,\ldots,T$.

Let A_{tt} be a (k_t+1)-vector of ones for $t = 1, \ldots, T$ and for $t < \tau$, let

$$A_{\tau t} = (a_{t\tau}^{1}, \ldots, a_{t\tau}^{k_t+1}).$$

For $t > \tau$ let $A_{\tau t}$ be a (k_t+1)-vector of zeroes. Finally, let

$$x = (x_1, \ldots, x_T), \qquad u = (u_1, \ldots, u_T), \text{ and}$$

$$A = \begin{bmatrix} A_{11} & & & \\ -A_{21} & A_{22} & & 0 \\ \vdots & & \ddots & \\ -A_{T1} & -A_{T2} & \cdots & A_{TT} \end{bmatrix}.$$

Then the investment selection model can be expressed as

$$\text{Maximize} \sum_{t=1}^{T} u_t \, x_{k_t+1}$$

subject to

$$Ax = b$$
$$x \geqq 0$$

where the matrix A is block triangular and Leontief and each diagonal block is (totally) Leontief.

Manne [90] proves the following "All-or-None" property of the optimal solution to the preceding budgeting model.

> If there exists an optimal solution to the capital budgeting model described above, then there exists an optimal solution in which
>
> $$(w_t)\left(\sum_{j=1}^{k_t} x_{jt}\right) = (x_{k_t+1})\left(\sum_{j=1}^{k_t} x_{jt}\right) = 0$$
>
> for $t = 1, \ldots, T$.

2.9.2 Multi-Facility Economic-Lot-Size Model [125,135]

A straightforward generalization of the economic-lot-size model (see Section 2.11) is the multi-facility version. "A facility is a marketing or production activity that stores or produces a single item" [125]. An item might be a physical good differentiated within its own classification by time or location. We consider a setting having N facilities and n time periods.

Let a_{ij}^{st} be the known and fixed amount of stock from facility s in period i needed to produce one unit at facility t in period j. We assume that $a_{ij}^{st} \geqq 0$ for all s,t (= 1, ..., N) and i,j (= 1, ..., n) and that $a_{ii}^{ss} < 1$ for i = 1, ..., n and s = 1, ..., N. Finally, to prevent current production from requiring inputs form future time periods we require that $a_{ij}^{st} = 0$ for $i > j$ (= 1, ..., n) with s = 1, ..., N.

Let x_i^s, y_i^s, and r_i^s be, respectively, the production, end-of-period inventory, and known nonnegative demand at facility s (= 1, ..., N) in period i (= 1, ..., n). Let $A_{ij} = (a_{ij}^{st})$ be the matrix of requirements at the N facilities in period i to produce one unit at the N facilities in period j. Let $x_i = (x_i^s)$, $y_i = (y_i^s)$ and $r_i = (r_i^s)$.

The balance equations in matrix form are:

2.9.1

$$Az = \begin{bmatrix} I-A_{11} & -I & -A_{12} & 0 & -A_{13} & \cdots & -A_{1n} \\ 0 & I & I-A_{22} & -I & -A_{23} & \cdots & -A_{2n} \\ 0 & 0 & 0 & I & I-A_{33} & \cdots & -A_{3n} \\ \cdot & \cdot & \cdot & \cdot & \cdot & & \cdot \\ \cdot & \cdot & \cdot & \cdot & \cdot & & \cdot \\ \cdot & \cdot & \cdot & \cdot & \cdot & & \cdot \\ 0 & 0 & 0 & 0 & 0 & \cdots & I-A_{nn} \end{bmatrix} \begin{bmatrix} x_1 \\ y_1 \\ x_2 \\ y_2 \\ x_3 \\ y_3 \\ \vdots \\ x_n \end{bmatrix} = \begin{bmatrix} r_1 \\ r_2 \\ r_3 \\ \cdot \\ \cdot \\ \cdot \\ r_n \end{bmatrix}$$

In 2.9.1 each column has exactly one positive element (recall $a_{ii}^{ss} < 1$). Let

$$y_i = e \qquad i = 1, \ldots, n-1.$$

If

$$(I-A_{11})x_1 = e$$
$$x_1 \geqq 0$$

has a solution, then the constraint matrix in Equation (2.9.1) is Leontief since, setting $x_i = 0$ for $i = 2, \ldots, n$, would give us $z \geqq 0$ and $Az > 0$. Notice that under these conditions, each block diagonal matrix is Leontief (although possibly not totally Leontief) and that A is upper block triangular.

The above model can be extended to include inventory shrinkage (that is, partial shrinkage) and backlogging of unsatisfied demand in much the same manner as will be discussed under the economic-lot-size model [see Section 2.11].

An application of the above model is the arborescence multi-echelon model [125]. Let $a_{ii}^{st} = 1$ if facility s supplies facility t in period i (= 1, ..., n). Otherwise let $a_{ii}^{st} = 0$. In the arborescence model, there is, at most, one (predecessor) supplier for each facility. We assume that there are no time lags in shipments.

For example, consider the following distribution system:

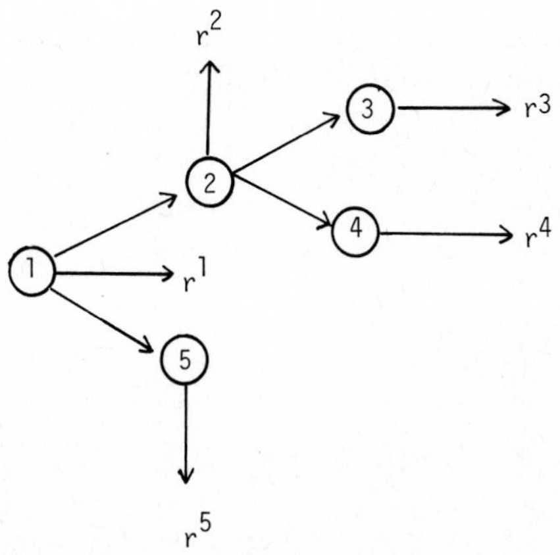

The resulting balance equations for a two period problem are:

$$Az = \begin{bmatrix} 1 & -1 & 0 & 0 & -1 & -1 & 0 & 0 & 0 & 0 & 0 & 0 & 0 & 0 & 0 \\ 0 & 1 & -1 & -1 & 0 & 0 & -1 & 0 & 0 & 0 & 0 & 0 & 0 & 0 & 0 \\ 0 & 0 & 1 & 0 & 0 & 0 & 0 & -1 & 0 & 0 & 0 & 0 & 0 & 0 & 0 \\ 0 & 0 & 0 & 1 & 0 & 0 & 0 & 0 & -1 & 0 & 0 & 0 & 0 & 0 & 0 \\ 0 & 0 & 0 & 0 & 1 & 0 & 0 & 0 & 0 & -1 & 0 & 0 & 0 & 0 & 0 \\ 0 & 0 & 0 & 0 & 0 & 1 & 0 & 0 & 0 & 0 & 1 & -1 & 0 & 0 & -1 \\ 0 & 0 & 0 & 0 & 0 & 0 & 1 & 0 & 0 & 0 & 0 & 1 & -1 & -1 & 0 \\ 0 & 0 & 0 & 0 & 0 & 0 & 0 & 1 & 0 & 0 & 0 & 0 & 1 & 0 & 0 \\ 0 & 0 & 0 & 0 & 0 & 0 & 0 & 0 & 1 & 0 & 0 & 0 & 0 & 1 & 0 \\ 0 & 0 & 0 & 0 & 0 & 0 & 0 & 0 & 0 & 1 & 0 & 0 & 0 & 0 & 1 \end{bmatrix} \begin{bmatrix} x_1^1 \\ x_1^2 \\ x_1^3 \\ x_1^4 \\ x_1^5 \\ y_1^1 \\ y_1^2 \\ y_1^3 \\ y_1^4 \\ y_1^5 \\ x_2^1 \\ x_2^2 \\ x_2^3 \\ x_2^4 \\ x_2^5 \end{bmatrix} = \begin{bmatrix} r_1^1 \\ r_1^2 \\ r_1^3 \\ r_1^4 \\ r_1^5 \\ r_2^1 \\ r_2^2 \\ r_2^3 \\ r_2^4 \\ r_2^5 \end{bmatrix}.$$

"A facility s is called a wholesale facility if $r_i^s = 0$ for every i and is called a retail (outlet) facility otherwise" [12]. In the above, it is readily determined that A is dynamic and totally Leontief.

2.10 Optimization Over Leontief Substitution Systems

In Section 2.6 we demonstrated that totally Leontief problems could be solved by an iterative procedure. In essence we had converted a linear program into an equivalent transient Markov decision process. In so doing we required that $M = N$, that is, the set of all class Z matrices formed from the constraint matrix were also class K matrices.

In general, a Leontief matrix satisfies

1. $M \subseteq N$

2. At least one $J \in N$ gives $A_J \in K$.

Since $M \neq N$, in general, we might suspect that the results of Section 2.6 would not apply to the general Leontief Substitution system. This, unfortunately, is the case.

For example, consider the following Leontief Substitution problem:

$$\text{Max} \quad 2x_1 + 3x_2 - 6x_3 - 3x_4 - x_5$$

subject to

$$x_1 + x_2 - 2x_3 - x_4 = 6$$

$$-2x_1 - x_2 + x_3 + x_4 + x_5 = 5$$

$$x_i \geqq 0 \qquad i = 1, \ldots, 5.$$

For the above problem

$$N_1 = \{1,2\}, \qquad N_2 = \{3,4,5\},$$

$$N = \{(1,3), (1,4), (1,5), (2,3), (2,4), (2.5)\}.$$

It is readily verified that

$$M = \{(1,5), (2,5)\}.$$

The optimal solution is

$$x_2 = 6,$$

$$x_5 = 11 \qquad \text{with} \qquad J^* = (2,5)$$

Suppose we tried to use Algorithm 1 to solve this problem with an initial guess of $v^{0'} = (0,0)$. The sequence of solution vectors would be

2.10.1 $$\overset{v^0}{\begin{bmatrix}0\\0\end{bmatrix}}, \quad \overset{v^1}{\begin{bmatrix}3\\-1\end{bmatrix}}, \quad \overset{v^2}{\begin{bmatrix}2\\-1\end{bmatrix}}, \quad \overset{v^3}{\begin{bmatrix}2\\-1\end{bmatrix}}, \quad \text{STOP} \quad J^* = (2,5)$$

If the initial guess were $v^{0'} = (0,3)$ we would obtain

$$\overset{v^0}{\begin{bmatrix}0\\3\end{bmatrix}}, \quad \overset{v^1}{\begin{bmatrix}8\\-1\end{bmatrix}}, \quad \overset{v^2}{\begin{bmatrix}2\\10\end{bmatrix}}, \quad \overset{v^3}{\begin{bmatrix}22\\-1\end{bmatrix}}, \quad \overset{v^4}{\begin{bmatrix}2\\38\end{bmatrix}}, \quad \text{no convergence.}$$

The above illustrates that, in general, iterative methods for the Leontief case appear to have convergence dependent on the initial guess.

Another problem with Leontief Substitution Systems is that they are not totally bounded (except when $M = N$ which is the Totally Leontief case). Hence, although a Leontief Substitution System always has a feasible solution, it may not have a bounded optimum.

The following theorem provides a sufficient condition under which iterative methods will solve the general Leontief problem. The condition is easily satisfied in a computational setting.

<u>Theorem 2.10.1</u>

Suppose a given Leontief Substitution System has a bounded optimal solution. Let v^* be the optimal solution vector to the dual problem. If $v^0 \leqq v^*$ then

$$\lim_{n\to\infty} \mathcal{L}(\mathcal{J}^n(v^0)) \to v^*.$$

Proof.

See Chapter 4.

We again note that $v^0 \leqq v^*$ is not a necessary condition for convergence. In Example 2.10.1 the vector $v^{0'} = (0,0)$ does not satisfy $v^0 \leqq v^*$ but did converge to v^*.

We can modify Algorithm 3 to solve the general Leontief problem by restricting suboptimality tests and cheap iterations to J for $J \in M$. Also, at the end of the process we must determine which $J \in N^\infty$ gives $A_J' \in K$.

There appears to be no easy procedure for determining whether a given Leontief Substitution System has an unbounded optimal solution.

2.11 Some Leontief Substitution Systems

A few Leontief models are given below. Again, most of these were summarized in [125]. Some related models can be found in [79, 129].

2.11.1 Single-Product Economic-Lot-Size Models

The investment selection model (of Section 2.9) is a special case of a more general problem [125]. Let $r_1, \ldots, r_n$ be the known non-negative requirements for a single product in periods 1, ..., n. Let x_i be the amount produced in period i. Denote by y_i and w_i, respectively, the amounts of inventory on hand and backlogged demand at the end of period i. Let $\alpha_i > 0$ be the amount of stock generated in period i+1 from one unit stored in period i. Let $\beta_i \geqq 0$ be the amount of backlogged demand generated in period i+1 from one unit backlogged in period i. Material balance is dictated by

2.11.1 $$x_i + \alpha_{i-1}y_{i-1} + w_i - y_i - \beta_{i-1}w_{i-1} = r_i \qquad i = 1, \ldots, n$$

where $y_0 = w_0 = y_n = w_n = 0$. For example, let n = 3 and consider the following constraint set.

$$Az = \begin{bmatrix} 1 & 1 & -1 & 0 & 0 & 0 & 0 \\ 0 & -\beta_1 & \alpha_1 & 1 & 1 & -1 & 0 \\ 0 & 0 & 0 & 0 & -\beta_2 & \alpha_2 & 1 \end{bmatrix} \begin{bmatrix} x_1 \\ w_1 \\ y_1 \\ x_2 \\ w_2 \\ y_2 \\ x_3 \end{bmatrix} = \begin{bmatrix} r_1 \\ r_2 \\ r_3 \end{bmatrix}.$$

Notice that A has exactly one positive element per column. Let each x_i, i = 1, ..., n component of z be positive and all other elements zero. Then Az > 0. Hence A is Leontief.

Veinott [125] lists several alternative interpretations of the single-product economic-lot-size model. Some are:

1. Reservoir Control

Let:

r_i = amount of (known) inflows of water in period i (i = 1, ..., n)

x_i = amount of water withdrawals from the reservoir at the end of period i (i = 1, ..., n)

w_i = amount of water in the reservoir at the end of period i (i = 1, ..., n)

y_i = amount of water that must be borrowed from external sources in period i (i = 1, ..., n).

2. Batch Queueing [128]

Let:

r_i = amount of (known) service required in period i (i = 1, ..., n)

x_i = amount of service provided in period i (i = 1, ..., n)

y_i = amount of future service completed by period i (i = 1, ..., n)

w_i = amount of accumulated requirements for service in period i (i = 1, ..., n).

3. Product Assortment

Let

r_i = product requirement for product i (i = 1, ..., n)

x_i = amount of product i produced for i = 1, ..., n where inventories of product i may be used to satisfy requirements for any product $j \geqq i$

y_i = amount by which production of products 1, ..., i exceeds the requirements for those products

w_i = amount by which products 1, ..., i fall short of the requirements for those products.

2.11.2 Single-Product Warehousing Model [12, 125, 128]

Suppose that there is a given upper bound on the amount of inventory capacity in each period. Let this be represented by w_i. As a variation of the economic-lot-size problem, we might consider the determination of production, inventory and sales (here r_i is a decision variable) in each period subject to the known limit of storage availability. Assume that there is no backlogging or inventory shrinkage.

Let ordering preceed selling in each period. Balance equations for each period are:

2.11.2 $$x_i + y_{i-1} - y_i = r_i \qquad i = 1, \ldots, n$$

with

$$r_0 = y_0 = 0.$$

Let u_i be the excess warehouse capacity in period i after ordering but before selling. Then the capacity constraints on storage are:

2.11.3 $$x_i + y_{i-1} + u_i = w_i \qquad i = 1, \ldots, n.$$

Consider as an example, a three period problem:

$$\begin{bmatrix} 1 & -1 & -1 & 0 & 0 & 0 & 0 & 0 & 0 & 0 & 0 \\ 0 & 0 & 1 & 1 & -1 & -1 & 0 & 0 & 0 & 0 & 0 \\ 0 & 0 & 0 & 0 & 0 & 1 & 1 & -1 & 0 & 0 & 0 \\ 1 & 0 & 0 & 0 & 0 & 0 & 0 & 0 & 1 & 0 & 0 \\ 0 & 0 & 1 & 1 & 0 & 0 & 0 & 0 & 0 & 1 & 0 \\ 0 & 0 & 0 & 0 & 0 & 1 & 1 & 0 & 0 & 0 & 1 \end{bmatrix} \begin{bmatrix} x_1 \\ r_1 \\ y_1 \\ x_2 \\ r_2 \\ y_2 \\ x_3 \\ r_3 \\ u_1 \\ u_2 \\ u_3 \end{bmatrix} = \begin{bmatrix} 0 \\ 0 \\ 0 \\ w_1 \\ w_2 \\ w_3 \end{bmatrix}.$$

The above problem does not have a Leontief constraint matrix since some columns have no positive element (r_i's) while others have two positive elements (x_i's, y_i's). However, this problem is (hidden) Leontief and can be converted to a Leontief problem by elementary operations. Perform the following operations on Equation (2.11.2) and (2.11.3):

1. For each i = 2, ..., n, replace Equation (2.11.3) by

$$(x_i+y_{i-1}+u_i) - (x_{i-1}+y_{i-2}+u_{i-1}) + (x_{i-1}+y_{i-2}-y_{i-1}-r_{i-1}) = w_i - w_{i-1}$$

2. For i = 1, ..., n, replace each Equation (2.11.2) by its negative.

Under the above transformation, the three period example becomes:

$$Az = \begin{bmatrix} -1 & 1 & 1 & 0 & 0 & 0 & 0 & 0 & 0 & 0 & 0 \\ 0 & 0 & -1 & -1 & 1 & 1 & 0 & 0 & 0 & 0 & 0 \\ 0 & 0 & 0 & 0 & 0 & -1 & -1 & 1 & 0 & 0 & 0 \\ 1 & 0 & 0 & 0 & 0 & 0 & 0 & 0 & 1 & 0 & 0 \\ 0 & -1 & 0 & 1 & 0 & 0 & 0 & 0 & -1 & 1 & 0 \\ 0 & 0 & 0 & 0 & 0 & 0 & 1 & 0 & 0 & -1 & 1 \end{bmatrix} \begin{bmatrix} x_1 \\ r_1 \\ y_1 \\ x_2 \\ r_2 \\ y_2 \\ x_3 \\ r_3 \\ u_1 \\ u_2 \\ u_3 \end{bmatrix} = \begin{bmatrix} 0 \\ 0 \\ 0 \\ w_1 \\ w_2-w_1 \\ w_3-w_2 \end{bmatrix} = b.$$

The matrix A is readily determined to be Leontief. The system $Az = b$, $z \geqq 0$ is a Leontief Substitution System if b is non-negative.

As a closing statement, it is possible to combine the multi-facility lot-size model and the warehouse model into a single model [125].

2.11.3 General Comments

In many applications the difference between a pre-Leontief, Leontief, or totally Leontief Substitution System is reflected in the degree of impositions placed upon the system. For example, consider the economic lot-size-model. In that model inventory shrinkage parameters $\alpha_i > 0$ and backlog shrinkage parameters $\beta_i \geqq 0$ were defined and used in balancing equations of the form

$$x_i + \alpha_{i-1}y_{i-1} - y_i - \beta_{i-1}w_{i-1} + w_i = r_i \qquad i = 1, \ldots, n.$$

Consider a three period problem. The constraint set takes the form:

$$Az = \begin{bmatrix} 1 & -1 & 1 & 0 & 0 & 0 & 0 \\ 0 & \alpha_1 & -\beta_1 & 1 & -1 & 1 & 0 \\ 0 & 0 & 0 & 0 & \alpha_2 & -\beta_2 & 1 \end{bmatrix} \begin{bmatrix} x_1 \\ y_1 \\ w_1 \\ x_2 \\ y_2 \\ w_2 \\ x_3 \end{bmatrix} = \begin{bmatrix} r_1 \\ r_2 \\ r_3 \end{bmatrix}$$

$$z \geqq 0.$$

If we relaxed the condition $\alpha_i > 0$ to $\alpha_i \geqq 0$, then A is pre-Leontief. Requiring each $\alpha_i > 0$ gives that A is Leontief [see Section 2.11.1]. To give A totally Leontief requires that

$$\alpha_1 - \beta_1 > 0$$

$$\alpha_2 - \beta_2 > 0.$$

Thus, the imposition of conditions in a model can affect the degree of the system (i.e., pre-Leontief, Leontief or totally Leontief). (Of course, these same ideas can be applied to the general m-period economic lot size problem, resulting in several possible classifications of the problem.)

2.12 Illustration of the Composite Algorithm

To illustrate the composite algorithm (Algorithm 3) given in Section 2.8, a detailed example is now presented. It should be noted though that the efficiency of the iterative algorithm over any form of the Simplex procedure will usually hold only for large problems. Thus, the following example should be considered for illustrative purposes and not as a demonstration of computational superiority.

Consider the iterative procedure given in Theorem 2.4.3 where

$$v^{n+1} = (I - Q)^{-1}(P_J - Q)v^n + (I - Q)^{-1}c_J \quad \text{for} \quad J \in M$$

and

$$P_J \geqq Q \quad \text{for all } J \in M.$$

We choose Q diagonal to simplify inversion of I - Q.

To illustrate the algorithm, consider the following contrived totally Leontief problems.

Max	x_{11}	x_{12}	x_{13}	x_{21}	x_{22}	x_{23}	x_{31}	x_{32}	x_{33}	b
Objective	1.31	2.62	1.79	2.14	2.19	3.06	2.14	0.98	1.06	
Subject to	.87	.54	.79	-.30	-.26	-.15	-.30	-.13	-.29	1.41
	-.41	-.13	-.31	.74	.70	.90	-.20	-.30	-.28	2.63
	-.33	-.37	-.22	-.20	-.30	-.40	.67	.77	.71	1.51

$$x_{ij} \geqq 0, \qquad i,j = 1,2,3.$$

Step 0

Compute Q and specify v^0, I, ε, n, and M^0.

(a) Q Determination

Let

$$q_{ij} = \begin{cases} 0 & i \neq j \\ \min_{J \in M} (P_J)_{ii} & i = j. \end{cases}$$

Then

$$q_{11} = \text{Min}\ \{0.13,\ 0.46,\ 0.21\} = 0.13,$$

$$q_{22} = \text{Min}\ \{0.26,\ 0.30,\ 0.10\} = 0.10,$$

$$q_{33} = \text{Min}\ \{0.33,\ 0.23,\ 0.29\} = 0.23.$$

Thus

$$Q = \begin{bmatrix} 0.13 & 0 & 0 \\ 0 & 0.10 & 0 \\ 0 & 0 & 0.23 \end{bmatrix}.$$

(b) Parameters

Let

$$v^o = 0$$

$$I = 1$$

$$\varepsilon = 10^{-5}$$

$$n = 0.$$

Since the system is totally Leontief, we have

$$M^o = M = \{x_{11}, x_{12}, x_{13}\} \times \{x_{21}, x_{22}, x_{23}\} \times \{x_{31}, x_{32}, x_{33}\}.$$

Go to Step 2 and begin iteration 1.

Step 2

Solve

$$v^1 = \underset{J \varepsilon M^o}{\text{Max}}\ (I - Q)^{-1}[(P_J - Q)v^o + c_J].$$

$$v_1^1 = \text{Max} \begin{cases} \frac{1}{0.87}(1.31) = 1.50575 \\ \frac{1}{0.87}(2.62) = 3.01149 \\ \frac{1}{0.87}(1.79) = 2.05747 \end{cases}$$

$$v_2^1 = \text{Max} \begin{cases} \frac{1}{0.90}(2.14) = 2.37778 \\ \frac{1}{0.90}(2.19) = 2.43333 \\ \frac{1}{0.90}(3.06) = 3.40000 \end{cases}$$

$$v_3^1 = \text{Max} \begin{cases} \frac{1}{0.77}(2.14) = 2.77922 \\ \frac{1}{0.77}(0.98) = 1.27273 \\ \frac{1}{0.77}(1.06) = 1.37662 \end{cases}$$

$$v^1 = \begin{bmatrix} 3.01149 \\ 3.40000 \\ 2.77922 \end{bmatrix} \quad \text{with} \quad J = (x_{12}, x_{23}, x_{31}).$$

Step 3

We use the bounds given in Theorem 2.8.3 part 5 and the suboptimal column elimination procedure of Corollary 2.8.2.1. It is readily determined that the mimimum row sum $\underline{\alpha}$ is 0.55844 and that the maximum row sum $\overline{\alpha}$ is 0.95402.

Also

$$v^1 - v^o = \begin{bmatrix} 3.01149 \\ 3.40000 \\ 2.77922 \end{bmatrix}.$$

Thus

$$a = 2.77922$$

$$b = 3.40000$$

$$\underline{\alpha} = 0.55844$$

$$\overline{\alpha} = 0.95402$$

$$\alpha = 0.55844$$

$$\beta = 0.95402.$$

The sub-optimality tests are of the form:

$$\text{If} \quad t_1 = e_i' \left([I - Q]^{-1}([P_{J(x_{ij})} - Q]\, v^n + c_{J(x_{ij})})\right) <$$

$$e_i' \left(v^n + \frac{a}{1-\alpha} e - [I - Q]^{-1}(P_{J(x_{ij})} - Q) \frac{b}{1-\beta} e\right) = t_2$$

then x_{ij} is sub-optimal. Here $J(x_{ij})$ is equal to J with the ith position of J replaced by x_{ij}. The resulting test values are:

Column	t_1	t_2	Decision
x_{11}	1.50575	133.07686	sub-optimal
x_{12}	3.01149	-51.23142	
x_{13}	2.05750	87.56917	sub-optimal
x_{21}	2.37778	-149.82252	
x_{22}	2.43333	-179.40252	
x_{23}	3.40000	-31.50252	
x_{31}	2.77922	-34.32074	
x_{32}	1.27273	-2.16856	
x_{33}	1.37662	-21.45987	

Thus

$$M^1 = \{x_{12}\} \text{ X } \{x_{21}, x_{22}, x_{23}\} \text{ X } \{x_{31}, x_{32}, x_{33}\}.$$

Since $|M^1| = 9 \neq 1$, go to Step 4.

<u>Step 4</u>

$$|v' - v^o| = \begin{bmatrix} 3.01149 \\ 3.40000 \\ 2.77922 \end{bmatrix} > 10^{-5}e. \quad \text{Go to Step 1.}$$

<u>Step 1</u>

Begin Iteration 2.

Here we solve

$$v^2 = (I - Q)^{-1}[(P_J - Q)v^1 + c_J]$$

$$v^3 = (I - Q)^{-1}[(P_J - Q)v^2 + c_J]$$

$$v_1^2 = \frac{1}{0.87}(2.62 + 0.33(3.01149) + 0.13(3.40000) + 0.37(2.77922))$$

$$v_2^2 = \frac{1}{0.90}(3.06 + 0.15(3.01149) + 0.0(3.40000) + 0.40(2.77922))$$

$$v_3^2 = \frac{1}{0.77}(2.14 + 0.30(3.01149) + 0.20(3.40000) + 0.10(2.77922))$$

or

$$v^2 = \begin{bmatrix} 5.84380 \\ 5.13713 \\ 5.19658 \end{bmatrix}.$$

Likewise

$$v^3 = \begin{bmatrix} 8.20577 \\ 6.68356 \\ 7.06522 \end{bmatrix}.$$

<u>Step 2</u>

$$v_1^4 = \frac{1}{0.87}(2.62 + 0.33(8.20577) + 0.13(6.68356) + 0.37(3.06522)) = 10.12747$$

$$v_2^4 = \text{Max}\begin{cases} \frac{1}{0.90}(2.14 + 0.30(8.20577) + 0.16(6.68356) + 0.20(3.06522)) = 7.87127 \\ \frac{1}{0.90}(2.19 + 0.26(8.20577) + 0.20(6.68256) + 0.30(3.06522)) = 8.64420 \\ \frac{1}{0.90}(3.06 + 0.15(8.20577) + 0.0(6.68356) + 0.40(3.06522)) = 7.90773 \end{cases}$$

$$= \quad 8.64420$$

$$v_3^4 = \text{Max}\begin{cases} \frac{1}{0.77}\,(2.14 + 0.30(8.20577) + 0.20(6.68356) + 0.10(3.06522)) \\ \qquad = 8.62982 \\ \frac{1}{0.77}\,(0.98 + 0.13(8.20577) + 0.30(6.68356) + 0.0(3.06522)) \\ \qquad = 5.26210 \\ \frac{1}{0.77}\,(1.06 + 0.29(8.20577) + 0.28(6.68356) + 0.06(3.06522)) \\ \qquad = 7.44803 \end{cases}$$

$$= \quad 8.62982.$$

That is

$$v^4 = \begin{bmatrix} 10.12747 \\ 8.64420 \\ 8.62982 \end{bmatrix}, \qquad J = (x_{12}, x_{22}, x_{31}).$$

Step 3

$$v^4 - v^3 = \begin{bmatrix} 1.92170 \\ 1.96064 \\ 1.56460 \end{bmatrix}.$$

Thus

$$\begin{aligned} a &= 1.56460 \\ b &= 1.96064 \\ \underline{\alpha} &= 0.55844 \\ \overline{\alpha} &= 0.94502 \\ \alpha &= 0.55844 \\ \beta &= 0.94502 \end{aligned}$$

and we get

Column	t_1	t_2	Decision
x_{12}	10.12747	-15.23397	
x_{21}	7.87127	-5.16744	
x_{22}	8.64420	-22.22499	
x_{23}	7.90773	63.06278	sub-optimal
x_{31}	8.62982	-13.51783	
x_{32}	5.26210	5.02259	sub-optimal
x_{33}	7.44803	-6.10190	

Thus

$$M^4 = \{x_{12}\} \times \{x_{21}, x_{22}\} \times \{x_{31}, x_{33}\}.$$

Again, $|M^4| \neq 1$ and we go to Step 4.

Step 4

$|v^4 - v^3| > 10^{-5}e$, thus go to Step 1.

A summary of the solution of this problem is given below:

Iteration	v_1	v_2	v_3	$\lvert M^n \rvert$	J
1	3.01149	3.40000	2.77922	9	(x_{12},x_{23},x_{31})
2	10.12747	8.64420	8.62982	6	(x_{12},x_{22},x_{31})
3	14.58955	12.60143	12.41193	4	(x_{12},x_{22},x_{31})
6	20.67580	17.96225	17.51423	2	(x_{12},x_{22},x_{31})
9	22.36883	19.45348	18.93362	1	(x_{12},x_{22},x_{31})

STOP

We now need to compute the solution

$$\begin{bmatrix} 0.54 & -0.26 & -0.30 \\ -0.13 & 0.70 & -0.20 \\ -0.37 & -0.30 & 0.67 \end{bmatrix} \begin{bmatrix} x_{12} \\ x_{22} \\ x_{31} \end{bmatrix} = \begin{bmatrix} 1.41 \\ 2.63 \\ 1.51 \end{bmatrix}$$

to complete the solution.

We again point out that the above illustration employed a straightforward split of A'_J and a simple sub-optimality test. To achieve a faster convergent sequence we could use faster convergent splits such as the split of Theorem 2.4.3 with a Gauss-Seidel iteration. The complexity in this increases slightly but the bounds of Theorem 2.8.3 are not applicable. We then have to use more complicated procedures for bounds as cited in Section 2.8.

CHAPTER 3

Extensions of Leontief Models

In this chapter we look at various extensions of the Leontief model. For example, we consider problems that do not have a Leontief Substitution System for a constraint set but which are Leontief to within a nonsingular transformation. We also consider integrality constraints, and non-linear objective functions. Applications of the various extensions are presented.

3.1 Hidden Leontief Substitution Systems

Saigal [109] presented a generalization of Leontief Substitution Systems that characterize constraint sets that do not appear to be Leontief Substitution Systems but can be shown to be equivalent to Leontief Substitution Systems. The following property of a Leontief matrix is fundamental.

Theorem 3.1.1

If A is Leontief, then there is a partition $A = (A_1, A_2, \ldots, A_m)$ such that if A^i is the submatrix of A formed by dropping all columns in A_i, $A^i x > 0$, $x \geqq 0$ has no solution, for each $i = 1, 2, \ldots, m$.

Proof.

See Chapter 5.

For example, consider an input-output model with substitution. Let A^i correspond to the submatrix of A formed by all firms which output good i. Then $A^i x > 0$, $x \geqq 0$ has no solution. In other words, no firm is left to output good i. Thus $(A^i x)_i \not> 0$ for all $x \geqq 0$.

Let $C = \{y: y \geqq 0\}$. Another interesting property of Leontief Substitution Systems is given in the following theorem.

Theorem 3.1.2

Let A_J be a basis of a Leontief matrix A. If $A_J x_J = b$, $x_J \geqq 0$ has a solution for some $b > 0$, then it has a solution for all $b \in C$.

Proof.

Under the conditions of the theorem, $A_J \in K$ by Theorem 2.3.4 part 1. Then $A_J^{-1} \geqq 0$ and $A_J^{-1} b \geqq 0$ for all $b \in C$.

Q.E.D.

It seems reasonable that the above two properties (i.e., Theorems 3.1.1 and 3.1.2) could be extended to include non-Leontief problems. For example, consider Figure 3.1.1. Here we are looking at the requirement space for a four variable linear program. Suppose b is to be selected from set C. The constraint matrix $A = (A_1, A_2)$ is partitioned as in Theorem 3.1.1 and is is clear that the ideas of Theorem 3.1.2 are also applicable, yet the problem is not Leontief.

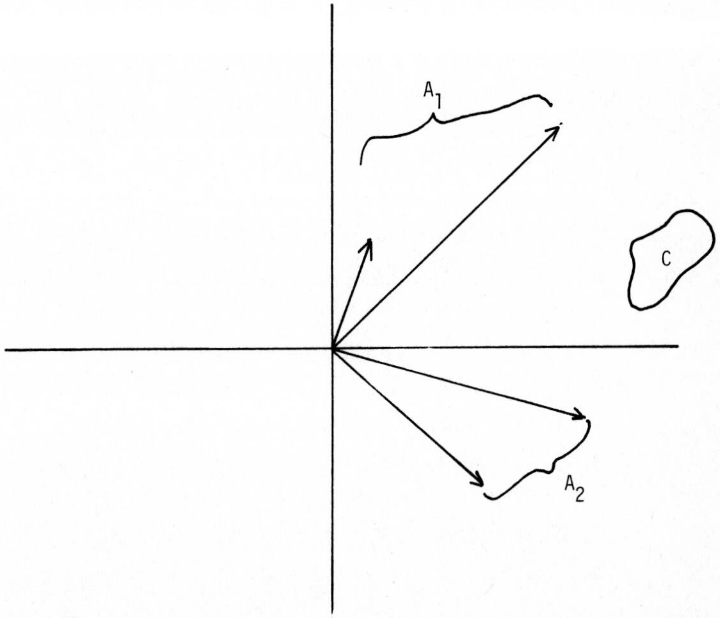

Figure 3.1.1. Requirement Space for a Non-Leonteif Problem

Along these lines, Saigal [109] has given two new definitions of Leontief type systems and some related properties.

Definition 3.1.1 (Generalized Leontief)

Let C be a subset of R^m with non-empty interior and let A be a full row rank m by n matrix. A is generalized Leontief with respect to C if

1. there is a basis B such that $C \subset \text{cone}(B)$: and
2. for each basis of A such that $C \cap \text{cone}(B) \neq \emptyset$, $C \subset \text{cone}(B)$.

In the above, $\text{cone}(B) = \{y: y = Bx,\ x \geqq 0\}$. The set of all m by n generalized Leontief matrices with respect to C is denoted by L(C).

Definition 3.1.2 (Hidden Leontief)

A matrix $A \in L(C)$ is called hidden Leontief if there exists a nonsingular matrix D such that DA is Leontief and $Db \geqq 0$ for all $b \in C$.

The following result characterizes a class of hidden Leontief systems. Below, int(C) means the interior of set C.

Theorem 3.1.3

Let A be an m by n full row rank matrix with $A = (\bar{A}, \bar{\bar{A}})$ where $\bar{\bar{A}}$ may be vacuous and $\bar{A}$ has full row rank. Let C be a convex subset of R^m with non-empty interior. Then the following are equivalent:

1. $\bar{A} \in L(C)$ and is hidden Leontief and every extreme point of X(b), $b \in C$, has zero components associated with the columns of $\bar{\bar{A}}$.
2. There exists a simplicial cone $T = \{x: Dx \geqq 0\}$ such that $\bar{A} \in L(T)$, $D\bar{A}$ is Leontief, $C \subset T$, and no feasible basis of X(b), $b \in \text{int}(C)$, contains a column of $\bar{\bar{A}}$.
3. There exists a partition $A = (A_1, A_2, \ldots, A_m)$ and a simplicial cone T such that $C \subset T$. Also, if A^i is the submatrix formed by dropping the columns A_i from A:

   (i) for each $i = 1, \ldots, m$, $\text{cone}(A^i) \cap \text{int}(T) = \emptyset$; and

   (ii) there is at least one column of A_i, call it B_i, for each $i = 1, \ldots, m$ where $\text{cone}(B_i, A^i) \cap \text{int}(T) \neq \emptyset$.

Proof.

See Chapter 5.

Example 3.1.1

To illustrate Theorem 3.1.1, consider the following numerical example. Let

$$A = \begin{bmatrix} 3 & -3 & 5 & -4 \\ 1 & -1 & 5 & -3 \end{bmatrix}$$

$$C = \left\{ \begin{bmatrix} x_1 \\ x_2 \end{bmatrix} : \quad (x_1+2)^2 + (x_2-3)^2 \leqq 1 \right\}.$$

Figure 3.1.2 illustrates the requirement space for $Ax = b$, $x \geqq 0$ and the set C.

A has full row rank and we can partition A as $A = (A_1, A_2)$ where $A_1 = (a_1, a_3)$ and $A_2 = (a_2, a_4)$. In Figure 3.1.2 we see the simplicial cone T given by

$$T = \{y: y = Dx, x \geqq 0\}$$

where

$$D = \begin{bmatrix} -1 & -3 \\ 4 & 2 \end{bmatrix}$$

and that $C \subset T$.

Also, $A_1 = A^2$ gives $\text{cone}(A^2) \cap \text{int}(T) = \emptyset$ and $A_2 = A^1$ gives cone $(A^1) \cap \text{int}(T) = \emptyset$. Finally, $\text{cone}(a_2, A^2) \cap \text{int}(T) \neq \emptyset$ and $\text{cone}(a_3, A^1) \cap \text{int}(T) \neq \emptyset$. We have then that A satisfies part 3 of Theorem 3.1.3 and, hence, that A satisfies parts 1 and 2 of Theorem 3.1.3.

In the next section we look at a class of problems that are hidden Leontief. Once we determine the matrix D we can use the results of Chapter 2 and solve the problems using recursive solution procedures.

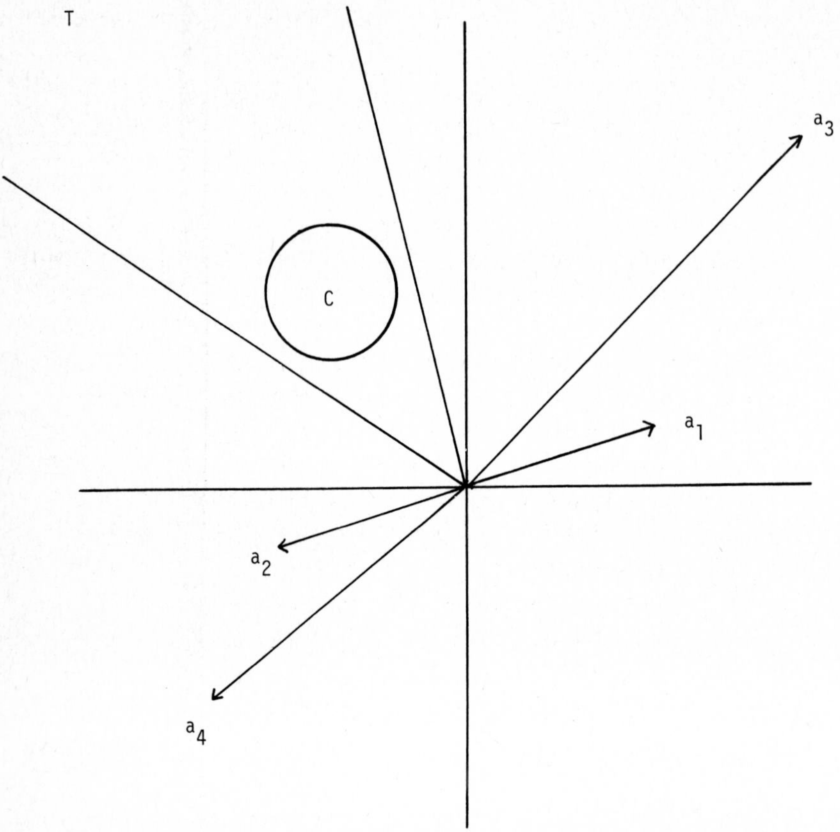

Figure 3.1.2 Illustration of Theorem 3.1.3

3.2 An Application Exploiting Hidden Leontief Properties

Suppose a system is observed at successive time periods. At each such stage the system is found to be in one of a finite number of states S. For any state $i \in S$ observed at stage t (= 0, 1, 2,...), an action $a \in A_i$ is taken. Each A_i is assumed to be non-empty and finite. If state $i \in S$ is observed at stage t and action $a \in A_i$ taken then an expected profit c_{ia} is earned immediately and the probability that state j is observed in the next stage is $P_{ij}(a)$. A decision J is a vector valued function that specifies an action for each state. That is, for each $i \in S$, $J_i \in A_i$. Let M be the set of all decisions. For each decision $J \in M$ we associate with it an m by 1 vector of expected profits c_J and an m by m matrix of transition probabilities P_J where m is the cardinality of S. We assume that $P_J e = e$ for all $J \in M$. We also assume that each P_J for $J \in M$ has one ergodic chain (i.e., P_J is irreducible for each $J \in M$) which must be aperiodic. The above model was given by Howard [61].

Consider for the time being the behavior of the system if the same decision $J \in M$ is used at each stage. The total expected reward for using J for the first n stages is v^n, defined by

$$v^n = c_J + P_J c_J + \ldots + P_J^{n-1} c_J$$

or

$$v^n = \sum_{\ell=0}^{n-1} P_J^{\ell} c_J .$$

It can be shown (see, for example, [61,71]) that

$$\sum_{\ell=0}^{n-1} P_J^{\ell} = nP_J^* + S_J + T_n$$

where $\lim_{n \to \infty} T_n = 0$, and $\lim_{\ell \to \infty} P_J^{\ell} = P_J^* = e\pi'$.

Here π is the unique vector of limiting state probabilities. Then

$$\begin{aligned} v^n &= nP_J^* c_J + S_J c_J + T_n c_J \\ &= ne\pi' c_J + S_J c_J + T_n c_J \\ &= neg_J + w_J + T_n c_J \end{aligned}$$

where

$$g_J = \pi' c_J$$

and

$$w_J = S_J c_J.$$

In the above, g_J is called the gain rate and w_J the bias of decision J. In the limit, the total expected profit for state i is $ng_J+(w_J)_i$. We see that the limiting values of v_i^n for decision J approaches a line with slope g_J and intercept $(w_J)_i$. Denardo [22] gives a good description of the above and points out that an optimizer faced with a long horizon might choose the decision which first gives the highest gain and then, for those decisions which give the highest gain, choose the one giving the highest bias.

There are several methods for finding a gain optimal decision [26] but we will focus on a method originally given by Koehler, Whinston, and Wright [73] which uses a linear programming procedure given by Manne [89]. That formulation is:

3.2.1 $$\text{Max} \sum_{i\varepsilon S} \sum_{a\varepsilon A_i} c_{ia} x_{ia}$$

subject to

$$\sum_{i\varepsilon S} \sum_{a\varepsilon A_i} x_{ia} = 1$$

3.2.2 $$\sum_{i\varepsilon S} \sum_{a\varepsilon A_i} (\delta_{ij} - P_{ij}(a)) x_{ia} = 0, \qquad j \varepsilon S$$

$$x_{ia} \geqq 0, \qquad i \varepsilon S,\ a \varepsilon A_i$$

where

$$\delta_{ij} = \begin{cases} 0 & \text{if } i \neq j \\ 1 & \text{if } i = j. \end{cases}$$

Let x_{ia}^* for $i \varepsilon S$, $a \varepsilon A_i$, be the optimal solution. Define

$$y_{ia} = \frac{x_{ia}^*}{\sum_{a\varepsilon A_i} x_{ia}^*} \qquad \text{for } i \varepsilon S \text{ and } a \varepsilon A_i$$

and let $J^* = (a_1, a_2, \ldots, a_m)$ where $a_i \in A_i$ and $y_{ia_i} = 1$. (It can be shown that such a J^* and corresponding y_{ia} exist which give a non-randomized solution [26]. Also, (3.2.1) yields these.)

One of the constraints of Equation 3.2.2 is redundant. Hence we will remove the equation corresponding to j = m and rewrite the above as:

3.2.3
$$\text{Max} \sum_{i \in S} \sum_{a \in A_i} c_{ia} x_{ia}$$

subject to

$$\sum_{i \in S} \sum_{a \in A_i} x_{ia} = 1$$

3.2.4
$$\sum_{i \in S} \sum_{a \in A_i} B_{ia} x_{ia} = \begin{bmatrix} 0 \\ \vdots \\ 0 \end{bmatrix}$$

$$x_{ia} \geqq 0, \qquad i \in S,\ a \in A_i$$

where

$$B_{ia} = \begin{bmatrix} -P_{i1}(a) \\ \vdots \\ 1 - P_{ii}(a) \\ \vdots \\ -P_{i,m-1}(a) \end{bmatrix}.$$

Let $x_1 = (x_{ia})$ be a vector containing x_{ia}, $i \in S$, $a \in A_i$, for all $i \neq m$. Let $x_2 = (x_{ma})$, $a \in A_m$. In matrix notation, Equation 3.2.3 and 3.2.4 become:

3.2.5
$$\text{Max} \ c_1' x_1 + c_2' x_2$$

subject to

$$\begin{bmatrix} e_1' & e_2' \\ B_1 & B_2 \end{bmatrix} \begin{bmatrix} x_1 \\ x_2 \end{bmatrix} = \begin{bmatrix} 1 \\ 0 \end{bmatrix}$$

$$x_1, x_2 \geqq 0.$$

In Equation 3.2.5, B_1 is pre-Leontief as can be seen by Equation 3.2.4, the definition of B_{ia}, and the partitioning giving x_1. Also, $B_2 \leqq 0$. To demonstrate that Equation 3.2.5 has a hidden Leontief constraint set we will construct a nonsingular matrix D that gives

$$D\begin{bmatrix} e_1' & e_2' \\ B_1 & B_2 \end{bmatrix}$$

Leontief and

$$D\begin{bmatrix} 1 \\ 0 \end{bmatrix} \geqq 0 .$$

Consider the following problem:

3.2.6 $\quad \text{Min } y'e$

subject to

$$B_1'y \geqq e.$$

The dual to Equation 3.2.6 is:

$$\text{Max } e'x$$

subject to

$$B_1x = e$$

$$x \geqq 0$$

which is a pre-Leontief constrained linear program. In fact we can make a stronger statement as shown in the following theorem.

Theorem 3.2.1

B_1, as given in Equation 3.2.5, is totally Leontief.

Proof.

See Chapter 5.

By Theorem 3.2.1, y is well defined and, since y is determined by some class K matrix, $y > 0$. The vector y is an $m - 1$ by 1 vector where y_i can be interpreted as the longest expected time until state m is observed given state i.

Notice that the vector y can be found using matrix iterative procedures as described in Chapter 2.

Let

$$D = \begin{bmatrix} 1 & -y' \\ 0 & I \end{bmatrix}.$$

Then

3.2.7 $$D\begin{bmatrix} e_1' & e_2' \\ B_1 & B_2 \end{bmatrix} = \begin{bmatrix} e_1' - y'B_1 & e_2' - y'B_2 \\ B_1 & B_2 \end{bmatrix} \equiv A$$

and

$$D\begin{bmatrix} 1 \\ 0 \end{bmatrix} = \begin{bmatrix} 1 \\ 0 \end{bmatrix}.$$

Furthermore D is nonsingular,

$$e_1' - y'B_1 \leqq 0,$$

and

$$e_2' - y'B_2 > 0.$$

Thus, A is pre-Leontief. Again, we can make a stronger statement as given in the following theorem.

Theorem 3.2.2

The matrix A, as given in Equation 3.2.7, is totally Leontief.

Proof.

See Chapter 5.

To solve the gain optimal problem we may first determine the vector y (by solving a totally Leontief problem), transform the original constraint set, and then solve another totally Leontief linear program. The gain optimal decision is any $J \in M^{\infty}$ for the problem:

3.2.8 $$\text{Max } c_1'x_1 + c_2'x_2$$

subject to

$$A\begin{bmatrix} x_1 \\ x_2 \end{bmatrix} = \begin{bmatrix} 0 \\ 1 \end{bmatrix}, \qquad x_1, x_2 \geqq 0.$$

Surprisingly, we can then use Equation 3.2.8 to solve the bias optimal problem. To do this we use results given by Denardo [23]. Consider first, though, the case where expected profits are discounted by β, $0 \leqq \beta < 1$. We have

$$v_\beta^n(J) = \sum_{\ell=0}^{n-1} \beta^\ell P_J^\ell c_J.$$

Blackwell [9] examined the behavior of v_β^n for β sufficiently close to 1. A decision $J^* \varepsilon M$ is called β-optimal [9, 182] if

$$v_\beta^\infty(J^*) \geqq v_\beta^\infty(J) \qquad \text{for all } J \varepsilon M.$$

A decision J^* is called optimal if it is β-optimal for all β sufficiently close to 1 [93]. Blackwell [9] showed that β-optimal decisions exists and Miller and Veinott [93] demonstrated the existence of optimal decisions. Blackwell [9] showed that

$$v_\beta^\infty(J) = \frac{g(J)e}{(1-\beta)} + w_J + o(1).$$

Veinott [126] gave a procedure for finding a bias optimal decision in this case while Miller and Veinott [93] generalized Veinott's [126] procedure to find an optimal decision. Jeroslow [63, 64] presented a solution procedure which uses asymptotic linear programming.

From the above we have that an optimal decision is a gain optimal and bias optimal decision, that a bias optimal decision is gain optimal, but that a gain optimal decision may not be bias optimal or optimal.

To find a bias optimal decision using Denardo's [23] procedure, we solve a sequence of linear programs. To find an optimal decision we continue this procedure. The first linear program is used to find gain optimal decisions. The totally Leontief problem given in Equation 3.2.8 can be used to find gain optimal decisions. That is, any $J \varepsilon M^\infty$ is gain optimal.

The optimal solution to the dual of Equation 3.2.1 is an m+1 by 1 vector

$$\begin{bmatrix} v \\ g_{J^*} \end{bmatrix}.$$

Denardo's second linear program uses this vector to determine a gain optimal decision for a restricted and altered version of Equation 3.2.1. When all gain optimal decisions have on ergodic chain, as was assumed, then the second problem finds the optimal bias. Let

$$B_i = \{a \varepsilon M_i : v_i + g_{J*} - c_{ia} - \sum_{J=1}^{m} P_{ij}(a) v_j = 0\}, \qquad i = 1, \ldots, m.$$

For the altered problem the decision space is $\overline{M} = \mathop{X}_{i=1}^{m} B_i$ and $- v_i$ replaces c_{ia}. If $B_i = \emptyset$ for some i, then an altered state space is produced. In any case, Problem 3.2.8 is transformed by changing the objective function and by removing columns or rows. The resulting structure is a Leontief Substitution System. Hence once we have found the hidden Leontief structure we can still use this structure in finding bias optimal and all optimal decisions for sufficiently small discount rates. The advantage is that the methods of Chapter 2 are applicable in solving such problems.

3.3 Integral Leontief Substitution Systems

In this section we consider the additional constraints on the decision variables of integrality. More explicitly we address the problem:

$$\begin{aligned} &\text{Max } c'x \\ &\text{subject to} \\ &\quad Ax = b \\ &\quad x \geqq 0 \quad \text{integer.} \end{aligned}$$

Let A and b be integral and $X(A, b) = \{x: Ax = b, x \geqq 0\}$. Veinott and Dantzig [127] generalized a result due to Hoffman and Kruskal [60] in giving the following:

Theorem 3.3.1

If A is an integral matrix having linearly independent rows, the following are equivalent.

(1) Every basis is unimodular.

(2) The extreme points of X(A, b) are integral for all integral b.

(3) Every basis has an integral inverse.

Proof.

See Chapter 5.

It is well-known that if A is totally unimodular (i.e., each nonsingular submatrix of A has a determinant equal to +1 or -1), then the extreme points of X(A, b) are integral. The converse is not generally true. For example, consider the set packing problem [43] where A consists of zeros and ones and b consists of a vector of ones. With slack variables included in x, the problem is:

$$\begin{aligned} &\text{Max } c'x \\ &\text{subject to} \\ &\quad x \in X(A, b) \\ &\quad 0 \leqq x \leqq e \quad \text{integer.} \end{aligned}$$

This problem has integral extreme points if A is balanced (see Berge [6]) and in the more general case when A is perfect (see Padberg [98]). In both cases A may not be totally unimodular.

Another case where X(A, b) has only integer extreme points but does not necessarily have A totally unimodular arises when A is Leontief, $b \geqq 0$ where A and b are integral and each A_J for $J \in M$ has determinant of A_J equal to +1. From Veinott [124] we have the following theorem which follows immediately from Theorems 2.5.3 and 3.3.1:

<u>Theorem 3.3.2</u>

If A is an integral Leontief matrix, the following are equivalent.

(1) A_J^{-1} is integral for each A_J, $J \in M$.

(2) $\det A_J = 1$ for each A_J, $J \in M$.

(3) The extreme points of X(A, b) are integral for every non-negative integral b.

Proof.

(1)$\Rightarrow$(2)

For each $J \in M$, $A_J \in K$ and, hence, $\det(A_J) > 0$ (see Theorem 2.3.4). Since A_J and A_J^{-1} are integral, $\det(A_J)$ and $\det(A_J^{-1})$ are nonzero integers. Now $\det(A_J)\det(A_J^{-1}) = 1$, hence, with the above, $\det(A_J) = \det(A_J^{-1}) = 1$.

(2)$\Rightarrow$(3)

Since every extreme point of X(A, b) is determined by an A_J, $J \in M$ by Theorem 2.5.3, then with $\det(A_J) = 1$, using Cramer's rule (for example [96]), it follows that each extreme point is integral.

(3)$\Rightarrow$(1)

e_i is an integral non-negative b. Therefore $A_J^{-1}e_i$ is integral. Hence the ith column of A_J^{-1} is integral for any $J \in M$.

Q.E.D.

As an example, consider the following (recursive) totally Leontief problem with integrality requirements:

$$\text{Max } c'x$$

subject to

$$Ax = \begin{bmatrix} 1 & 1 & 0 & 0 & 0 & 0 \\ -3 & -2 & 1 & 1 & 0 & 0 \\ -1 & -4 & 0 & -2 & 1 & 1 \end{bmatrix} \begin{bmatrix} x_1 \\ x_2 \\ x_3 \\ x_4 \\ x_5 \\ x_6 \end{bmatrix} = \begin{bmatrix} 2 \\ 1 \\ 3 \end{bmatrix} = b$$

$$x_j \geqq 0 \text{ and integer for } i = 1, \ldots, 6.$$

Notice that A is not totally unimodular since the nonsingular submatrix

$$\begin{bmatrix} -3 & -2 \\ -1 & -4 \end{bmatrix}$$

does not have determinant +1 or -1. By Theorem 3.3.2, though, it is readily apparent that the system has only integer extreme points since each A_J, $J \in M$ takes the form

$$A_J = \begin{bmatrix} 1 & 0 & 0 \\ * & 1 & 0 \\ * & * & 1 \end{bmatrix}.$$

The determinant of a lower or upper triangular matrix is the product of its diagonal elements. Clearly $\det(A_J) = 1$ for every $J \in M$ and hence, each extreme point of $X(A, b)$ is integral.

3.4 Some Integral Leontief Problems

Some applications discussed in earlier sections can be viewed as integral Leontief problems. In this section we briefly review one of those applications and consider the conversion of regular integer linear programs to integral Leontief problems and the inherent problems therein.

3.4.1 Transshipment Problems

In Section 2.7 we considered the shortest path problem and transshipment matrices in general. A transshipment matrix, A, is a matrix having at most, two non-zero elements per column, a +1 and a -1. The following theorem, as stated in [105], was given in [60] and is here presented without proof.

Theorem 3.4.1

A matrix A is totally unimodular if it satisfies the following five conditions:

(1) All entries of A are 0, $\pm$ 1.

(2) The rows of A can be partitioned into two disjoint sets T_1 and T_2.

(3) Every column of A contains at most two non-zero entries.

(4) If any column of A contains two non-zero entries of the same sign, then one is in a row of T_1 and the other in a row of T_2.

(5) If any column of A contains two non-zero entries of opposite sign, then they are both in rows of T_1 or both in rows of T_2.

Clearly, a transshipment matrix is totally unimodular. Hence a Leontief problem of the form

$$\text{Max } c'x$$

$$\text{subject to}$$

$$Ax = b \geqq 0$$

$$x \geqq 0 \quad \text{integer}$$

where A is a transshipment matrix has only integral extreme points and is just a linear program.

3.4.2 Equivalent Constrained Recursive Systems

Nanda [95] proposed an algorithm for transforming a general integer linear program containing only 0, $\pm$ 1 elements into an equivalent integer linear program having an integral recursive Leontief Substitution System with each diagonal block consisting of a row of ones with the addition of possible side constraints consisting of upper and lower bounds on the variables. Kappauf [69] provided conditions necessary for the algorithm to work and concluded with several observations on the practicality of Nanda's procedure.

Consider a bounded integer linear program of the form:

3.4.1

$$\begin{aligned} &\text{Max } c'x \\ &\text{subject to} \\ &Ax = b \\ &x \geqq 0. \end{aligned}$$

Suppose T is a square unimodular matrix and h an integral vector. Let

$$x = Tz + h.$$

Substituting this into (3.4.1) gives

3.4.2

$$\begin{aligned} &\text{Max } c'Tz + c'h \\ &\text{subject to} \\ &ATz = b - Ah \\ &Tz \geqq -h \\ &z \text{ integral.} \end{aligned}$$

From Bradley [10] (recently extended by Faaland [31]) we have:

Theorem 3.4.2

For each square unimodular matrix T and integral vector h, there is a problem equivalent to (3.4.1) of the form given in (3.4.2).

Proof.

See Bradley [10].

With the above theorem, Nanda [95] attempted to convert a general bounded integer program having only 0, $\pm$ 1 elements in A to a lower recursive Leontief Substitution System having diagonal blocks consisting of a row of ones. For example, with m = 3 and n = 6, the following matrix is a lower recursive Leontief matrix having diagonal blocks consisting of a row of ones:

$$A = \begin{bmatrix} 1 & 1 & 0 & 0 & 0 & 0 \\ -2 & -2 & 1 & 1 & 0 & 0 \\ -1 & -2 & -3 & -2 & 1 & 1 \end{bmatrix}.$$

As mentioned in Section 3.3, using Theorem 3.3.2, problems having recursive Leontief Substitution System with a matrix as defined above have only integral extreme points. Furthermore, the recursive nature allows a two pass solution procedure. That procedure is:

Pass 1

Compute

3.4.3 $$\pi_m = \operatorname*{Max}_{m_k \varepsilon M_m} c_{m_k}$$

$$\pi_i = \operatorname*{Max}_{i_k \varepsilon M_i} \{c_{i_k} - \sum_{j=i+1}^{m} a_{ji_k} \pi_j\}, \quad i = m-1, \ldots, 1.$$

Let i_k^* be the index $i_k \varepsilon M_i$ for each i = 1, ..., m solving 3.4.3. Then the m-tuple $J^* = (1_k^*, 2_k^*, \ldots, m_k^*)$ indexes the optimal primal basis.

Pass 2

The optimal primal values are found by solving $A_{J^*} x_{J^*} = b$ with all other $x_i = 0$. Since A_{J^*} is lower triangular, the vector x_{J^*} is given by:

3.4.4 $$x_{1_k^*} = b_1$$

$$x_{i_k^*} = b_i - \sum_{j=1}^{i-1} a_{ij_k^*} x_{j_k^*}, \quad i = 2, \ldots, m.$$

Returning to Nanda's procedure (as modified by Kappauf [69]), a bounded integer linear program having only 0, $\pm$ 1 elements in A can be converted to the form:

3.4.5 $$\text{Max } c'x$$

subject to

$$Ax = b \geqq 0$$

$$0 \leqq \ell \leqq x \leqq u$$

$$x \text{ integral}$$

where A is lower recursive Leontief with diagonal blocks consisting of a row of ones, and A, b, ℓ, and u are all integral.

A simple procedure [75] for converting any bounded integer linear program to the form given in (3.4.5) is as follows. Suppose the initial problem given is of the form

3.4.6 $$\text{Max } c'x$$

subject to

$$Ax = b$$

$$\ell \leqq x \leqq u$$

$$x \text{ integral.}$$

First redefine x and b so that $\ell \geqq 0$, then add the constraint

3.4.7 $$e'x \leqq r$$

where r is a sufficiently large number (perhaps determined by a linear programming solution of some relaxation of (3.4.6) with c set to e). Next add a slack variable s to (3.4.7) and subtract k_i times (3.4.7) from row i of Ax = b in (3.4.6) where k_i is the largest non-negative integer in row i of A. Finally, to each row add $D_i = \hat{b}_i$ as determined by

$$\hat{b}_i = \begin{cases} 0 & \text{if the new righthand side } (\text{RHS}_i) \text{ is non-negative} \\ -\text{RHS}_i & \text{if the new } \text{RHS}_i \text{ is negative.} \end{cases}$$

Note that $0 \leqq \hat{b}_i \leqq D_i \leqq \hat{b}_i$, $0 \leqq s \leqq r$ and $0 \leqq \ell \leqq x \leqq u$. Redefining x to include the s and D variables gives the form of problem 3.4.5.

For example, consider the integer program

$$\text{Max } 2x_1 + 3x_2$$

subject to

$$3x_1 + 2x_2 = 15$$
$$x_1 - x_2 = 2$$
$$1 \leqq x_1 \leqq 3$$
$$-1 \leqq x_2 \leqq 2$$
$$x_1,\ x_2 \text{ integer}.$$

Using the above procedure yields:

$$\text{Max } 2x_1 + 3\bar{x}_2$$

subject to

$$Ax = \begin{bmatrix} 1 & 1 & 1 & 0 & 0 \\ 0 & -1 & -3 & 1 & 0 \\ 0 & -2 & -1 & 0 & 1 \end{bmatrix} \begin{bmatrix} x_1 \\ \bar{x}_2 \\ s \\ D_1 \\ D_2 \end{bmatrix} = \begin{bmatrix} 5 \\ 2 \\ 0 \end{bmatrix} = b$$

$$\ell = \begin{bmatrix} 1 \\ 0 \\ 0 \\ 0 \\ 4 \end{bmatrix} \leqq \begin{bmatrix} x_1 \\ \bar{x}_2 \\ s \\ D_1 \\ D_2 \end{bmatrix} \leqq \begin{bmatrix} 3 \\ 3 \\ 5 \\ 0 \\ 4 \end{bmatrix} \leqq u$$

$$x_1,\ \bar{x}_2,\ s,\ D_1,\ D_2 \text{ integral}$$

and $x_2 = \bar{x}_2 - 1$ after $\bar{x}_2$ is determined.

Kappauf [69] correctly notes that Bradley's procedure (as utilized in the above) maps extreme points to extreme points and integral points to integral points. Hence, unless the initial problem can be solved by linear programming procedures, we can never hope that conversion to an equivalent problem will allow a linear programming procedure. We can, however (see [75]), hope that the resulting equivalent integer program is easier to solve. With that in mind, Koehler, Whinston, and Wright [75] give a branch and bound procedure for solving Equation 3.4.5 which takes advantage of the primary constraint structure (i.e., the recursive Leontief structure which permits solution by 3.4.3 and 3.4.4).

3.5 Concave Minimization over Leontief Substitution Systems

A large class of problems can be represented by minimizing a (non-linear) concave function over a Leontief Substitution System. Consider the following problem:

3.5.1
$$\text{Min } c(x)$$
subject to
$$Ax = b \geqq 0$$
$$x \geqq 0$$

where A is Leontief, $X(b) = \{x: Ax = b, x \geqq 0\}$, and $c(x)$ is concave on $X(b)$. It is well known [88] that, if it exists, the optimal solution occurs at an extreme point of $X(b)$. Thus, according to Theorem 2.5.3, the optimal solution to Problem (3.5.1) is determined by some class K basis of A. We assume in this section that a solution to 3.5.1 exists.

Many concave minimization applications over Leontief Substitution Systems have additional side constraints of the form $x_i x_j = 0$ for selected pairs (i,j). For example, consider the single product economic-lot-size model of Section 2.11. Let

- r_i = known demand in period i (= 1, ..., n)
- x_i = amount produced in period i (= 1, ..., n)
- y_i = amount of inventory on hand at the end of period i (= 1, ..., n)
- w_i = amount of backlogged demand at the end of period i (= 1, ..., n)
- α_i = positive amount of stock generated in period i+1 from one unit of ending inventory at period i
- β_i = nonnegative amount of backlogged demand generated in period i+1 from one unit backlogged in period i.

Material balance equations are:

$$x_i + \alpha_{i-1} y_{i-1} + w_i - y_i - \beta_{i-1} w_{i-1} = r_i, \qquad i = 1, \ldots, n$$

with $y_0 = w_o = y_n = w_n = 0$. Since each extreme point of $X(r)$ for this problem is associated with a square Leontief matrix, it is readily apparent that

$$x_i y_{i-1} = 0$$

$$x_i w_i = 0$$

$$y_{i-1} w_i = 0 \qquad i = 1, \ldots, n.$$

We might impose [125] an additional constraint of the form:

$$y_i w_i = 0 \qquad i = 1, \ldots, n-1$$

which states that in no period will we allow simultaneous positive amounts of backlogged demand and inventory. This is truly an additional constraint placed on the economic-lot-size problem.

Veinott [124] developed the following notation for describing a class of restrictions of the form $x_i x_j = 0$. Let E^n be a Euclidean space of dimension n. Let r_i be {0} or E^1 and

$$R = \mathop{X}_{i=1}^{n} r_i$$

Let U be the class of all 2^n subsets of R and V the class of all unions of sets in U. For example, with n = 2, we have:

$$R_1 = \{0\} \times \{0\}$$
$$R_2 = \{0\} \times E^1$$
$$R_3 = E^1 \times \{0\}$$
$$R_4 = E^1 \times E^1$$
$$U = \{R_1, R_2, R_3, R_4\}$$
$$V = \{R_1, R_2, R_3, R_4\}$$

Notice that V = U. Similarly, let r_i' be {0} or E^1 - {0} with

$$R' = \mathop{X}_{i=1}^{n} r_i'.$$

Let U' be the class of all 2^n subsets of R' and V' the class of all unions of sets in U'. Again, as an example consider n = 2. Here:

$$R_1' = \{0\} \times (E^1 - \{0\})$$
$$R_2' = \{0\} \times \{0\}$$

$$R_3' = (E' - \{0\}) \times \{0\}$$

$$R_4' = (E^1 - \{0\}) \times (E^1 - \{0\})$$

$$U' = \{R_1', R_2', R_3', R_4'\}$$

$$V' = \{R_1', R_2', R_3', R_4', R_1' \cup R_2', \text{etc.}\}.$$

Notice that $V \subset V'$ and V is the class of sets in V' that are closed [124].

Suppose that $n = 3$ and $x_1 x_3 = 0$ is required. Then $S = \{(x_1, x_2, x_3): x_1 x_3 = 0\} \in V$ because

$$S = (\{0\} \times E^1 \times E^1) \cup (E^1 \times E^1 \times \{0\}).$$

Also, $S \in V'$ since $V \subset V'$.

The following result is due to Veinott [124]:

Theorem 3.5.1

If $S \in V'$, the following are equivalent:

(i) x is an extreme point of $\text{conv}(X(b) \cap S)$.

(ii) $x \in S$ and x is an extreme point of $X(b)$.

Proof.

See Chapter 5.

In the above, $\text{conv}(X(b) \cap S)$ means the convex hull of $X(b) \cap S$. The above theorem implies that extreme points of $\text{conv}(X(b) \cap S)$ for $S \in V'$ are determined by class K matrices.

Example 3.5.1

Let

$$A = \begin{bmatrix} 1 & 1 & -1 & 0 \\ -1 & 0 & 1 & 1 \end{bmatrix} \qquad b = \begin{bmatrix} 1 \\ 1 \end{bmatrix}$$

with

$$S = \{x: x_2 x_3 = 0\}.$$

We have

$$M = \{(1,4),\ (2,3),\ (2,4)\}$$

which gives the set of extreme points of X(b) as

$$\{x:\ x_J = A_J^{-1}b,\ x_{\bar{J}} = 0,\ J \in M\}$$

$$= \left\{ \begin{bmatrix} 1 \\ 0 \\ 0 \\ 2 \end{bmatrix}, \begin{bmatrix} 0 \\ 2 \\ 1 \\ 0 \end{bmatrix}, \begin{bmatrix} 0 \\ 1 \\ 0 \\ 1 \end{bmatrix} \right\}.$$

Notice that $\left\{ \begin{bmatrix} 1 \\ 0 \\ 0 \\ 2 \end{bmatrix}, \begin{bmatrix} 0 \\ 1 \\ 0 \\ 1 \end{bmatrix} \right\} \varepsilon\ S$. Hence, the extreme points of conv(X(b) ∩ S) are

$$\left\{ \begin{bmatrix} 1 \\ 0 \\ 0 \\ 2 \end{bmatrix}, \begin{bmatrix} 0 \\ 1 \\ 0 \\ 1 \end{bmatrix} \right\}.$$

(In the above $\bar{J}$ is the complement of J).

Let T ε V be the set $\{x:\ x_i x_j = 0,\ i,j \in N_\ell,\ i \neq j, \text{ and } \ell = 1, \ldots, m\}$. That is, T is the set of all vectors having, at most, only one non-zero component for each set N_ℓ, $\ell = 1, \ldots, m$, of component identifications. (Recall $N_\ell = \{j:\ a_{\ell j} > 0\}$). In various applications [125], the following result due to Veinott [124] is important.

Theorem 3.5.2

If A is Leontief, $b \geqq 0$, S ε V', and X(b) ∩ S ∩ T is bounded, then the following are equivalent:

(i) x is an extreme point of conv(X(b) ∩ S).

(ii) x ε X(b) ∩ S ∩ T.

Proof.

See Chapter 5.

Example 3.5.2

Consider the following:

$$A = \begin{bmatrix} 1 & 1 & -1 & 0 \\ -1 & 0 & 1 & 1 \end{bmatrix}, \quad b = \begin{bmatrix} 1 \\ 1 \end{bmatrix},$$

with

$$S = \{x: x_2x_3 = 0\}.$$

We have also that

$$T = \{x: x_1x_2 = 0,\ x_3x_4 = 0\}.$$

The point $x' = (1, 0, 0, 2) \in X(b) \cap S \cap T$ and x is also an extreme point of $\text{conv}(X(b) \cap S)$. We can show that $X(b) \cap S \cap T$ is bounded so we would expect this result by Theorem 3.5.2. Consider the case where $b = \begin{bmatrix} 0 \\ 0 \end{bmatrix}$. The cone $C = \left\{ \begin{bmatrix} 1 \\ 0 \\ 1 \\ 0 \end{bmatrix} \lambda,\ \lambda \geqq 0 \right\}$ is such that $x \in C$ and $x \in X(b) \cap S \cap T$ but no such non-zero x is an extreme point of $\text{conv}(X(b) \cap S)$.

We now return to Problem (3.5.1) and consider the solution when additional constraints of the form $x_ix_j = 0$ are imposed. The following is due to Zangwill [136] (as presented by Veinott [124]):

Theorem 3.5.3

If $S \in V$, $c(\cdot)$ is concave on $X(b)$, and $c(\cdot)$ achieves its minimum on $X(b) \cap S$, then $c(\cdot)$ achieves its minimum on $X(b) \cap S$ at an extreme point of $\text{conv}(X(b) \cap S)$.

Proof.

Let x minimize $c(\cdot)$ over $X(b) \cap S$. Since $x \in S$ and $S \in V$, $x \in R$ for some $R = \overset{n}{\underset{i=1}{X}} r_i$. Hence x minimizes $c(\cdot)$ over the closed ($S \in V$ is closed) convex polyhedral set $X(b) \cap R$. Since $X(b)$ is bounded from below, $X(b) \cap R$ is bounded from below, then $X(b) \cap R$ (and thus $X(b) \cap S$) achieves its minimum at an extreme point [88] y of $X(b) \cap R$. Thus by Theorem 3.5.1, y is an extreme point of $X(b)$ and with $y \in R \subset S$, y is an extreme point of $\text{conv}(X(b) \cap S)$.

Q.E.D.

We can easily extend the above results to include the case where $c(\cdot)$ is quasi-concave [50, 100, 116]. $c(\cdot)$ is quasi-concave over a convex set if, for any two points x^1 and x^2 in the set, we have

$$c(\lambda x^1 + (1-\lambda)x^2) \geqq \min \{c(x^1), c(x^2)\}$$

with $0 \leqq \lambda \leqq 1$.

3.6 Some Concave Minimization Problems

Many applications already discussed (in Sections 2.7, 2.9, and 2.11) can be readily viewed under a concave cost structure. In this section we briefly mention a simple problem with a dynamic Leontief structure and a problem involving a fixed cost structure.

3.6.1 Single-Product Economic-Lot-Size Model

The single-product economic-lot-size model was discussed in Section 2.11 and briefly in Section 3.5. Consider the model with the additional side constraints that

$$\begin{aligned} y_{i-1}x_i &= 0 & i &= 2, \ldots, n \\ x_iw_i &= 0 & i &= 1, \ldots, n-1 \\ y_{i-1}w_i &= 0 & i &= 2, \ldots, n-1 \\ y_iw_i &= 0 & i &= 1, \ldots, n-1. \end{aligned}$$

The first three additional constraints are constraints of the form represented by T in Section 3.5. The remaining constraint is represented by S in Section 3.5.

According to Theorem 3.5.3 we need only search the extreme points of $X(r)$ to determine the minimum (if it exists) of a concave function over $X(r) \cap S \cap T$. Veinott [125] points out a special case where the objective function $c(\cdot)$ is of the form

$$c(z) = \sum_{i=1}^{n} c_i(x_i, y_i, w_i) \qquad z = \begin{bmatrix} x \\ y \\ w \end{bmatrix}$$

where $c_i(\cdot, \cdot, \cdot)$ is concave on the non-negative orthant for each i. Under such conditions these exists an efficient dynamic programming procedure for finding the optimal solution over $X(r) \cap S \cap T$ [91, 130, 134]. Some related types of problems can be found in [34, 35, 36, 68, 81, 83, 84, 110].

3.6.2 Fixed Cost Minimization over Leontief Substitution Systems

Consider the problem [74]

$$\text{Min } c(x)$$

subject to

$$Ax = b > 0$$
$$x \geqq 0$$

where A is m by n and totally Leontief, x is n by 1, b is m by 1, and $c(\cdot)$ is a quasi-concave function of the form:

$$c(x) = \sum_{i=1}^{n} f_i(x_i)$$

where

$$f_i(x_i) = \begin{cases} c_i x_i + d_i & \text{if } x_i > 0 \qquad (d_i \geqq 0) \\ 0 & \text{if } x_i = 0. \end{cases}$$

The above problem is a fixed cost minimization over a totally Leontief Substitution System.

Associate with each continuous variable x_i a binary variable y_i and reformulate the problem as:

3.6.1 $$\text{Min } c'x + d'y$$

Subject to

$$Ax = b > 0$$
$$x - \ell y \leqq 0$$
$$x \geqq 0$$
$$y \in Y$$

where

$$Y = \{y\text{: } y \text{ is binary and } \sum_{j \in M_i} y_j = 1,\ i = 1, 2, \ldots, m\}$$

with

$$\ell > x_i$$

for all possible x_i in any $x \in X(b)$. The requirement that

$$\sum_{j \in M_i} y_j = 1 \qquad i = 1, 2, \ldots, m$$

is a result directly apparent from Theorem 2.5.3 and the fact that $c(\cdot)$ is quasi-concave.

The problem given in 3.6.1 can be reformulated as:

3.6.2
$$\min_{y \in Y} d'y + \begin{bmatrix} \text{Min } c'x \\ \text{subject to} \\ Ax = b > 0 \\ x \leqq \ell y \\ x \geqq 0 \end{bmatrix}$$

For a given $y \in Y$ the inner problem has only one solution and that is

$$x_J = A_J^{-1} b \qquad x_{\bar{J}} = 0$$

where $J = \{j: y_j = 1\}$ (which we will refer to later as $J(y)$).

Using Bender's [4] partitioning procedure, Problem (3.6.2) is equivalent to

3.6.3
$$\text{Min } z + d'y$$

subject to

$$z \geqq b'\pi_1^i + \ell y'\pi_2^i \qquad i = 1, 2, \ldots, k$$

$$y \in Y$$

where K is the number of inner problems solved and π_1^i, π_2^i are solutions to the dual of the ith inner program given y^i. It is straigntforward to show that [see Section 5.6]

$$\pi_1^i = c'_{J(y^i)} A^{-1}_{J(y^i)} \qquad i = 1, \ldots, k$$

$$\pi_2^i = [c - A'\pi_1^i]^- \qquad i = 1, \ldots, k$$

where $[z]^-$ is a vector of $[z_i]^-$ for $i = 1, 2, \ldots, n$ and $[z_i]^- = \min(0, z_i)$ unless $y_i = 1$ in which case $[z_i]^- = 0$.

The extension of Problem (3.6.1) to allow A to be Leontief and $b \geqq 0$ is made in a natural manner. We note that the efficiency of the above solution procedure depends primarily on the ease of solving 3.6.3.

As an illustration, consider the problem:

Min f(x, t)

Subject to

$$\begin{bmatrix} 1 & -1 & 0 & 0 & 0 & -1 & 0 & 0 & 0 & 0 \\ 0 & 1 & 1 & -1 & 0 & 0 & 0 & -1 & 0 & 0 \\ 0 & 0 & 0 & 1 & 1 & 0 & 0 & 0 & 0 & -1 \\ 0 & 0 & 0 & 0 & 0 & 1 & -1 & 0 & 0 & 0 \\ 0 & 0 & 0 & 0 & 0 & 0 & 1 & 1 & -1 & 0 \\ 0 & 0 & 0 & 0 & 0 & 0 & 0 & 0 & 1 & 1 \end{bmatrix} \begin{bmatrix} x_1^1 \\ t_1^1 \\ x_2^1 \\ t_2^1 \\ x_3^1 \\ x_1^2 \\ t_1^2 \\ x_2^2 \\ t_2^2 \\ x_3^2 \end{bmatrix} = \begin{bmatrix} 3 \\ 4 \\ 2 \\ 1 \\ 2 \\ 1 \end{bmatrix}$$

$$x_i^j \geqq 0 \quad \text{for} \quad i = 1, 2, 3, \quad j = 1, 2;$$

$$t_i^j \geqq 0 \quad \text{for} \quad i = 1, 2, \quad j = 1, 2;$$

where

$$f(x, t) = \sum_{i=1}^{3} \sum_{j=1}^{2} f_i^j (x_i^j) + \sum_{i=1}^{2} \sum_{j=1}^{2} f_i^j (t_i^j)$$

and

$$f_i^j (x_i^j) = \begin{cases} c_i^j x_i^j + d_i^j & \text{if} \quad x_i^j > 0 \\ 0 & \text{if} \quad x_i^j = 0 \end{cases}$$

$$i = 1, 2, 3, \quad j = 1, 2;$$

and

$$f_i^j\,(t_i^j) = \begin{cases} c_i^j\, t_i^j + d_i^j & \text{if} \quad t_i^j > 0 \\ 0 & \text{if} \quad t_i^j = 0 \end{cases}$$

$$i = 1,\ 2, \qquad j = 1,\ 2.$$

Let

$$c_{x^1} = \begin{bmatrix} 3 \\ 2 \\ 4 \end{bmatrix}, \qquad d_{x^1} = \begin{bmatrix} 1 \\ 3 \\ 1 \end{bmatrix},$$

$$c_{x^2} = \begin{bmatrix} 5 \\ 4 \\ 7 \end{bmatrix}, \qquad d_{x^2} = \begin{bmatrix} 2 \\ 6 \\ 4 \end{bmatrix},$$

$$c_{t^1} = \begin{bmatrix} 1 \\ 3 \end{bmatrix}, \qquad d_{t^1} = \begin{bmatrix} 2 \\ 1 \end{bmatrix},$$

$$c_{t^2} = \begin{bmatrix} 5 \\ 3 \end{bmatrix}, \qquad d_{t^2} = \begin{bmatrix} 3 \\ 7 \end{bmatrix},$$

where $c_{x^i} = (c_j^i)$ associated with x_j^i. The remaining notation follows in like manner.

Examining the problem structure gives:

$$M_1 = \{x_1^1\} \qquad M_4 = \{x_1^2\}$$

$$M_2 = \{t_1^1,\ x_2^1\} \qquad M_5 = \{t_1^2,\ x_2^2\}$$

$$M_3 = \{t_2^1,\ x_3^1\} \qquad M_6 = \{t_2^2,\ x_3^2\}\ .$$

Assume $\ell = 100$ is appropriately large.

To start the solution procedure let y^1 correspond to the optimal linear program solution of the inner problem ignoring $x \leqq \ell y$. $J(y^1) = (x_1^1, x_2^1, x_3^1, x_1^2, x_2^2, t_3^2)$. The outer problem becomes

$$\text{Min } z + d_x'\, y_x + d_t'\, y_t$$

Subject to

$$z \geqq 54 \qquad \text{and} \qquad (y_x,\ y_t)' \in Y.$$

The two alternative optimal solutions to the above problem are:

$$J(y^2) = (x_1^1, t_1^1, t_2^1, x_1^2, t_1^2, x_3^2)$$

$$J(y^2) = (x_1^1, t_1^1, x_3^1, x_1^2, t_1^2, x_3^2).$$

Using the first gives a second outer problem of:

$$\text{Min } z + d_x{}'y_x + d_t{}'y_t$$

Subject to

$$z \geqq 54$$

$$z \geqq 87 - 200y_{x_2^1} - 300y_{x_3^1} - 500y_{x_2^2}$$

$$(y_x, y_t)' \in Y.$$

Continuing as above, and using all alternative optima, the following was found:

Iteration	$J(y^i)$	Added Constraint
3	$(x_1^1, t_1^1, x_3^1, x_1^2, t_1^2, x_3^2)$	$z \geqq 78 - 200x_2^1 - 500x_2^2$
4	$(x_1^1, x_2^1, x_3^1, x_1^2, t_1^2, x_3^2)$	$z \geqq 70 - 700x_2^2$
	$(x_1^1, x_2^1, t_2^1, x_1^2, t_1^2, x_3^2)$	$z \geqq 73 - 100x_2^2 - 700x_2^2$
5	$(x_1^1, t_1^1, t_2^1, x_1^2, x_2^2, x_3^2)$	$z \geqq 77 - 200x_2^1 - 300x_3^1 - 300t_2^2$
	$(x_1^1, t_1^1, x_3^1, x_1^2, x_2^2, x_3^2)$	$z \geqq 68 - 200x_2^1$
6	$(x_1^1, x_2^1, t_2^1, x_1^2, x_2^2, x_3^2)$	$z \geqq 59 - 100x_3^1 - 300t_2^2$
	$(x_1^1, x_2^1, x_3^1, x_1^2, x_2^2, x_3^2)$	$z \geqq 56 - 200t_2^2$
7	$(x_1^1, x_2^1, x_3^1, x_1^2, x_2^2, x_3^3)$	

-STOP-

(In the right side of the above table x_i^j and t_i^j represent, respectively, $y_{x_i^j}$ and $y_{t_i^j}$).

CHAPTER 4

Extended Discussion of Leontief Systems I

In this chapter we present definitions and proofs not included in earlier chapters. We also include results not required in earlier chapters which are required to complete proofs in this chapter.

4.1 Notation

There are several definitions for norms. In general we wish to measure the deviation between vectors or matrices. A vector norm or matrix norm is used to measure such a deviation. Let $||\cdot||$ be a vector or matrix norm. Some commonly used norms are:

$$||A|| = \sum_{i,j} |a_{ij}|.$$

$$||A||_1 = \max_{1 \leqq j \leqq n} \sum_{i=1}^{n} |a_{ij}|, \quad \text{A is square.}$$

$$||A||_\infty = \max_{1 \leqq i \leqq n} \sum_{j=1}^{n} |a_{ij}|, \quad \text{A is square.}$$

$$||A|| = \left(\sum_{i,j} a_{ij}^2\right)^{\frac{1}{2}}.$$

$$||A||_2 = \max_{x'x = 1} (x'A'Ax)^{\frac{1}{2}}.$$

In general, norms satisfy [30]:

1. $||A|| \geqq 0.$
2. $||A|| = 0$ if and only if $A = 0.$
3. $||\lambda A|| = |\lambda| \cdot ||A||$ for $\lambda \in R.$
4. $||AB|| \leqq ||A|| \cdot ||B||.$
5. $||A+B|| \leqq ||A|| + ||B||.$

In showing certain convergence properties, it is usually convenient to speak of the spectral radius of a matrix.

Definition 4.1.1 (Spectrum of a Matrix)

Given an n by n matrix A, the spectrum of A, denoted by $\sigma(A)$, is the set of its eigenvalues. That is,

$$\sigma(A) = \{\lambda_1, \lambda_2, \ldots, \lambda_n\}$$

where λ_i, i = 1, ..., n, are the roots of the characteristic equation

$$\det(A - \lambda I) = 0.$$

Definition 4.1.2 (Spectral Radius)

The spectral radius of an n by n matrix A, denoted by $\rho(A)$, is the greatest modulus of its eigenvalues. That is,

$$\rho(A) = \max_{1 \leqq i \leqq n} |\lambda_i|, \qquad \lambda_i \in \sigma(A).$$

The spectral radius is the radius of the smallest disk in the complex plane with center at the origin which contains all the eigenvalues of A.

Theorem 4.1.1

For an arbitrary n by n matrix A,

$$||A|| \geqq \rho(A)$$

where $||\cdot||$ is one of the various matrix norms.

Proof.

Since $Ax = \lambda x$ where $\lambda \in \sigma(A)$ and x is an eigenvector of A, we have

$$||Ax|| = ||\lambda x||.$$

Noting the properties of norms,

$$||A|| \cdot ||x|| \geqq |\lambda| \; ||x||.$$

But $|\lambda| = \rho(A)$ for some $\lambda \in \sigma(A)$. Hence

$$||A|| \geqq \rho(A).$$

Q.E.D.

We note then that $1 > ||A||$ implies $1 > \rho(A)$.

Example 4.1.1

Consider

$$A = \begin{bmatrix} 1 & -2 & 1 \\ -2 & 4 & -2 \\ 1 & -2 & 1 \end{bmatrix}.$$

Note that A is a symmetric matrix and hence that all eigenvalues of A must be real numbers (see [52] for a proof of this). We have

$$\sigma(A) = \{6, 0, 0\}$$

and

$$\rho(A) = 6.0 .$$

Note that $||A|| \geqq 6.0$.

Consider the following two definitions of particular subspaces.

Definition 4.1.3 (Null Space)

The null space of an m by n matrix A, written N(A), is defined as

$$N(A) = \{x\colon Ax = 0,\ x \in R^n\}.$$

Definition 4.1.4 (Range Space)

The range space of a m by n matrix A, written R(A), is defined as

$$R(A) = \{y\colon y = Ax,\ x \in R^n\}.$$

Example 4.1.2

The null space of

$$A = \begin{bmatrix} 1 & 2 & 1 \\ 0 & 1 & 1 \\ 1 & -1 & 2 \end{bmatrix}$$

can be found by solving the homogeneous system

$$Ax = 0.$$

The solution is the set of all vectors spanned by

$$\begin{bmatrix} 1 \\ -1 \\ 1 \end{bmatrix}.$$

That is,

$$N(A) = \{x: x = \lambda \begin{bmatrix} 1 \\ -1 \\ 1 \end{bmatrix}, \lambda \in R\}.$$

The last notational construct we wish to point out involves submatrices. If A is n by n, let N denote the integers {1, ..., n} and $M \subset N$. Then A(M) is a submatrix of A formed by crossing out rows and columns in M^c (the complement of M).

Example 4.1.3

Let n = 4, M = {2,4}, and

$$A = \begin{bmatrix} 1 & 4 & 0 & 1 \\ 6 & 2 & -1 & 4 \\ -3 & -1 & 0 & 3 \\ 2 & -2 & 1 & 1 \end{bmatrix}.$$

Then A(M) is

$$\begin{bmatrix} 2 & 4 \\ -2 & 1 \end{bmatrix}.$$

Such matrices are called principal submatrices of A corresponding to M [32].

4.2 Matrix Iterative Analysis

Lemma 4.2.1

Let A be a given n by n matrix. Let $L_{K_i}(\lambda_i)$ denote a K_i by K_i matrix of the form:

$$L_{K_i}(\lambda_i) = \begin{bmatrix} \lambda_i & 1 & & 0 \\ & \lambda_i & 1 & \\ & & \ddots & 1 \\ 0 & & & \lambda_i \end{bmatrix}.$$

Then there exists an n by n non-singular matrix T such that

$$TAT^{-1} = \begin{bmatrix} L_{K_1}(\lambda_1) & & 0 \\ & \ddots & \\ 0 & & L_{K_r}(\lambda_r) \end{bmatrix} = \tilde{A}$$

where $K_1 + K_2 + \ldots + K_r = n$ and λ_i are the distinct eigenvalues of A with multiplicity K_i. $\tilde{A}$ is called the Jordan form of A.

The proof of the above lemma is quite involved and can be found in MacLane and Birkhoff [85].

Example 4.2.1 (Jordan Form)

Consider

$$A = \begin{bmatrix} 1 & -2 & 1 \\ -2 & 4 & -2 \\ 1 & -2 & 1 \end{bmatrix}.$$

We have

$$\sigma(A) = \{6, 0, 0\}.$$

An eigenvector x_1 associated with the eigenvalue $\lambda = 6$ is

$$x_1' = (1, -2, 1).$$

(That is, x_1 generates the null space of $A - 6I$).

The two eigenvectors corresponding to $\lambda = 0$ ($\lambda = 0$ has multiplicity 2, $K_2(0) = 2$) are

$$x_2' = (2,\ 1,\ 0)$$

and

$$x_3' = (1,\ -2,\ -5).$$

Normalizing each eigenvector gives

$$u_1' = \left[\frac{1}{\sqrt{6}},\ -\frac{2}{\sqrt{6}},\ \frac{1}{\sqrt{6}}\right] \quad \text{for } x_1,$$

$$u_2' = \left[\frac{2}{\sqrt{5}},\ \frac{1}{\sqrt{5}},\ 0\right] \quad \text{for } x_2,$$

$$u_3' = \left[\frac{1}{\sqrt{30}},\ \frac{-2}{\sqrt{30}},\ \frac{-5}{\sqrt{30}}\right] \quad \text{for } x_3.$$

Let

$$T = \begin{bmatrix} \frac{1}{\sqrt{6}} & \frac{2}{\sqrt{5}} & \frac{1}{\sqrt{30}} \\ \frac{-2}{\sqrt{6}} & \frac{1}{\sqrt{5}} & \frac{-2}{\sqrt{30}} \\ \frac{1}{\sqrt{6}} & 0 & \frac{-5}{\sqrt{30}} \end{bmatrix}^{-1},$$

$$L_{K_1}(\lambda = 6) = \begin{bmatrix} 6 \end{bmatrix},$$

and

$$L_{K_2}(\lambda = 0) = \begin{bmatrix} 0 & 1 \\ 0 & 0 \end{bmatrix}.$$

Then

$$TAT^{-1} = \begin{bmatrix} 6 & 0 & 0 \\ 0 & 0 & 1 \\ 0 & 0 & 0 \end{bmatrix} = \begin{bmatrix} L_{K_1}(6) & 0 \\ 0 & L_{K_2}(0) \end{bmatrix}.$$

Example 4.2.2 (Jordan Form)

Consider

$$A = \begin{bmatrix} 3 & 1 & 1 \\ 5 & 7 & 0 \\ 0 & 0 & 1 \end{bmatrix}.$$

Note that A is not a symmetric matrix. We have

$$\sigma(A) = \{1, 2, 8\}.$$

Eigenvectors associated with the eigenvalues in $\sigma(A)$ are:

$$x_1' = (-6, 5, 7) \quad \text{for } \lambda = 1,$$

$$x_2' = (1, -1, 0) \quad \text{for } \lambda = 2,$$

$$x_3' = (1, 5, 0) \quad \text{for } \lambda = 8.$$

Consider

$$T = (x_1, x_2, x_3)^{-1}$$

$$= \begin{bmatrix} -6 & 1 & 1 \\ 5 & -1 & 5 \\ 7 & 0 & 0 \end{bmatrix}^{-1}.$$

Then

$$TAT^{-1} = \begin{bmatrix} 1 & 0 & 0 \\ 0 & 2 & 0 \\ 0 & 0 & 8 \end{bmatrix}.$$

We have $L_{K_1}(\lambda = 1) = [1]$,

$$L_{K_2}(\lambda = 2) = [2],$$

and

$$L_{K_3}(\lambda = 8) = [8].$$

Example 4.2.3 (Jordan Form)

Consider the matrix

$$A = \begin{bmatrix} 3 & 0 & 0 \\ 0 & 4 & \sqrt{3} \\ 0 & \sqrt{3} & 6 \end{bmatrix}.$$

We have $\sigma(A) = \{7, 3, 3\}$. Eigenvectors associated with $\sigma(A)$ are

$$x_1' = (0, 1/2, \sqrt{3}/2) \quad \text{for} \quad \lambda = 7,$$

$$x_2' = (0, -\sqrt{3}/2, 1/2) \quad \text{for} \quad \lambda = 3,$$

$$x_3' = (1, 0, 0) \quad \text{for} \quad \lambda = 3.$$

Let

$$T = \begin{bmatrix} 0 & 0 & 1 \\ 1/2 & -\sqrt{3}/2 & 0 \\ \sqrt{3}/2 & 1/2 & 0 \end{bmatrix}^{-1}.$$

Then

$$TAT^{-1} = \begin{bmatrix} 7 & 0 & 0 \\ 0 & 3 & 0 \\ 0 & 0 & 3 \end{bmatrix}.$$

We have $L_{K_1}(\lambda = 7) = [7]$ and

$$L_{K_2}(\lambda = 3) = \begin{bmatrix} 3 & 0 \\ 0 & 3 \end{bmatrix}.$$

Using the Lemma 4.2.1, we prove the following important result.

Theorem 2.2.1

The infinite power of an n by n matrix A is zero if and only if $\rho(A) < 1$. That is, A is convergent if and only if its spectral radius is strictly less than one. (Oldenburger [97])

Proof.

($\Rightarrow$) By Lemma 4.2.1, there exists a nonsingular matrix T such that

$$TAT^{-1} = \tilde{A}.$$

By direction computation

$$(TAT^{-1})^m = TA^mT^{-1} = \tilde{A}^m.$$

Also

$$\tilde{A}^m = \begin{bmatrix} L^m_{K_1}(\lambda_1) & & 0 \\ & \ddots & \\ 0 & & L^r_{K_r}(\lambda_r) \end{bmatrix}.$$

Furthermore, the i,j^{th} component of $L^m_{K_\ell}(\lambda_\ell)$, denoted $d^m_{ij}(\ell)$, is

$$d^m_{ij}(\ell) = \begin{cases} 0 & \text{for } j < i \\ 0 & \text{for } m+i < j \leqq K_\ell \\ \binom{m}{j-i} \lambda_\ell^{m-j+1} & \text{for } i \leqq j \leqq \mathrm{Min}(K_\ell, m+i). \end{cases}$$

Now, if TA^mT^{-1} is convergent, then $\tilde{A}$ is convergent. But if $\tilde{A}^m$ is convergent, then each $L_{K_i}(\lambda_i)$ must be convergent. Hence, in each of the diagonal matrices $L_{K_i}(\lambda_i)$ the following inequality must hold:

$$|\lambda_i| < 1.$$

Clearly, if $|\lambda_i| < 1$ for $i = 1, \ldots, n$, then

$$\rho(A) = \max_{1 \leqq i \leqq n} |\lambda_i| < 1.$$

($\Leftarrow$) If $\rho(A) < 1$, then the diagonal elements of each $L_{K_i}(\lambda_i)$ satisfy $|\lambda_i| < 1$. It follows that

$$\lim_{m \to \infty} d^m_{ij}(\ell) = 0 \qquad i,j = 1, \ldots, K_\ell; \quad \ell = 1, \ldots, r.$$

Therefore, $\tilde{A}$ is convergent and since

$$A^m = A^{-1}\tilde{A}^mT,$$

A is convergent.

Q.E.D.

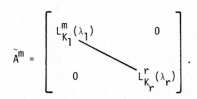

4.3 Class Z and K Matrices

To prove the various theorems in Section 2.3, we require some preliminary definitions and theorems.

Definition 4.3.1 (Irreducible Matrix)

An n by n matrix A is called reducible if there exists an n by n permutation matrix P such that

$$PAP' = \begin{bmatrix} A_{11} & A_{12} \\ 0 & A_{22} \end{bmatrix}$$

where A_{11} is an r by r submatrix and A_{22} is an (n-r) by (n-r) submatrix with $1 \leqq r < n$. If no such permutation exists, then A is called irreducible.

Example 4.3.1

$$A = \begin{bmatrix} 1 & -1 \\ 0 & 3 \end{bmatrix}$$ is a reducible matrix.

Let

$$P = P' = \begin{bmatrix} 1 & 0 \\ 0 & 1 \end{bmatrix}.$$

Then

$$PAP' = \begin{bmatrix} A_{11} & A_{12} \\ 0 & A_{22} \end{bmatrix}$$

with $A_{11} = [1]$, $A_{12} = [-1]$, and $A_{22} = [3]$.

Example 4.3.2

$$A = \begin{bmatrix} 0 & 0 & 1 & 1 \\ 0 & 0 & 1 & -1 \\ 1 & -1 & 0 & 0 \\ 1 & 1 & 0 & 0 \end{bmatrix}$$

is an irreducible matrix. That is, there exists no n by n permutation matrix P such that P and A satisfy Definition 4.3.1.

Example 4.3.3

$$A = \begin{bmatrix} 1 & 2 & 0 \\ 6 & 7 & 0 \\ 5 & 2 & 3 \end{bmatrix} \quad \text{is a reducible matrix.}$$

Let

$$P = \begin{bmatrix} 0 & 0 & 1 \\ 0 & 1 & 0 \\ 1 & 0 & 0 \end{bmatrix}.$$

Then

$$PAP' = \begin{bmatrix} A_{11} & A_{12} \\ \begin{matrix} 0 \\ 0 \end{matrix} & A_{22} \end{bmatrix}$$

where $A_{11} = [3]$, $A_{22} = \begin{bmatrix} 7 & 6 \\ 2 & 1 \end{bmatrix}$, and $A_{12} = [2, 5]$.

Note that A_{11} and A_{22} are both irreducible matrices.

Example 4.3.4

$$A = \begin{bmatrix} 1 & -1 & 2 & 3 & 0 & 1 & 0 \\ 2 & 4 & 6 & 7 & 1 & -1 & 0 \\ 9 & 5 & 7 & 3 & 2 & -1 & 0 \\ 2 & -1 & 1 & 0 & 1 & 2 & -1 \\ 0 & 0 & 0 & 0 & 1 & -1 & 0 \\ 0 & 0 & 0 & 0 & 3 & 5 & 7 \\ 0 & 0 & 0 & 0 & 1 & -1 & 1 \end{bmatrix}$$

is a reducible matrix.

Let $P = I$ (7 by 7 identity matrix). Then

$$PAP' = \begin{bmatrix} A_{11} & A_{12} \\ 0 & A_{22} \end{bmatrix}$$

with

$$A_{11} = \begin{bmatrix} 1 & -1 & 2 & 3 \\ 2 & 4 & 6 & 7 \\ 9 & 5 & 7 & 3 \\ 2 & -1 & 1 & 0 \end{bmatrix} \quad \text{and} \quad A_{22} = \begin{bmatrix} 1 & -1 & 0 \\ 3 & 5 & 7 \\ 1 & -1 & 1 \end{bmatrix}.$$

Note that both A_{11} and A_{22} are irreducible matrices.

We now give a description of the algorithm of Fox and Landi [40] for determining the irreducible submatrices of a given n by n matrix $M = (m_{ij})$.

Let $B^{(1)} = (b_{ij})$ be the Boolean representation of M. That is,

$$b_{ij} = \begin{cases} 1 & \text{if } m_{ij} \neq 0 \\ 0 & \text{if } m_{ij} = 0 \end{cases}$$

for all $i,j = 1, \ldots, n$.

Using the terminology of Markov chains we call each i and j (the indices of the elements b_{ij} in $B^{(1)}$) states and say that two states i and j <u>communicate</u> if there exists two sequences of pairs of states, say

$$(i_1, i_2), (i_2, i_3), \ldots, (i_{n-1}, i_n)$$

and

$$(j_1, j_2), (j_2, j_3), \ldots, (j_{m-1}, j_m)$$

with $i = i_1 = j_m$ and $j = i_n = j_1$ such that

$$\prod_{k=1}^{n-1} b_{i_k i_{k+1}} = 1 \quad \text{and} \quad \prod_{k=1}^{m-1} b_{j_k j_{k+1}} = 1.$$

Continuing we say that

(1) a state i is <u>absorbing</u> if and only if $b_{ii} = 1$ and $b_{ij} = 0$ for all $j \neq i$;

(2) if state j is absorbing and $b_{ij} = 1$, then state i is said to be a transient state;

(3) if state j is transient and $b_{kj} = 1$, then state k is also transient;

(4) if state i communicates with state j and state j communicates with state k, then state i communicates with state k.

The Fox and Landi algorithm requires that $B^{(1)}$ is searched for a set of communicating states. Next the rows and columns of $B^{(1)}$ that correspond to the set of communicating states are replaced by a single state representing the union of the states in the communicating set, forming a new matrix $B^{(2)}$ of smaller dimensionality. The matrix $B^{(2)}$ is searched in the same manner as $B^{(1)}$ for communicating states, and so forth. The irreducible submatrices of M are identified when a set of communicating states collapses into an absorbing state.

We now give the Fox and Landi algorithm followed by an example.

ALGORITHM (Fox and Landi)

Step 1

Define the single element sets $S_i = \{i\}$ for each state i ($i=1, 2, \ldots, n$). Search the main diagonal of $B^{(1)}$, using (1) and label each absorbing state as an "A". If a state j is absorbing, then label every state with $b_{ij} = 1$ as a "T", a transient state. Let $n = 0$. (Note in the example following Step 4 that none of the states are absorbing.) Go to Step 2.

Step 2

If all the states are labeled, then stop; otherwise go to Step 3.

Step 3

If $n = 0$, then construct a chain of states beginning by searching any row, say row i_0, which corresponds to an unlabeled state, for a 1. That is,

(3*) search unlabeled row i_0 for a 1 which occurs in, say, position i_1. Next extend the chain of states $\{i_0, i_1, \ldots, i_n\}$ by searching row i_n (initially $n = 1$) for a 1, say $b_{i_n i_{n+1}} = 1$; if state i_{n+1} is transient, label each state in the set $(S_{i_0} \cup S_{i_1} \cup \ldots \cup S_{i_n})$ transient and set $n = 0$ and go to Step 2; if state i_{n+1} has not been labeled transient and $i_{n+1} = i_k$ for some $k \leqq n$ (a closed loop), go to Step 4; otherwise, replace n by $n+1$ and extend the chain again.

Step 4

Replace row i_k by the union of the rows $i_k, i_{k+1}, \ldots, i_n$. Replace column i_k by the union of the columns $i_k, i_{k+1}, \ldots, i_n$. Delete rows and columns $i_{k+1}, i_{k+2}, \ldots, i_n$ from the matrix. Let $S_{i_k} = (S_{i_k} \cup S_{i_{k+1}} \cup \ldots \cup S_{i_n})$. If state i_k is absorbing, then label each state in S_{i_k} ergodic, "E", label each state with $b_{hi_k} = 1$ transient, set $n = 0$ and go to Step 2. If state i_k is not absorbing, set $n = k$, $i_0 = k$, and go to 3* in Step 3.

Note that once all the states are labeled, we can say that M is irreducible if the only set of ergodic states is $\{1, 2, \ldots, n\}$. Otherwise M is a reducible matrix containing irreducible submatrices associated with the ergodic subsets of $\{1, 2, \ldots, n\}$.

Example 4.3.5

Consider the following Boolean matrix $B^{(1)}$ constructed from the matrix A given in Example 4.3.4.

$$B^{(1)} = \begin{array}{c} \\ 1 \\ 2 \\ 3 \\ 4 \\ 5 \\ 6 \\ 7 \end{array} \begin{array}{c} \begin{array}{ccccccc} 1 & 2 & 3 & 4 & 5 & 6 & 7 \end{array} \\ \begin{bmatrix} 1 & 1 & 1 & 1 & 0 & 1 & 0 \\ 1 & 1 & 1 & 1 & 1 & 1 & 0 \\ 1 & 1 & 1 & 1 & 1 & 1 & 0 \\ 1 & 1 & 1 & 0 & 1 & 1 & 1 \\ 0 & 0 & 0 & 0 & 1 & 1 & 0 \\ 0 & 0 & 0 & 0 & 1 & 1 & 1 \\ 0 & 0 & 0 & 0 & 1 & 1 & 1 \end{bmatrix} \end{array} .$$

Note that no states are absorbing. We have

$$B^{(2)} = \begin{array}{c} \\ 1,2 \\ 3 \\ 4 \\ 5 \\ 6 \\ 7 \end{array} \begin{array}{c} \begin{array}{cccccc} 1,2 & 3 & 4 & 5 & 6 & 7 \end{array} \\ \begin{bmatrix} 1 & 1 & 1 & 1 & 1 & 0 \\ 1 & 1 & 1 & 1 & 1 & 0 \\ 1 & 1 & 0 & 1 & 1 & 1 \\ 0 & 0 & 0 & 1 & 1 & 0 \\ 0 & 0 & 0 & 1 & 1 & 1 \\ 0 & 0 & 0 & 1 & 1 & 1 \end{bmatrix} \end{array} ,$$

$$B^{(3)} = \begin{array}{c} \\ 1,2,3 \\ 4 \\ 5 \\ 6 \\ 7 \end{array} \begin{array}{c} \begin{array}{ccccc} 1,2,3 & 4 & 5 & 6 & 7 \end{array} \\ \begin{bmatrix} 1 & 1 & 1 & 1 & 0 \\ 1 & 0 & 1 & 1 & 1 \\ 0 & 0 & 1 & 1 & 0 \\ 0 & 0 & 1 & 1 & 1 \\ 0 & 0 & 1 & 1 & 1 \end{bmatrix} \end{array} ,$$

and

$$B^{(4)} = \begin{array}{c} \\ 1,2,3,4 \\ 5 \\ 6 \\ 7 \end{array} \begin{array}{c} \begin{array}{cccc} 1,2,3,4 & 5 & 6 & 7 \end{array} \\ \begin{bmatrix} 1 & 1 & 1 & 1 \\ 0 & 1 & 1 & 0 \\ 0 & 1 & 1 & 1 \\ 0 & 1 & 1 & 1 \end{bmatrix} \end{array}$$

where the matrices $B^{(2)}$, $B^{(3)}$, and $B^{(4)}$ were constructed by successive applications of Step 3.

Continuing,

$$B^{(5)} = \begin{array}{r} \\ 1,2,3,4 \\ 5,6 \\ 7 \end{array} \begin{array}{c} \begin{array}{ccc} \begin{matrix}1,2\\3,4\end{matrix} & 5,6 & 7 \end{array} \\ \begin{bmatrix} 1 & 1 & 1 \\ 0 & 1 & 1 \\ 0 & 1 & 1 \end{bmatrix} \end{array}$$

and

$$B^{(6)} = \begin{array}{r} \\ 1,2,3,4 \\ 5,6,7 \end{array} \begin{array}{c} \begin{array}{cc} 1,2,3,4 & 5,6,7 \end{array} \\ \begin{bmatrix} 1 & 1 \\ 0 & 1 \end{bmatrix} \end{array} \begin{array}{c} T \\ A \end{array}.$$

Note that in this example all the states remained unlabeled until matrix $B^{(6)}$ was computed. We have

$$A = \begin{bmatrix} A_{11} & A_{12} \\ 0 & A_{22} \end{bmatrix}$$

where the column vectors in A_{22} correspond to the set of ergodic states: 5, 6, and 7. The column vectors forming A_{11} are 1, 2, 3, and 4. Also, A_{22} is an irreducible matrix.

We now turn to a discussion of class Z matrices and some related results. Consider $A \in Z$. Then $A \in Z$, as noted in Chapter 2, can be written as

$$A = I - B$$

where $B \geqq 0$. In light of Section 2.2 we would like to know whether $\rho(B) < 1$. We now turn to Perron's [99] theorem on positive matrices and its generalization by Frobenius [41]. See [104] for a geometric view of the Frobenius theorem and references to several other proofs and generalizations of the Perron-Frobenius results. The following statements and proofs of the Perron-Frobenius theorem are taken from Debreu and Herstein [21] and Varga [122].

<u>Theorem 4.3.2</u> (Perron-Frobenius Theorem)

Let M be an n by n non-negative irreducible matrix.

Then:

1. M has a positive real eigenvalue, r, equal to its spectral radius.
2. Associated with r is an eigenvector $x > 0$.

3. r increases when any element of M increases.
4. r is a simple eigenvalue of M.

Proof.

(1) Note that if $x \geq 0$ then $Mx \geq 0$. If not, at least one column of M would consist of zeros and M would not be irreducible. Hence $e'Mx > 0$ for all $x \geq 0$. Consider the simplex $S = \{x \varepsilon R^n: x \geq 0, x'e = 1\}$ and the mapping $T:S \to S$ defined by:

$$T(x) = \frac{1}{\alpha(x)} Mx \quad \text{where } \alpha(x) > 0.$$

Clearly $\alpha(x) > 0$ exists for every $x \varepsilon S$ (for example $\alpha(x) = e'Mx > 0$). Now T is a continuous transformation of S into S and hence, by the Brouwer fixed point theorem, there exists a unique $x_0 \varepsilon S$, such that $T(x_0) = x_0 = (1/\alpha(x_0))Mx_0$. Let $r = \alpha(x_0)$. Note that r is an eigenvalue of M and x_0 its associated eigenvector. To prove that $r = \rho(M)$ first consider the proof of part (2).

(2) From the above we have $x_0 \geq 0$, $r > 0$. Let x_0 and M be similarly permuted so that:

$$\tilde{M} = \begin{bmatrix} M_{11} & M_{12} \\ M_{21} & M_{22} \end{bmatrix}, \qquad \tilde{x}_0 = \begin{bmatrix} \varepsilon \\ 0 \end{bmatrix}, \qquad \varepsilon > 0.$$

Then

$$\tilde{M}\tilde{x}_0 = r\tilde{x}_0$$

or

$$M_{11}\varepsilon = r\varepsilon$$

and

$$M_{21}\varepsilon = 0$$

which implies that $M_{21} = 0$, or that M is reducible, a contradiction. Therefore, $x_0 > 0$. Returning now to complete the proof of (1), consider M'. Since M is irreducible and non-negative, so also is M'. Hence we can find an eigenvector x_1 and associated eigenvalue r, of M' where $r_1 > 0$ and $x_1 > 0$. Then

$$M'x_1 = r_1x_1$$

and

$$M'x_1 = |M'x_1| = |r_1x_1| = r_1x_1.$$

Consider

$$My = \lambda y \qquad \text{with} \qquad \lambda \in \sigma(M),\ y \neq 0.$$

Then

$$M|y| = |M|\,|y| \geqq |My| = |\lambda y| = |\lambda|\cdot|y|.$$

Now

$$|y|'M'x_1 = r_1|y|'x_1$$

and

$$x_1'\ M|y| \geqq |\lambda|x_1'|y|$$

or

$$r_1|y|'x_1 \geqq |\lambda|x_1'\ |y|.$$

Now since $x_1 > 0$ and $|y| \geq 0$, $x_1'\ |y| > 0$.
Therefore

$$r_1 \geqq |\lambda|.$$

We know that since $Mx_0 = rx_0$, $r \in \sigma(M)$. Hence $r_1 \geqq r$. Repeating the argument with M replacing M' we find $r \geqq r_1$. Noting that $\sigma(M) = \sigma(M')$ we conclude that r is the spectral radius of M.

(3) Let $N \geq M$ (which means at least one element of N is strictly greater than a corresponding element of M). Since N' and M are non-negative and irreducible we know from parts (1) and (2) that there exists x_1 and r_1, x_0, and r such that:

$$N'x_1 = r_1x_1 \quad \text{with} \quad r_1 > 0,\ \ x_1 > 0,$$

and

$$Mx_0 = rx_0 \quad \text{with} \quad r > 0,\ \ x_0 > 0.$$

Also, since $N \geq M$,

$$Nx_0 \geq Mx_0 .$$

Hence

$$x'_1Nx_0 > x_1'Mx_0 = rx_1'x_0.$$

But

$$x_0'N'x_1 = r_1x_0'x_1.$$

Hence

$$r_1x_0'x_1 > rx_0'x_1.$$

Since $x_0'x_1 > 0$, then $r_1 > r$.
But, noting the proof of part (2), $\rho(N) = r_1$ and $\rho(M) = r$. Thus $\rho(N) > \rho(M)$.

(4) To prove that r is a simple eigenvalue of M (i.e., an eigenvalue of multiplicity one) consider any principal square submatrix B of M. (A principle square submatrix of a n x n matrix M is any matrix obtained by crossing out any j rows and the corresponding j columns of M, where $1 \leq j < n$.)
Let P be a permutation matrix such that

$$PMP' = \begin{bmatrix} B & M_{12} \\ M_{21} & M_{22} \end{bmatrix}$$

and let

$$C = \begin{bmatrix} B & 0 \\ 0 & 0 \end{bmatrix}.$$

Clearly, $0 \leqq C \leqq PMP'$ and, by Part (3) above, $|\lambda| < \rho(M)$ for $\lambda \in \sigma(C)$. Thus $\det(tI - B)$ with $t \geqq \rho(M)$ cannot be zero. Also, $\det(tI - B) = t^n + O(t^n)$, so $\lim_{t\to\infty} \det(tI - B) \to +\infty$ and $\det(tI - B) \neq 0$ for $t \geqq \rho(M)$ and is continuous so it must be that $\det(tI - B) > 0$. Now $\phi(t) = \det(tI - M)$ and $\phi'(t)$ is the sum of the determinants of (n-1) by (n-1) principal submatrices of tI - M (see MacLane and Birkhoff [85].) Thus $\phi'(t) > 0$ for $t \geqq r$. Thus r cannot have multiplicity greater than one.

Q.E.D.

The Perron-Frobenius Theorem can be generalized to reducible non-negative matrices. Continuity arguments can be used to extend the results of Theorem 4.3.2 to reducible matrices by noting that any reducible matrix can be made irreducible by replacing all zero entries by a small positive perturbation. The generalized results are given in the following theorem.

Theorem 4.3.3

Let M be an n by n non-negative matrix. Then

1. M has a non-negative real eigenvalue, r, equal to its spectral radius.

2. Associated with r is an eigenvector $x \geqq 0$.

3. r does not decrease when any element of M increases.

Corollary 4.3.2.1

If M is an n by n irreducible non-negative matrix, then either

$$Me = \rho(M)e$$

or

$$\underset{1 \leqq i \leqq n}{\text{Min}} \left[\sum_{j=1}^{n} m_{ij} \right] < \rho(M) < \underset{1 \leqq i \leqq n}{\text{Max}} \left[\sum_{j=i}^{n} m_{ij} \right].$$

Proof.

If $Me = \alpha e$ (i.e. all row sums equal), then obviously $\alpha \in \sigma(M)$ and $\rho(M) \geqq \alpha$. With $\rho(M)$ there exists $x > 0$ such that:

$$M'x = \rho(M)x.$$

But

$$e'M'x = \alpha e'x = \rho(M)e'x \quad \text{and} \quad e'x > 0.$$

Hence $\alpha = \rho(M)$.

Now consider the case where $Me \neq \rho(M)e$. Let B be a non-negative matrix such that B + M gives a matrix where every row sums to the maximum row sum of M. Then

$$(B + M)e = \rho(B + M)e.$$

Noting Theorem 4.3.2 Part 3 and the above, the maximum row sum of M equals $\rho(B + M)$ and satisfies $\rho(B + M) > \rho(M)$. Similarly, M could be decreased to a matrix having all row sums equal to the minimum row sum of M.

Q.E.D.

It is to be noted that Corollary 4.3.2.1 is also true for column sums.

We now give an example of Theorem 4.3.3 and Corollary 4.3.2.1.

Example 4.3.6

Let $$M = \begin{bmatrix} .23799 & .61770 & .04431 \\ .57132 & .01250 & .31619 \\ .20796 & .03901 & .65305 \end{bmatrix}.$$

Since M is positive, M is irreducible. We have

$$\sigma(M) = \{0.9000, -0.45766, 0.46119\}.$$

Note that Me = 0.9 . Thus, e is an eigenvector for $\rho(M) = 0.9$.

Consider now the following general properties of matrices (as given by Fiedler and Ptak [32]).

Definition 4.3.2 (Dominant Principal Diagonal)

An n by n matrix A is said to have dominant principal diagonal if

$$|a_{ii}| > \sum_{k \neq i} |a_{ik}| \quad \text{for} \quad i = 1,\ldots,n.$$

Theorem 4.3.4

If A is an n by n matrix with dominant principal diagonal, then

$$\rho(I - D^{-1}A) < 1$$

where D is the diagonal of A.

Proof.

Let $\lambda \in \sigma(I - D^{-1}A)$ and $x \neq 0$ be its associated eigenvector. Then

$$x - D^{-1}Ax = \lambda x.$$

Let i be such that

$$|x_i| \geqq |x_j|, \qquad j = 1,\ldots,n.$$

Then

$$|x_i| > 0$$

and

$$\lambda x_i = x_i - \frac{1}{a_{ii}} \sum_{j=1}^{n} a_{ij} x_j$$

which gives

$$|\lambda||x_i| = |\lambda x_i| = \Big|\sum_{\substack{j=1 \\ j\neq i}}^{n} \frac{a_{ij}}{a_{ii}} x_j\Big| \leqq \sum_{\substack{j=1 \\ j\neq i}}^{n} \frac{|a_{ij}|}{|a_{ii}|} |x_j| < |x_i|.$$

Therefore, $|\lambda| < 1$. Since λ was an arbitrary eigenvalue of $I - D^{-1}A$, $\rho(\lambda) < 1$.

Q.E.D.

Let M_i denote the set $\{1,2,...,i\}$.

Theorem 4.3.5

For an n by n matrix A the following are equivalent:

1. $\det A(M_i) > 0$ for $i = 1, ..., n$.
2. There exists a lower triangular matrix T_1 and an upper triangular matrix T_2 both with positive diagonal elements such that $A = T_1T_2$.

Proof.

We shall show that (1)⟹(2) by induction.

For $n = 1$, (2) readily follows.

Assume (2) is true for all matrices of order less than $n > 1$.

Let:

$$A = \begin{bmatrix} A_{n-1} & a \\ b' & a_{nn} \end{bmatrix}$$

satisfy condition (1). Then $\det A > 0$, $\det A_{n-1} > 0$, and

$$\det A = (\det A_{n-1})(a_{nn} - b' A_{n-1}^{-1} a) > 0.$$

Hence $a_{nn} - b'A_{n-1}^{-1}a > 0$.

We are given that (2) is true for matrices of order less than or equal to n-1. Hence

$$A_{n-1} = \tilde{T}_1\tilde{T}_2$$

for some lower triangular matrix $\tilde{T}_1$ and upper triangular matrix $\tilde{T}_2$, both with positive diagonal elements.

Then

$$A = T_1T_2$$

with

$$T_1 = \begin{bmatrix} \tilde{T}_1 & 0 \\ b'\tilde{T}_2^{-1} & 1 \end{bmatrix}, \qquad T_2 = \begin{bmatrix} \tilde{T}_2 & \tilde{T}_1^{-1}a \\ 0 & a_{nn} - b'A_{n-1}^{-1}a \end{bmatrix},$$

where T_1 and T_2 satisfy (2).

(2)⟹(1)

Note that T_1 and T_2 are, respectively, lower and upper triangular. Thus, for $A = T_1T_2$,

$$\det(A(M_i)) = \sum_{j=1}^{i} (T_1)_{jj}(T_2)_{jj}.$$

But $(T_1)_{jj}$ and $(T_2)_{jj}$ are positive. Hence $\det(A(M_i)) > 0$ for $i = 1,\ldots,n$.

Q.E.D.

Theorem 4.3.6

Let $A \in Z$ and n by n. Suppose

$$A = T_1T_2$$

where $T_1(T_2)$ is a lower (upper) triangular matrix with positive diagonal elements. Then $T_1 \in Z$ and $T_2 \in Z$.

Proof.

Let $T_1 = (r_{ij})$ and $T_2 = (s_{ij})$.

Then:

$$r_{ij} = 0 \quad \text{for} \quad i < j \text{ and } r_{ii} > 0 \qquad i,j = 1,\ldots,n$$

$$s_{ij} = 0 \quad \text{for} \quad i > j \text{ and } s_{ii} > 0 \qquad i,j = 1,\ldots,n.$$

For $i + j = 3$, $r_{21} \leqq 0$ and $s_{12} \leqq 0$, since $a_{12} = r_{11}s_{12}$ and $a_{21} = r_{21}s_{11}$. Now, using induction on $i + j$, let $i + j > 3$ with $i \neq j$ and consider $r_{k\ell} \leqq 0$ and $s_{k\ell} \leqq 0$ for $k \neq \ell$ and $k + \ell < i + j$. Then for $i < j$:

$$a_{ij} = r_{ii}s_{ij} + \sum_{k<i} r_{ik}s_{kj}$$

which implies that $s_{ij} \leqq 0$. Similarly for $i > j$, we find $r_{ij} \leqq 0$. Thus the off diagonals of T_1 and T_2 are non-positive. Hence $T_1 \in Z$ and $T_2 \in Z$.

Q.E.D.

Definition 4.3.2 (Class P)

The set of all matrices fulfilling the properties of the following theorem are said to form class P.

Theorem 4.3.7

For an n by n matrix A, the following properties are equivalent:

1. All principal minors of A are positive.

2. For $x \neq 0$ and $y = Ax$, there exists an index ℓ such that $x_\ell y_\ell > 0$.

3. For $x \neq 0$ there exists a diagonal matrix D_x with positive diagonal such that

$$x'A'D_x x > 0.$$

4. For $x \neq 0$ there exists a diagonal matrix $H_x \geqq 0$ such that

$$x'A'H_x x > 0.$$

5. Every real eigenvalue of A(M) is positive where $M \subseteq \{1,2,\ldots,n\}$.

Proof.

(1)⟹(2)

Let $x \neq 0$ and $y = Ax$ with $x_i y_i \leqq 0$ for $i = 1,2,\ldots,n$. Let $M = \{i: x_i \neq 0\} \neq \emptyset$. Let x(M) be the vector formed from x using the components with subscripts listed in M. Consider $z = A(M)x(M)$ where z is y(M). Since $x_i y_i \leqq 0$, then $z_i x(M)_i \leqq 0$ and there exists a diagonal matrix $D \geqq 0$ of the same order as A(M) such that $z = -Dx(M)$.

In other words:

$$(A(M) + D)x(M) = 0.$$

Since $x(M) \neq 0$, $N(A(M) + D) \neq \{0\}$ and $A(M) + D$ is singular. Now A has all principal minors positive and $D \geqq 0$ and diagonal. Thus $A(M) + D$ has all principal minors positive. This implies that $A(M) + D$ is nonsingular, a contradiction. Thus $x_i y_i > 0$. (In the above $N(\cdot)$ is a null space. See Definition 4.1.3.)

(2)⟹(3)

For $x \neq 0$, and $y = Ax$, let ℓ be the index such that $x_\ell y_\ell > 0$ and $\varepsilon > 0$ and small enough so that

$$x_\ell y_\ell + \varepsilon \sum_{j \neq \ell} x_j y_j > 0$$

Then set $d_{\ell\ell} = 1$, $d_{jj} = \varepsilon$ for $j \neq \ell$ and $d_{ij} = 0$ for $i \neq j$, $i,j = 1,\ldots,n$. Then the desired D_x is (d_{ij}).

(3)⟹(4)

Obvious from the construction of D_x in (2)⟹(3).

(4)⟹(5)

Let $0 \neq M \subseteq \{1,2,\ldots,n\}$ and $\lambda \in \sigma(A(M))$ be a real eigenvalue with eigenvector $x(M)$. Construct an n by 1 vector x from $x(M)$ by the following procedure.

Let $M = \{i_1, i_2, \ldots, i_k\}$. Set

$$x_{i_j} = x(M)_j \quad \text{for} \quad j = 1, \ldots, k$$

and

$$x_j = 0 \quad \text{for} \quad j \in M^c \quad (M^c \text{ is the complement of } M).$$

From (4) we have a diagonal matrix $H_x \geqq 0$ such that

$$0 < x'A'H_x x = x(M)'A(M)'H_x(M)x(M)$$

$$= \lambda\, x(M)'H_x(M)x(M)$$

$$= \lambda\, x'H_x x.$$

But $x'H_x x \geqq 0$, hence $\lambda > 0$.

(5)⟹(1)

For $\lambda \in \sigma(A(M))$ then $\lambda > 0$ if λ is real and the product of all the non-real eigenvalues is positive. Hence,

$$\prod_i \lambda_i > 0 \quad \text{for } \lambda_i \in \sigma(A(M)).$$

But $\prod_i \lambda_i = \det(A(M)) > 0$.

Q.E.D.

We now offer a slight modification of a result given by Fiedler and Ptak [32].

Theorem 2.3.3

Suppose $A \in Z$, $\sigma(A)$ contains at least one real eigenvalue and each real eigenvalue of A is positive. Let $B \in Z$ fulfill the inequality $A \leqq B$. Then,

1. Both A^{-1} and B^{-1} exist and $A^{-1} \geqq B^{-1} \geqq 0$.
2. each real eigenvalue of the matrix B is positive.
3. $\det(B) \geqq \det(A) > 0$.

Proof.

(1) Since $B \in Z$, we can find an $\alpha > 0$ so that $I - \alpha B \geqq 0$. Since $B \geqq A$, then

$$I - \alpha A \geqq I - \alpha B \geqq 0.$$

Now, by Theorem 4.3.3

$$\det(I - \alpha A - \rho(I - \alpha A)I) = 0$$

or

$$\det((1 - \rho(I - \alpha A))I - \alpha A) = 0.$$

Thus

$$\frac{(1 - \rho(I - \alpha A))}{\alpha} \in \sigma(A).$$

But $\rho(I - A)$ is real, α is real and all real eigenvalues of A are positive. Hence

$$\frac{1 - \rho(I - \alpha A)}{\alpha} > 0$$

or

$$1 > \rho(I - \alpha A).$$

Hence, by Theorems 2.2.1 and 2.2.2,

$$(I - (I - \alpha A))^{-1} = \sum_{\ell=0}^{\infty} (I - \alpha A)^{\ell}.$$

$I - \alpha A \geqq 0$ implies $(I - (I - \alpha A))^{-1} \geqq 0$.

But

$$A = \frac{1}{\alpha}(I - (I - \alpha A)).$$

Thus A is non-singular and

$$A^{-1} = \alpha(I - (I - \alpha A))^{-1} \geqq 0.$$

By Theorem 4.3.3

$$\rho(I - \alpha A) \geqq \rho(I - \alpha B) \geqq 0.$$

Thus $1 > (I - \alpha B)$ and $I - (I - \alpha B)$ is non-singular. Similarly, B is non-singular. Also, $B^{-1} \geqq 0$. Since $I - \alpha A \geqq I - \alpha B$, each term of the Neuman expansion (Theorem 2.2.2) has $(I - \alpha A)^{\ell} \geqq (I - \alpha B)^{\ell}$, or $A^{-1} \geqq B^{-1}$.

(2) For $\lambda \leqq 0$, $B - \lambda I \geqq A$ and by (1) above we have

$N(B - \lambda I) = \{0\}$. Hence λ cannot be in $\sigma(B)$.

(3) If A is of order 1, the result is obvious. Let the order of A be $n = k + 1$ where the result is true for all matrices of order less than or equal to k, $k \geqq 1$.
Let $M = \{1,2,...,n-1\}$. Then $A(M) \in Z$ and $B(M) \in Z$.
Also $A(M) \leqq B(M)$.
Let

$$\tilde{A} = \begin{bmatrix} A(M) & 0 \\ 0 & a_{nn} \end{bmatrix}.$$

Then $\tilde{A} \geqq A$ and $\tilde{A} \in Z$. Furthermore, by part 2 above, each real eigenvalue of $\tilde{A}$ is positive. By the construction of $\tilde{A}$, each real eigenvalue of A(M) is positive. By assumption we are given

$$\det(B(M)) \geqq \det(A(M)) > 0.$$

Since $A^{-1} \geqq B^{-1} \geqq 0$ (by part 1 above),

$$\frac{\det(A(M))}{\det(A)} \geqq \frac{\det(B(M))}{\det(B)} \geqq 0.$$

Hence $\det(A) > 0$ and $\det(B) > 0$. Furthermore

$$\det(B) \geqq \left[\frac{\det(A)}{\det(A(M))}\right]\left[\det(B(M))\right] \geqq \det(A) > 0.$$

Q.E.D.

Using theorems presented above, we now give Fiedler and Ptak's proof of Theorem 2.3.4 which characterizes class K matrices.

Theorem 2.3.4

For $A \in Z$, the following are equivalent:

1. There exists a vector $x \geqq 0$ such that $Ax > 0$.
2. There exists a vector $x > 0$ such that $Ax > 0$.
3. There exists a diagonal matrix D with positive diagonal elements such that $ADe > 0$.
4. There exists a diagonal matrix D with positive elements such that AD is a matrix with dominant positive principal diagonal.
5. For each diagonal matrix R where $R \geqq A$, then R is non-singular and $\rho(R^{-1}(P - A)) < 1$ where P is the diagonal of A.
6. If $B \in Z$ and $B \geqq A$, then B is non-singular.
7. Each real $\lambda \in \sigma(A)$ is positive and there is at least one real $\lambda \in \sigma(A)$.
8. All principal minors of A are positive.
9. There exists a strictly increasing sequence $\emptyset \neq M_1 \subset M_2 \subset M_3 \ \ldots \subset M_n$ (where M_i means M_i contains i distinct elements from $\{1,2,\ldots,n\}$) where $\det A(M_i) > 0$.
10. There exists a permutation matrix P such that $PAP^{-1} = LU$ where L is lower triangular with positive diagonal elements and $L \in Z$ and U is upper triangular with positive diagonal elements such that $U \in Z$.
11. A is non-singular and $A^{-1} \geqq 0$.
12. The real part of each $\lambda \in \sigma(A)$ is positive.
13. For each $x \neq 0$ there exists an index k such that $x_k y_k > 0$ for $y = Ax$.

Proof.

(1)⟹(2)

For $x \geqq 0$ where $Ax > 0$, choose $\varepsilon > 0$ small enough so that $A(x + \varepsilon e) > 0$. Then $x + \varepsilon e > 0$.

(2)⟹(3)

Given $x > 0$ where $Ax > 0$, let $d_{ii} = x_i$, for $i = 1,\ldots,n$ and $d_{ij} = 0$, for $i \neq j$, $i,j = 1,\ldots,n$. Then $D = (d_{ij})$ satisfies $Ax = ADe > 0$.

(3)⟹(4)

Let $W = AD$. Since $We = ADe > 0$,

$$|w_{ii}| \geqq w_{ii} > - \sum_{\substack{j=1 \\ j \neq i}}^{n} w_{ij} \quad \text{for } i = 1,\ldots,n.$$

Since $A \in Z$, $-w_{ij} = |w_{ij}|$. Hence W has a dominant principal diagonal. But $-w_{ij} \geqq 0$. Hence $w_{ii} > 0$.

(4)⟹(5)

For AD represented by elements w_{ij}, it is obvious from (4) that $w_{ii} > 0$ and $a_{ii} > 0$. By Theorem 4.3.4

$$\rho(I - H^{-1}AD) < 1$$

where H is the diagonal of AD. Let P be the diagonal of A, then $H = PD$. Thus

$$1 > \rho(I - H^{-1}AD) = \rho(I - D^{-1}P^{-1}AD) = \rho(D^{-1}(D - P^{-1}AD))$$

$$= \rho(D^{-1}(I - P^{-1}A)D) = \rho(I - P^{-1}A).$$

Now, let R be diagonal such that $R \geqq A$. Hence $r_{ii} \geqq a_{ii} > 0$. Therefore $\det(R) > 0$ and R is non-singular. Furthermore, $P^{-1} \geqq R^{-1}$ and $P - A \geqq 0$. By Theorem 4.3.3

$$\rho(R^{-1}(P - A)) \leqq \rho(P^{-1}(P - A)).$$

But $1 > \rho(I - P^{-1}A) = \rho(P^{-1}(P - A))$.
Hence $1 > \rho(R^{-1}(P - A))$.

(5)⟹(6)

Let R be the diagonal matrix of $B \in Z$ and P the diagonal matrix of A. Since $B \geqq A$, then $R \geqq P$, R^{-1} exists, has positive diagonal elements, and $\rho(R^{-1}(P - A)) < 1$. Now:

$$P - A \geqq R - B \geqq 0.$$

Therefore, $R^{-1}(P - A) \geqq R^{-1}(R - B) \geqq 0$.

Hence, by Theorem 4.3.3 and (5),

$$1 > \rho(R^{-1}(P - A)) \geqq \rho(R^{-1}(R - B)) = \rho(I - R^{-1}B).$$

By Theorems 2.2.1 and 2.2.2, $(I - I + R^{-1}B)^{-1}$ exists. Hence $(R^{-1}B)^{-1}$ exists implying B has full rank. Thus B^{-1} exists.

(6)$\Rightarrow$(7)

Let $\lambda \leqq 0$. Then $A - \lambda I \in Z$ and, from (6), $(A - \lambda I)^{-1}$ exists. Hence λ cannot be in $\sigma(A)$. Now choose $\lambda > 0$ so that $A - \lambda I \leqq 0$, that is, $\lambda I - A \geqq 0$. By Theorem 4.3.3, $\rho(\lambda I - A)$ is real and

$$\det[\lambda I - A - \rho(\lambda I - A)I] = 0.$$

Hence $\lambda - \rho(\lambda I - A) \in \sigma(A)$. But λ is real and $\rho(\lambda I - A)$ is real. Hence, there exists a real eigenvalue of A.

(7)$\Rightarrow$(8)

Each real $\lambda \in \sigma(A)$ satisfies $\lambda > 0$. Let B be a matrix formed by

$$b_{ij} = a_{ij} \text{ for } i,j \in M,$$

$$b_{ii} = a_{ii} \text{ for } i \notin M,$$

and

$$b_{ij} = 0 \text{ for } i \notin M \text{ or } j \notin M,$$

where M is a proper subset of $\{1,2,\ldots,n\}$. Then $B \geqq A$ and $B \in Z$. By Theorem 2.3.3, $\det(B) > 0$ and each real $\lambda \in \sigma(B)$ is positive. But

$$\det(B) = \det(A(M)) \prod_{i \notin M} a_{ii} > 0.$$

Hence,

$$\det(A(M)) > 0.$$

(8)$\Rightarrow$(9) Obvious.

(9)$\Rightarrow$(10) Follows from Theorems 4.3.5 and 4.3.6.

(10)⟹(11)

Since $A \in Z$ and $A = LU$ where L and U are, respectively, lower and upper triangular with positive diagonal elements, it is readily seen that $L^{-1} \geqq 0$ and $U^{-1} \geqq 0$. Hence $A^{-1} \geqq 0$.

(11)⟹(1)

Let $x = A^{-1}e \geqq 0$. Then $Ax > 0$.

(8)⟺(13) by Theorem 4.3.7.

(7)⟹ (12)

Let $\alpha > 0$ where $\alpha I - A \geqq 0$. By Theorem 4.3.3 $\rho(\alpha I - A) \geqq 0$. Let $\lambda \in \sigma(A)$ and $x \neq 0$ be the associated eigenvector. Then

$$Ax = \lambda x$$

and

$$\alpha Ix - Ax = \alpha Ix - \lambda x.$$

Hence, $\rho(\alpha I - A) \geqq |\alpha - \lambda|$.
Now, there exists a real $\lambda_0 \in \sigma(A)$ such that

$$\alpha - \lambda_0 = \rho(\alpha I - A).$$

Hence, $\alpha + \lambda_0 > \alpha$, since $\lambda_0 > 0$. Then:

$$\alpha > \alpha - \lambda_0 = \rho(\alpha I - A) \geqq |\alpha - \lambda|$$

which implies the real part of λ must be positive.

(12)⟹(7) obvious.

Q.E.D.

Finally we present the following Theorem given by Varga [122].

Theorem 4.3.8

(a) If M is an n by n non-negative matrix, then the following are equivalent:

1. $\alpha > \rho(M)$.
2. $\alpha I - M$ is non-singular and $(\alpha I - M)^{-1} \geqq 0$.

(b) Furthermore, if M is irreducible, the following are equivalent:

1. $\alpha > \rho(M)$.
2. $\alpha I - M$ is non-singular and $(\alpha I - M)^{-1} > 0$.

Proof.

(1a)⟹(2a)

Given $\alpha > \rho(M)$, let $G = \alpha(I - M/\alpha)$. (Note $\rho(M) \geqq 0$ by Theorem 4.3.3.)

Now $1 > \rho(M)/\alpha = \rho(M/\alpha)$. By Theorems 2.2.1 and 2.2.2, $I - M/\alpha$ is non-singular. Also, by Theorem 2.2.2,

$$G^{-1} = \frac{1}{\alpha}(I - M/\alpha)^{-1} = \frac{1}{\alpha}(I + M/\alpha + M^2/\alpha^2 + \ldots).$$

Since $M \geqq 0$ so are its powers, hence $G^{-1} \geqq 0$, or

$$1/\alpha(I - M/\alpha)^{-1} \geqq 0. \quad \text{Hence } (\alpha I - M)^{-1} \geqq 0.$$

(2a)⟹(1a)

Let $(\alpha I - M)$ be non-singular and $(\alpha I - M)^{-1} \geqq 0$.

Let $x \geq 0$ be the eigenvector associated with $\rho(M)$. That is,

$$Mx = \rho(M)x.$$

Then

$$(\alpha I - M)x = (\alpha - \rho(M))x$$

or

$$\frac{x}{\alpha - \rho(M)} = (\alpha I - M)^{-1}x \geq 0.$$

Since $x \geq 0$ it follows that $\alpha > \rho(M)$.

(b) The proof of (b) follows that of (a). It should be noted (without proof) that the irreducibility of M implies there exists a finite integer K such that $M^K > 0$. (See Varga [122].) Hence $(\alpha I - M)^{-1} > 0$.

Q.E.D.

4.4 Class K Matrices and Matrix Iterative Techniques

Section 2.4 was self contained. We note here that many other types of isotone splits and related issues may be found in [101, 121, 122, 132].

4.5 Leontief Substitution Systems

The theorems and proofs of this section were given or generalized by Veinott [124]. To simplify several results we use the following term given by Veinott [124].

Definition 4.5.1 (Trivial Row)

The ith row (column) of an m by n matrix A is called trivial if for every non-negative vector x for which $Ax \geqq 0$, the ith component of $Ax(x)$ is zero; otherwise the ith row (column) is called non-trivial.

Lemma 4.5.1

If a column of a pre-Leontief matrix is non-trivial and the column contains only non-positive elements in the trivial rows of the matrix, then those non-positive elements are all zero.

Proof.

Let A be pre-Leontief with $a_{ij} < 0$ for the ith row trivial and j^{th} column non-trivial. We have $x \geqq 0$ with $x_j > 0$ since column j is non-trivial. Since row i is trivial

$$\sum_{\ell=1}^{n} a_{i\ell}\, x_\ell = 0.$$

Let

$$y_i = x_i \text{ for } i \neq j$$

and

$$y_j = x_j - \varepsilon \text{ with } \varepsilon > 0.$$

Then $y \geqq 0$ and for an appropriate ε, $Ay \geqq 0$ and $y \geqq 0$. For row i

$$\sum_{\ell=1}^{n} a_{i\ell}x_\ell - a_{ij}\,\varepsilon \geqq 0.$$

But $\sum_{\ell=1}^{n} a_{i\ell}x_\ell = 0$ and $a_{ij} < 0$. Therefore row i is non-trivial which is a contradiction.

Q.E.D.

Theorem 2.5.1

If A is pre-Leontief, then one can partition A, after suitably permuting its rows and columns, so that

$$A = \begin{bmatrix} A_1 & A_3 \\ 0 & A_2 \end{bmatrix}$$

where A_1 is Leontief, A_2 is sub-Leontief, and each positive element of A_3 appears above a trivial column of A_2. Some of the submatrices may be vacuous.

Proof:

First permute A so that the trivial rows and columns are last. Then permute the non-trivial columns of A so that the non-trivial columns of A which have a positive element in some non-trivial row appear first. We obtain

$$A = \begin{bmatrix} A_1 & A_3 \\ A_4 & A_2 \end{bmatrix}.$$

Then A_1 has positive elements in its columns, (A_1, A_3) has non-trivial rows, and $\begin{bmatrix} A_1 \\ A_4 \end{bmatrix}$ has non-trivial columns.

(1) A_1 is Leontief and $A_4 = 0$.

There exists an $x \geqq 0$ with $(A_1, A_3)x > 0$ and $Ax \geqq 0$. By appropriately partitioning x, we may write

$$A_1x_1 + A_3x_2 > 0.$$

Now, by construction, $A_3x_2 \leqq 0$ since every positive element of A_3 lies in a trivial column. Thus $A_1x_1 > 0$ which implies A_1 is Leontief. Furthermore, by Lemma 4.5.1, $A_4 = 0$.

(2) A_2 is Sub-Leontief.

Assume A_2 is not sub-Leontief. Then there exists an $x_2 \geqq 0$ such that $A_2x_2 \geq 0$. Since A_1 is Leontief, there exists an $x_1 \geqq 0$ such that $A_1x_1 + A_3x_2 \geqq 0$. Now, since $A_4 = 0$, we have

$$A \begin{bmatrix} x_1 \\ x_2 \end{bmatrix} \geqq 0 \quad \text{and} \quad \begin{bmatrix} x_1 \\ x_2 \end{bmatrix} \geqq 0$$

and for some trivial row we have $A \begin{bmatrix} x_1 \\ x_2 \end{bmatrix}$ is positive. Hence there is a contradition and A_2 is sub-Leontief.

(3) Each positive element of A_3 lies above a trivial column of A_2.

Suppose the jth column of $\begin{bmatrix} A_3 \\ A_2 \end{bmatrix}$ has a positive element in A_3. Now the jth column of A_2 cannot be a null vector because, noting part (1) above, we would be able to choose some $x_{2j} > 0$ to give $A_1x_1 + A_3x_2 > 0$ and $A \begin{bmatrix} x_1 \\ x_2 \end{bmatrix} \geqq 0$. This would imply that column j is non-trivial. Hence the jth column of A_2 contains at least one negative component. By Lemma 4.5.1 the jth column of A_2 must be trivial.

Q.E.D.

We now show that a pre-Leontief Substitution System is equivalent to a Leontief Substitution System and that each extreme point of the Leontief Substitution System is associated with a class K matrix.

Theorem 4.5.2

The following are equivalent:

1. A is a square Leontief matrix permuted to class Z.
2. A is pre-Leontief with no vanishing rows, and the columns of A are linearly independent and non-trivial.
3. A is pre-Leontief with no vanishing rows, A' is pre-Leontief, the columns of A are non-trivial, and X(0) is bounded.
4. $A \in K$.

Proof.

(1)$\Rightarrow$(4)

Since A is Leontief, there exists an $x \geqq 0$ such that $Ax > 0$. By Theorem 2.3.4, $A \in K$.

(4)$\Rightarrow$(1)

$A \in K$ implies $A \in Z$ and there exists an $x \geqq 0$ such that $Ax > 0$.

(4)$\Rightarrow$(2)

Since $A \in K$, there exists an $x > 0$ such that $Ax > 0$, (Theorem 2.3.4). Therefore, the columns of A are non-trivial. Furthermore, A is non-singular.

(4)$\Rightarrow$(3)

Since the columns of A are linearly independent $N(A) = \{0\}$. Hence $X(0) = \{0\}$ and is bounded. Since A has non-trivial columns there exists an $x > 0$ such that $Ax \geqq 0$. Hence A cannot have a row with no positive element (A has no vanishing row). If A is m by n, having one positive element per row requires $n \geqq m$. But the columns of A linearly independent implies $m \geqq n$. Thus $m = n$ and at least one positive element per row implies only one positive element per column. Hence A' is pre-Leontief.

(3)$\Rightarrow$(1)

Since the columns of A are non-trivial there exists an $x > 0$ such that $Ax \geqq 0$. If A were sub-Leontief $A(\lambda x) = 0$ for $\lambda \geqq 0$ and x for $Ax = 0$ would not be bounded. Thus A is not sub-Leontief. If A is Leontief it is square since A' is pre-Leontief. Assume A is pre-Leontief, then A may be partitioned as in Theorem 2.5.1. Since A' is pre-Leontief, A_1 is square and $A_3 \leqq 0$. Also, A_3 must have at least one column or else A has a vanishing row. Now, from above, $A_1 \in K$ and $A_1^{-1}A_3 \leqq 0$. Thus $-A_1^{-1}A_3 \geqq 0$. Let $x \geqq 0$ $y_2 = x_2 \neq 0$

and $y_1 = -A_1^{-1}A_3y_2$. Thus $Ay = \begin{bmatrix} A_3y_2 - A_3y_2 \\ A_2y_2 \end{bmatrix} = \begin{bmatrix} 0 \\ 0 \end{bmatrix}$ since A_2 is sub-Leontief. But y satisfies $A(\lambda y) = 0$ for $\lambda \geqq 0$ and, hence, y for $Ay = 0$ is unbounded. This contradiction implies A is not pre-Leontief.

Q.E.D.

Lemma 4.5.2

Suppose A is block triangular (i.e., $A_{ij} = 0$ for all $i < j$ or all $i > j$) with $A_{ij} \leqq 0$ for $i \neq j$. Then A is Leontief if and only if A_{ii} is Leontief for all i.

Proof. Let A satisfy $A_{ij} = 0$ for all $j > i$.

($\Rightarrow$) Assume A is Leontief. Then there exists an $x \geqq 0$ such that $Ax > 0$. We have

$$A_{NN}x_N > 0$$

$$A_{N-1,N-1}x_{N-1} + A_{N-1,N}x_N > 0$$

$$\vdots$$

$$\sum_{i=1}^{N} A_{1i}x_i > 0.$$

Thus, A_{NN} is Leontief. Also, since A_{NN} is Leontief, $A_{N-1,N} \leqq 0$ and $A_{N-1,N-1}$ is therefore Leontief, and so forth.

($\Leftarrow$) Assume A_{ii} Leontief for all i. Since A_{NN} is Leontief, there exists an $x_N \geqq 0$ such that $A_{NN}x_N > 0$. Then, since $A_{N-1,N-1}$ is Leontief, there exists and $x_{N-1} \geqq 0$ where $A_{N-1,N-1}x_{N-1} > 0$, or $A_{N-1,N-1}x_{N-1} + A_{N-1,N}x_N > 0$ and so forth. Hence, there exists an $x \geq 0$ such that $Ax > 0$.

Q.E.D.

In the following, let J be a subset of {1, ..., n} and $\bar{J}$ its complement.

<u>Theorem 2.5.3</u>

If A is an m by n Leontief matrix, then x is an extreme point of $S = \{Ax = b;\ x \geqq 0;\ b \geqq 0\}$ if and only if x is determined by an m by m Leontief matrix.

Proof.

($\Rightarrow$) Assume x is an extreme point of S. If x = 0, the result holds trivially. Assume $x \geq 0$. Let A_J be the sub-matrix of A where J consists of the i where x_i are positive. Then $x_{\bar{J}} = 0$. Note that the non-positive rows of A_J must be zero rows. Permute A_J and b so that

$$A_J = \begin{bmatrix} A_1 \\ 0 \end{bmatrix} \quad \text{and} \quad b = \begin{bmatrix} b_1 \\ b_2 \end{bmatrix}.$$

Then $b_2 = 0$. Now A_1 has linearly independent columns and non-vanishing rows. Furthermore, since $x_J > 0$, the columns of A_1 are non-trivial. Hence, by Theorem 4.5.2, A_1 is square Leontief.

Now, since A is Leontief there is an m by m Leontief matrix C where

$$C = \begin{bmatrix} C_1 & C_3 \\ C_4 & C_2 \end{bmatrix}$$

with $C_3 \leqq 0$, $C_4 \leqq 0$ and C_1 has the same number of rows and columns as A_1. Hence

$$D = \begin{bmatrix} A_1 & C_3 \\ 0 & C_2 \end{bmatrix}$$

is Leontief. Since C is Leontief so is C_2 (see Lemma 4.5.2).

Hence, D is square (m by m) Leontief and x is determined by D.

($\Leftarrow$) Assume x is determined by an m by m Leontief matrix. Then $A_J x_J = b$ can be permuted so that $PA_J \varepsilon K$. By Theorem 2.3.4, $A_J^{-1} \geqq 0$ and

$$x_J = A_J^{-1} P^{-1} Pb \geqq 0.$$

Hence the positive components of x_J are associated with linearly independent columns and

$$x = \begin{bmatrix} x_J \\ x_{\bar{J}} \end{bmatrix}$$

with $x_{\bar{J}} = 0$ is feasible. Hence x is an extreme point (see [44]).

Q.E.D.

Theorem 2.5.2

For the system

$$Ax = b, \quad x \geqq 0, \text{ and } \quad b \geqq 0,$$

where A is pre-Leontief and partitioned as in Theorem 2.5.1 with $b_2 = 0$ and $b_1 \geqq 0$, the following are equivalent:

1. x is an extreme point.
2. $x_2 = 0$ and x_1 is an extreme point of $A_1 x_1 = b_1$, $x_1 \geqq 0$.

Proof.

(1)$\Rightarrow$(2)

We have

$$A_1 x_1 + A_3 x_2 = b_1$$
$$A_2 x_2 = b_2$$
$$x \geqq 0, \; b \geqq 0,$$

or x_1 is an extreme point of $b_1 - A_3 x_2$ determined by a full order Leontief sub-matrix (Theorem 2.5.3) of A_1.

Suppose $x_2 \neq 0$. Then $x_{1\bar{J}} = 0$ and

$$x = \begin{bmatrix} x_{1J} \\ \\ x_2 \end{bmatrix} = \frac{1}{2}\begin{bmatrix} A_J^{-1}b_1 \\ \\ 0 \end{bmatrix} + \frac{1}{2}\begin{bmatrix} A_J^{-1}(b_1 - 2A_3x_2) \\ \\ 2x_2 \end{bmatrix}$$

where A_J is the sub-matrix of A_1 giving x_1. Thus x is a strict convex combination of two distinct elements of $\{x: Ax = b, x \geqq 0, b \geqq 0\}$, so x is not an extreme point. Hence, $x_2 = 0$ or else a contradiction.

(2)$\Rightarrow$(1)

Let x not be an extreme point with $x_2 = 0$. Thus $x = \lambda y + (1 - \lambda)z$ for y and z extreme points and $0 < \lambda < 1$. Now y_2 and z_2 must be zero and y_1 and z_1 are extreme points of $A_1y_1 = b_1, y_1 \geqq 0$ and $A_1z_1 = b_1$, $z_1 \geqq 0$, respectively. Hence x_1 is not an extreme point of $A_1x_1 = b_1$, $x_1 \geqq 0$ which is a contradiction.

Q.E.D.

Theorem 2.5.4

The following are equivalent for A Leontief:

1. A is totally Leontief.
2. M = N.
3. X(b) is bounded for all $b \geqq 0$.

Proof.

(3)$\Rightarrow$(1)

If A is Leontief, there exists at least one $A_J \in K$, $J \in N$. Since X(0) is nonempty and bounded, by the dual theorem [53] there exists a y such that $y'A > 0$. Then $y'A_J > 0$ and $y'A_JA_J^{-1} \geqq 0$. Thus $y \geqq 0$ and $y'A > 0$.

(1)$\Rightarrow$(2)

Since $M \subseteq N$ we must show $N \subseteq M$. Choose A_J, $J \in N$. A totally Leontief implies that there exists a $y \geqq 0$ such that $y'A > 0$ or $y'A_J > 0$. Since class K is closed under transposition, $A_J \in K$ (Theorem 2.3.4). Hence $J \in M$. Thus M = N.

(2)$\Rightarrow$(3)

Choose $b > 0$ and $c > 0$ and solve the linear program Max c'x subject to $x \in X(b)$. Assume X(b) is unbounded. Then the simplex procedure will give a basis A_J, $J \in N$ (note by Theorem 2.5.3 a feasible basis is a square Leontief matrix) and a column a of A not contained in A_J for which

$$A_J^{-1} a = y \leqq 0.$$

That is $A_J y = a$. Suppose column i of A_J has a positive element in the same row as does a. Replace column i of A_J by a to get A_J^*. Then $J^* \in N$. Suppose $y_i = 0$. Then A_J^* is singular and $J^* \notin M$ which is a contradiction. Then since $y \leqq 0$, $y_i < 0$. Form A_J^{*-1} by performing a Gaussian elimination with pivoting on y_i which also gives $x_i = (A_J^{-1} b)_i / y_i$. We have $A_J^{-1} b > 0$ and $A_J^{*-1} b > 0$ but $x_i < 0$ since $y_i < 0$. This contradiction implies $y_i > 0$ which contradicts $y \leqq 0$. Hence X(b) is bounded. Since X(b) is bounded for one b, by the duality theorem, X(b), is bounded for all $b \geqq 0$.

Q.E.D.

4.6 Optimization Over Totally Leontief Substitution Systems

In this section we use results due to Veinott [123] which generalize work of Blackwell [8, 9], Denardo [24], and Shapley [112]) to prove Theorem 2.6.2. We note an alternative approach using M-functions [106,113] but forego this in favor of Veinott's results. Let $\pi = (J_1, J_2, \ldots)$ where J_i denotes the column identifications composing basis A'_{J_i} chosen at iteration i of Equation 2.6.7. Let π^n denote the first n components of π, i.e., $\pi^n = (J_1, J_2, \ldots, J_n)$, and let $J^\infty = (J, J, \ldots)$. For $\pi_1 = (J_1^{\,1}, J_2^{\,1}, \ldots)$ and $\pi_2 = (J_1^{\,2}, J_2^{\,2}, J_3^{\,2}, \ldots)$, let $(\pi_1^{\,n}, \pi_2) = (J_1^{\,1}, J_2^{\,1}, \ldots, J_n^{\,1}, J_1^{\,2}, J_2^{\,2}, \ldots)$ (i.e., for the first n steps we follow $\pi_1^{\,n}$, and π_2 afterwards for steps n+1, n+2, ... We refer to π as a policy. Let $P_J = R_J^{-1}S_J$ and $r_J = R_J^{-1}c_J$. We assume the ith row of P_J and the ith component of r_J do not depend on the ith entry of J. Finally for $\pi = (J_1, J_2, \ldots)$ define $P^N(\pi) = P_{J_1} P_{J_2} \ldots P_{J_N}$ with $P^0(\pi) = I$.

To illustrate the above notation consider the following example.

$$\text{Max } 2x_1 + 3x_2 - x_3$$

subject to

$$\begin{aligned} x_1 \qquad + x_3 &= 2 \\ -x_1 + x_2 \qquad &= 4 \\ x_1, x_2, x_3 &\geqq 0. \end{aligned}$$

The dual problem, as given in Equation (2.6.2), is

$$\text{Min } 2v_1 + 4v_2$$

subject to

$$\begin{aligned} v_1 - v_2 &\geqq 2 \\ v_2 &\geqq 3 \\ v_1 \qquad &\geqq -1 \end{aligned}$$

with $M = \{(1,2), (3,2)\} = \{J_1, J_2\}$. For each $J \in M$ choose $R_J = 2I$. Then

$$P_{J_1} = \frac{1}{2}\begin{bmatrix} 1 & 1 \\ 0 & 1 \end{bmatrix}, \qquad r_{J_1} = \frac{1}{2}\begin{bmatrix} 2 \\ 3 \end{bmatrix},$$

$$P_{J_2} = \frac{1}{2}\begin{bmatrix} 1 & 0 \\ 0 & 1 \end{bmatrix}, \qquad r_{J_2} = \frac{1}{2}\begin{bmatrix} -1 \\ 3 \end{bmatrix}.$$

Let $\pi = (J_1, J_2, J_1, J_1, \ldots)$. Then

$$P^2(\pi) = P_{J_1} P_{J_2} = \frac{1}{4}\begin{bmatrix} 1 & 1 \\ 0 & 1 \end{bmatrix}.$$

Let

$$v(\pi) = \sum_{\ell=1}^{\infty} P^{\ell-1}(\pi)\ r(\pi)_\ell$$

where $r(\pi)_\ell$ is r_{J_ℓ}.

Lemma 4.6.1

If $\sum_{\ell=0}^{\infty} P^\ell(\cdot)$ converges under $\pi_1 = (J_1^{\ 1}, J_2^{\ 1}, \ldots)$ and $\pi_2 = (J_1^{\ 2}, J_2^{\ 2}, \ldots)$, then

$$v(\pi_1) - v(\pi_2) = \sum_{\ell=0}^{\infty} P^\ell(\pi_1)\left[v(J^1_{\ell+1}, \pi_2) - v(\pi_2)\right].$$

Proof.

Note that

$$v(J^1_{\ell+1}, \pi_2) = r_{J_{\ell+1}} + P_{J_{\ell+1}}\ v(\pi_2).$$

Then

$$v(\pi_1^{\ \ell}, \pi_2) = \sum_{J=1}^{\ell} P^{j-1}(\pi_1)\ r(\pi_1)_j + P^\ell(\pi_1)v(\pi_2).$$

Now

$$\sum_{\ell=0}^{\infty} \left[v(\pi_1^{\ \ell+1}, \pi_2) - v(\pi_1^{\ \ell}, \pi_2)\right] =$$

$$v(\pi_1^{\ 1}, \pi_2) - v(\pi_2) + v(\pi_1^{\ 2}, \pi_2) - v(\pi_1^{\ 1}, \pi_2) + \ldots$$

$$= v(\pi_1) - v(\pi_2).$$

But

$$v(\pi_1^{\ \ell+1}, \pi_2) - v(\pi_1^{\ \ell}, \pi_2) = \sum_{j=1}^{\ell+1} P^{j-1}(\pi_1)r(\pi_1)_j + P^{\ell+1}(\pi_1)v(\pi_2)$$

$$- \sum_{j=1}^{\ell} P^{j-1}(\pi_1)r(\pi_1)_j - P^\ell(\pi_1)v(\pi_2)$$

$$= P^{\ell}(\pi_1)r(\pi_1)_{\ell+1} + P^{\ell+1}(\pi_1)v(\pi_2) - P^{\ell}(\pi_1)v(\pi_2)$$

$$= P^{\ell}(\pi_1)\left[r(\pi_1)_{\ell+1} + P_{J_{\ell+1}}v(\pi_2) - v(\pi_2)\right]$$

$$= P^{\ell}(\pi_1)\left[v(J^1_{\ell+1}, \pi_2) - v(\pi_2)\right].$$

Thus

$$v(\pi_1) - v(\pi_2) = \sum_{\ell=0}^{\infty} P^{\ell}(\pi_1)\left[v(J^1_{\ell+1}, \pi_2) - v(\pi_2)\right].$$

Q.E.D.

Note that if $\pi_1 = J^{\infty}$, then by Theorem 2.2.2, Lemma 4.6.1 reduces to

$$v(J^{\infty}) - v(\pi_2) = [I - P_J]^{-1}\,(v(J, \pi_2) - v(\pi_2)).$$

Lemma 4.6.2

Suppose $\rho(P_J) < 1$ for all $J \in M$. Then either $v(\bar{J}, J^{\infty}) - v(J^{\infty}) \geq 0$ for some $\bar{J} \in M$ or $v(J_i, J^{\infty}) - v(J^{\infty}) \leqq 0$ for all $J_i \in M$. Also,

1. $v(\bar{J}, J^{\infty}) - v(J^{\infty}) \geq 0$ implies $v(\bar{J}^{\infty}) \geq v(J^{\infty})$,

2. $v(J_i, J^{\infty}) - v(J^{\infty}) \leqq 0$ for all $J_i \in M$ if and only if $v(J_i^{\infty}) \leqq v(J^{\infty})$ for all $J_i \in M$.

Proof.

Suppose $e_j'(r_{J_i} + P_{J_i}v(J^{\infty}) - v(J^{\infty})) > 0$ for some $J_i \in M$ and $1 \leqq j \leqq m$. Then consider the $\bar{J} \in M$ where $\bar{J}$ differs from J in the jth component and this component is the jth component of J_i. Then

$$v(\bar{J}, J^{\infty}) - v(J^{\infty}) \geq 0.$$

1. By Lemma 4.6.1

$$v(\bar{J}^{\infty}) - v(J^{\infty}) = \sum_{\ell=0}^{\infty} P^{\ell}(\bar{J}^{\infty})(v(\bar{J}, J^{\infty}) - v(J^{\infty})) \geq 0$$

since $P^{\ell}(\bar{J}^{\infty}) \geqq 0$ for $\ell = 1, \ldots$ and $P^0(\bar{J}^{\infty}) = I$. Furthermore, $\bar{J}^{\infty}$ and J^{∞} converge since $\rho(P_J) < 1$ for all $J \in M$.

2. ($\Rightarrow$) Follows from Lemma 4.6.1 and $v(J_i, J^\infty) - v(J^\infty) \leqq 0$ for all $J_i \in M$ with $P_J \geqq 0$ and $\rho(P_J) < 1$ for all $J \in M$.

($\Leftarrow$) If $v(J_i^\infty) \leqq v(J^\infty)$ did not imply $v(J_i, J^\infty) \leqq v(J^\infty)$, then we could choose at least one term from

$$\sum_{\ell=0}^{\infty} P^\ell(J_i^\infty)(v(J_{i,\ell+1}, J^\infty) - v(J^\infty))$$

that would give $e_j'(v(J_{i,\ell+1}, J^\infty) - v(J^\infty)) > 0$ and, using part 1, would give a contradiction.

Q.E.D.

Veinott [123] credits Denardo [24] with the following generalization of results due to Shapley [112].

Corollary 4.6.2.1

If $\rho(P_J) < 1$ for all $J \in M$, there exists a $J \in M$ such that J^∞ maximizes $v(\cdot)$ over all J_i^∞, $J_i \in M$.

Proof:

Given $J_\ell \in M$, choose $J_{\ell+1} \in M$, if possible, so that

$$v(J_{\ell+1}, J_\ell^\infty) \geq v(J_\ell^\infty).$$

Then, by Lemma 4.6.2, $v(J_{\ell+1}^\infty) \geq v(J_\ell^\infty)$. If there is no such $J_{\ell+1}$ then

$$v(J_{\ell+1}, J_\ell^\infty) \leqq v(J_\ell^\infty) \quad \text{for all } J_{\ell+1} \in M$$

which implies

$$v(J_{\ell+1}^\infty) \leqq v(J_\ell^\infty). \quad (\text{i.e., } J_\ell^\infty \text{ maximizes } v(\cdot)).$$

Continue this process until no $J \in M$ satisfies the desired condition. The process will terminate in a finite number of steps since M is finite, i.e., we will find the maximizing J^∞.

Q.E.D.

The above corollary is the familiar policy improvement method of dynamic programming.

Let $v^* = \max_{J\varepsilon M} v(J^\infty)$. We now show that v^* is the unique fixed point of $\mathcal{L}(\cdot)$ as given in Equation (2.6.7). We note that $\mathcal{L}(\cdot)$ is isotone and that

$$\mathcal{L}^n(\cdot) = \mathcal{L}(\mathcal{L}^{n-1}(\cdot))$$

is also isotone. First we show that v^* is a unique fixed point of $\mathcal{L}$.

Corollary 4.6.2.2

$v^* = v(\bar{J}^\infty)$ is the unique fixed point of $\mathcal{L}$.

Proof:

1. v^* is a fixed point of .

Let $\bar{J} \varepsilon M$ be such that

$$v(J, \bar{J}^\infty) - v(\bar{J}^\infty) \leqq 0 \quad \text{for all } J \varepsilon M.$$

Then

$$r_J + P_J v(\bar{J}^\infty) \leqq v(\bar{J}^\infty) \text{ for all } J \varepsilon M.$$

That is

$$\mathcal{L}(v(\bar{J}^\infty)) \leqq v(\bar{J}^\infty).$$

But

$$r_{\bar{J}} + P_{\bar{J}}\, v(\bar{J}^\infty) = v(\bar{J}^\infty).$$

Hence

$$v(\bar{J}^\infty) = \mathcal{L}(v(\bar{J}^\infty)).$$

2. Suppose v is another fixed point. That is $v = P_J v + r_J$ for some $J \varepsilon M$. Then

$$v = (I - P_J)^{-1} r_J = v(J^\infty) \leqq v^*.$$

Also, if v is a fixed point of $\mathcal{L}$, then

$$v \geqq v(J^\infty) \quad \text{for all } J \varepsilon M,$$

and, in particular

$$v \geqq v(\bar{J}^\infty) = v^*.$$

Thus $v = v^*$.

Q.E.D.

Using the preceding corrollary, we have (from Veinott [123])

Corollary 4.6.2.3

If $\rho(P_J) < 1$ for all $J \varepsilon M$, then for any v,

$$\lim_{n\to\infty} \mathcal{L}^n(v) = v(\bar{J}^{\infty}) = v^*.$$

Also, if $\mathcal{L}(v) \geqq v$ $(\mathcal{L}(v) \leqq v)$, then $\mathcal{L}^n(v)$ approaches v* from below (above).

Proof.

Since $\mathcal{L}(\cdot)$ is isotone $\mathcal{L}(v) \geqq v$ $(\mathcal{L}(v) \leqq v)$ implies $\mathcal{L}^{n+1}(v) \geqq \mathcal{L}^n(v)$ $(\mathcal{L}^{n+1}(v) \leqq \mathcal{L}^n(v))$ for $n = 0, 1, \ldots$.

Let $\alpha = \text{Max}\ \{||v||, \text{Max}_{J\varepsilon M} ||r_J||\}$. Then, by Corollary 4.6.2.2, x_α is a unique fixed point of

$$x_\alpha = \text{Max}_{J\varepsilon M} \{\alpha e + P_J x_\alpha\}.$$

Then, by the choice of α,

$$x_{-\alpha} \leqq -\alpha e \leqq v \leqq \alpha e \leqq x_\alpha$$

and

$$x_{-\alpha} \leqq \mathcal{L}(x_{-\alpha}) \leqq \mathcal{L}(v) \leqq \mathcal{L}(x_\alpha) \leqq x_\alpha.$$

Thus

$$\mathcal{L}^n(x_{-\alpha}) \leqq \mathcal{L}^{n+1}(x_{-\alpha}) \leqq \mathcal{L}^{n+1}(v) \leqq \mathcal{L}^{n+1}(x_\alpha) \leqq \mathcal{L}^n(x_\alpha) \text{ for } n = 0, 1, \ldots .$$

$\mathcal{L}^n(x_\alpha)$ is bounded below by some vector x and $\mathcal{L}(\cdot)$ is continuous. Thus

$$x = \lim_{n\to\infty} \mathcal{L}(\mathcal{L}^n(x_\alpha)) = \mathcal{L}(x).$$

Hence, by Corollary 4.6.2.2, $x = v^*$. Similarly $\mathcal{L}^n(x_{-\alpha})$ is bounded above and, together, we have $\mathcal{L}^n(v) \to v^*$.

Q.E.D.

We continue with some further results due to Veinott [123].

Corollary 4.6.2.4

The following are equivalent:

1. $\rho(P_J) < 1$ for all $J \in M$.

2. $\sum_{\ell=0}^{\infty} P^{\ell}(\pi)$ converges uniformly in π.

3. $\max_{\pi} ||P^{\ell}(\pi)|| < 1$ for some $\ell \geq 1$.

Proof.

(3)⟹(2)⟹(1) Obvious.

(1)⟹(3)

Suppose $r_J = 0$ for all $J \in M$. Then

$$v^* = (I - P_J)^{-1} 0 = 0 \quad \text{for } J \in M.$$

Using $v^0 = e$, we have

$$v^n = \max_{\pi} P^n(\pi)e \to v^* \text{ as } n \to \infty.$$

That is, $\max_{\pi} ||P^{\ell}(\pi)|| < 1$ for some $\ell \geq 1$.

Q.E.D.

Corollary 4.6.2.5

$$\max_{J \in M} \rho(P_J) = \max_{\pi} \rho(P^{\ell}(\pi))^{1/\ell}, \quad \ell = 1, 2, \ldots .$$

Proof.

Using the Jordan canonical form it is readily shown that

$$\rho(P_J) = (\rho(P_J^{\ell}))^{1/\ell} \qquad \text{for } \ell = 1, 2, \ldots .$$

If the statement of the theorem is false then we can always choose an $\alpha > 0$ and small enough so that for some $\ell > 0$,

$$\rho(\alpha P_J) = \alpha\rho(P_J) < 1 < \alpha\rho(P^{\ell}(\pi))^{1/\ell} < \alpha^{\ell}\rho(P^{\ell}(\pi)) \text{ for all } J \in M.$$

Then it follows that

$$\left[\alpha^{\ell} P^{\ell}(\pi)\right]^m$$

cannot converge to the zero matrix as $m \to \infty$ (see Theorem 2.2.1). Thus

$$\sum_{j=0}^{\infty} (\alpha^j P^j(\pi^*))$$

diverges where $\pi^* = (\pi^\ell, \pi^\ell, \ldots)$. This contradicts Corollary 4.6.2.4 with αP_J replacing P_J.

Q.E.D.

Theorem 4.6.3

If $\rho(P_J) < 1$ for all $J \in M$ and π^* is a policy where $v(J, \pi^*) - v(\pi^*) \geq 0$ for some $J \in M$, then $v(J^\infty) \geq v(\pi^*)$. Also $v(J, \pi^*) - v(\pi^*) \leqq 0$ for all $J \in M$ if and only if $v(\pi) \leqq v(\pi^*)$ for all π.

Proof.

This result follows from Corollary 4.6.2.4 and similar steps as in Lemma 4.6.2.

Q.E.D.

Corollary 4.6.3.1

If $\rho(P_J) < 1$ for all $J \in M$, there exists a policy J^∞ for some $J \in M$ which maximizes $v(\cdot)$ over all policies.

Proof.

Using Theorems 4.6.3, Corollary 4.6.2.1, and Lemma 4.6.2, the result follows immediately.

Q.E.D.

Hence, according to Corollary 4.6.3.1, not only is $v(\cdot)$ optimized by some J^∞ over all J_i^∞ where $J_i \in M$ but $v(\cdot)$ is optimized by some J^∞ over all policies.

We now use results due to Cottle and Veinott [14] to show that v^* is the optimal solution to

$$\text{Min } b'v$$

subject to

$$A'v \geqq c$$

where A is totally Leontief and $b \geqq 0$. If v^* is a least element of $S = \{v: A'v \geqq c\}$ then v^* solves the above problem.

In the theorem we use the following two problems:

4.6.1 Min $b'v$
subject to

$$A'v \geqq c, \qquad S = \{v: A'v \geqq c\}.$$

4.6.2 Max $c'x$
subject to

$$Ax = b$$
$$x \geqq 0.$$

We state the general form of the theorem for use in future sections. (In the following A^+ represents a generalized inverse [5].)

Theorem 4.6.3

The following are equivalent:

1. $\bar{v}$ is the least element of S.
2. $\bar{v} \in S$ and there exists an m by n matrix $A^+ \geqq 0$ with $A^+A' = I$ and $A^+c = \bar{v}$.
3. There is an m by n matrix A^+ such that $x' = b'A^+$ is feasible for Problem (4.6.2) for all $b \geqq 0$, x is optimal for (4.6.2) for some positive b, and $\bar{v} = A^+c$.

The above conditions hold if, and provided $A'\bar{v} - c$ has at most m zero elements, only if either of the following holds:

4. $\bar{v} \in S$ and $\bar{v}$ is determined by a basis having a non-negative inverse.
5. $\bar{v}$ is determined by a basis that has a non-negative inverse and the basis is optimal for Problem (4.6.2) for some $b > 0$.

Proof.

(1)$\Longleftrightarrow$(2)

(1) holds if an only if for each i, $v = \bar{v}$ minimizes $e_i'x$ over S. By the duality theorem, this is so if and only if $\bar{v} \in S$ and for each i there exists a vector $y^i \geqq 0$ such that $Ay^i = e_i$ and $c'y^i = \bar{v}_i$. Let A^+ be the matrix formed by using $(y^i)'$ as row i for each i. Thus $A^+A' = I$, $A^+ \geqq 0$ and $A^+c = \bar{v}$.

(2)$\Longrightarrow$(3)

Given $\bar{v} \in S$ and $A^+ \geqq 0$ with $A^+A' = I$ and $A^+c = \bar{v}$, then $x' = b'A^+ \geqq 0$ for $b \geqq 0$ and $Ax = A(A^+)'b = b$. Thus $\bar{v}$ and x are feasible to (4.6.1) and (4.6.2) respectively. Furthermore

$$b'v = b'(A^+c) = x'c.$$

Thus by the optimality criterion of linear programming x is optimal to (4.6.2) for all $b \geqq 0$.

(3)$\Longrightarrow$(2)

$x' = b'A^+ \geqq 0$ for all $b \geqq 0$ implies $A^+ \geqq 0$. Also, since x is feasible for all $b \geqq 0$, then $Ax = A(A^+)'b = b$ for all $b \geqq 0$ implies $A^+A' = I$. To show that $\bar{v} \in S$, consider the following. Choose $\bar{b} > 0$ where $\bar{x}' = \bar{b}'A^+$ is optimal to (4.6.2). By the duality theorem there exists a $v \in S$ optimal to (4.6.1) for the given $\bar{b}$. By complementary slackness

$$\bar{x}'(A'v - c) = 0.$$

Now $\bar{x}_i = 0$ only if $x_i = 0$ for all $b \geqq 0$ since $A^+ \geqq 0$ and $\bar{b} > 0$. Thus

$$x'(A'v - c) = 0$$

for all $b \geqq 0$. This implies that

$$b'(v - A^+c) = 0$$

for all $b \geqq 0$. So

$$v = A^+c = \bar{v}$$

and $\bar{v} \in S$.

(2)$\Rightarrow$(4)

Since the rank of A^+A' is m, then $n \geqq m$. Permute, if required, the rows of (A', c) and corresponding columns of A^+ so that the first p components of $A'\bar{v} - c$ are zero and the last n - p are positive. By assumption $p \leqq m$. Partition A as (B, N) where B is m by p, and A^+ as (C, D) where C is p by n. Write

$$(A'\bar{v} - c)' = (0, y')$$

where $y > 0$. Then

$$\bar{v} - A^+c = 0 = A^+(A'\bar{v} - c) = Dy.$$

But $D \geqq 0$ and $y > 0$, hence $Dy = 0$ implies $D = 0$. From $A^+A' = I$ we have $CB' = I$ and rank CB' is $m \leqq p$. But $p \leqq m$. Hence $p = m$. Therefore B' has rank m and is non-singular. $B'^{-1} = C \geqq 0$ and B' determines $\bar{v}$.

(4)$\Rightarrow$(5)

Permute, if necessary, the rows of (A', c) so that A = (B, N) where B' is a basis, $B'^{-1} \geqq 0$, and $\bar{v}$ is determined by B'. Let

$$\bar{x} = (B^{-1}b, 0)'.$$

Then $\bar{v}$ and $\bar{x}$ are feasible for (4.6.1) and (4.6.2), and $b'\bar{v} = c'\bar{x}$ for all $c \geqq 0$. Hence by the duality theorem, B is optimal for (4.6.2) for all $c \geqq 0$.

(5)$\Rightarrow$(3)

Permute, if necessary, the rows of (A', c) so that A = (B, N) where B' is a basis, $(B')^{-1} \geqq 0$, and B is optimal to (4.6.2) for some $\bar{b}$. Let $A^+ = ((B')^{-1}, 0)$. Then $x = b'A^+$ is feasible for (4.6.2) for all $c \geqq 0$ because $(B')^{-1} \geqq 0$. Also $\bar{x} = \bar{b}'A^+$ is optimal for (4.6.2) and $A^+c = \bar{v}$ because $\bar{v}$ is determined by B'.

Q.E.D.

Thus we have that $v^* = \underset{J \varepsilon M}{\text{Max}}\ v(J^\infty)$ or

$$v^* = \underset{J \varepsilon M}{\text{Max}}\ (I - P_J)^{-1} r_J = \underset{J \varepsilon M}{\text{Max}}\ (A_J')^{-1} c_J.$$ (See page 171.)

Hence v^* is determined by a basis A_J' having a non-negative inverse ($A_J' \varepsilon K$).

Furthermore

$$A'_J\, v^* \geqq c_J \quad \text{for all } J \in M$$

implies $v^* \in \{v\colon A'v \geqq c\}$. Hence by Theorem 4.6.3 v^* is a least element of $\{v\colon A'v \geqq c\}$. Furthermore, $b \geqq 0$ implies v^* is optimal. At this point Theorem 2.6.2 has been verified.

4.7 Some Totally Leontief Substitution Systems

The following result is due to Veinott [124]:

Theorem 2.7.1

The constraint matrix arising from Equations (2.7.4) and (2.7.5) is Leontief if and only if there is no arc leading out of node k (the sink) and there is a chain to node k from every other node.

Proof.

(⟹) Assume matrix A in Equations (2.7.4) and (2.7.5) is Leontief. Since matrix A has one positive element per column, the (missing) row

$$\sum_{(k,j)\varepsilon A} x_{k,j} - \sum_{(j,k)\varepsilon A} x_{jk} = 0$$

has no positive elements. This is only so if there is no j such that $(k,j)\varepsilon A$. That is, no arc leads out of the sink, k. The ith row of matrix A is non-trivial which implies there is an $x \geqq 0$ for $Ax \geqq 0$ which gives

$$\sum_{(i,j)\varepsilon A} x_{ij} - \sum_{(j,i)\varepsilon A} x_{ji} > 0$$

which implies that there is a chain from i to k.

(⟸) Since there is no arc leading out of the sink and there is a chain to node k from every node we have immediately that A contains exactly one positive element per column and there exists a vector, $x \geqq 0$, giving $Ax > 0$.

Q.E.D.

The following follows readily.

Corollary 2.7.1.1

A in Equations (2.7.4) and (2.7.5) is sub-Leontief if and only if there is no arc leading into the sink, k. [124]

The following result characterizes a totally Leontief transshipment matrix.

Theorem 2.7.2

Call the matrix associated with 2.7.4 and 2.7.5 A. A is totally Leontief if and only if there is no arc leading out of node k (the sink), there is a chain to node k from every other node, and there are no cycles.

Proof.

From Theorem 2.7.2 A is Leontief if and only if there is no arc leading out of the sink and there is a chain to node k from every other node. A is not totally Leontief if and only if there is a column of A whose negative can be formed by sums of other columns. But this condition occurs if and only if the corresponding graph has at least one cycle.

Q.E.D.

4.8 Extensions of Algorithm 1

We now prove Theorem 2.8.4 and its corollary (given by Veinott [124]).

Theorem 2.8.4

A, as given in Equation (2.8.2), is totally Leontief if and only if each diagonal block is totally Leontief.

Proof.

($\Rightarrow$) Since A is totally Leontief there exists an $x \geqq 0$ and $y \geqq 0$ such that

$$Ax > 0 \text{ and } y'A > 0.$$

Or, partitioning x and y,

$$A_{N,N}x_N > 0,$$

$$A_{N-1,\, N-1}x_{N-1} > 0 - A_{N-1,N}x_N \geqq 0, \text{ and so forth.}$$

Similarly,

$y_1'A_{1,1} > 0,$

$y_2'A_{2,2} + y_1'A_{1,2} > 0$

or $y_2'A_{22} > 0 - y_1'A_{12} \geqq 0$, and so forth.

With each diagonal block having one position element per column, then $A_{i,i}$ $(i = 1, \ldots, n)$ is totally Leontief.

($\Leftarrow$) Since $A_{N,N}$ is totally Leontief, there exists an $x_N \geqq 0$ such that

$$A_{N,N}x_N > 0 \quad \text{and} \quad y_N'A_{NN} > 0.$$

Since $A_{N-1,N-1}$ is totally Leontief we can choose $x_{N-1} \geqq 0$ such that

$$A_{N-1,N-1}x_{N-1} > -A_{N-1,N}x_N \geqq 0, \quad \text{and so forth.}$$

Hence we can choose $x' = (x_1', \ldots, x_N') \geqq 0$ such that $Ax > 0$. Using similar arguments we can choose $y \geqq 0$ such that $y'A > 0$.

Q.E.D.

Corollary 2.8.4.1

A, as given in Equation (2.8.2), is Leontief if and only if each diagonal block is Leontief.

Theorem 2.8.5, as given below, was initially given by Dantzig [17].

Theorem 2.8.5

Consider the dual problem to that given in Equation (2.8.2). Then

$$\bar{v} = \begin{bmatrix} \bar{v}_1 \\ \vdots \\ \bar{v}_N \end{bmatrix}$$

solves (2.8.2) if and only if $\bar{v}_N$ solves

$$\text{Min } b_N' v_N$$

$$\text{subject to}$$

$$A_{NN}' v_N \geqq c_N$$

and $\bar{v}_i$, i = 1, ..., N-1, solves

$$\text{Min } b_i' v_i$$

$$\text{subject to}$$

$$A_{ii}' \, v_i \geqq c_i - \sum_{j=i+1}^{N} A_{ij}' \, \bar{v}_j .$$

Proof.

($\Longrightarrow$) If $\bar{v}$ solves the dual to Equation (2.8.2), then $\bar{v}$ is a least point of the set of all dual feasible points (Theorem 4.6.3). Since $b_i \geqq 0$ for i = 1, ..., N, then $\bar{v}_i$ solves each subproblem i for i = 1, ..., N.

($\Longleftarrow$) If $\bar{v}_i$ solves each subproblem i for i = 1, ..., N, then by Theorem 4.6.3, $\bar{v}_i$ is a least element of the set of all feasible vectors for subproblem i conditional upon solutions for subproblems i+1, ..., N. Now, for an arbitrary i, $-A_{ij}'$, j > i, is non-negative. Hence

$$c_i - \sum_{j=i+1}^{N} A_{ij}' \, \bar{v}_j \leqq c_i - \sum_{j=i+1}^{N} A_{ij}' \, v_j$$

where $\bar{v}_j$ is feasible to subproblem j. Hence, jointly, the vector $(\bar{v}_1, \ldots, \bar{v}_N)'$ gives the least vector feasible to the entire problem.

Q.E.D.

4.9 Dynamic Leontief Models

Section 2.9 was self-contained, and hence, no further discussion is required concerning dynamic Leontief models. The interested reader, though, is encouraged to refer to Veinott's paper [125] which discusses other dynamic Leontief models and presents algorithms for solving concave minimization problems over these dynamic Leontief Substitution Systems (see Section 3.5).

4.10 Optimization over Leontief Substitution Systems

The results in this section are due to Koehler [72]. Let $\mathcal{L}_F$ be the set of all fixed points of $\mathcal{L}(\cdot)$. Tarski [114] has shown that $\mathcal{L}_F$ is a lattice. (See [1] and [7] for a discussion of lattices and their properties.) Assume that a given linear program has a bounded optimal solution and a dual solution v*. Then we have

Theorem 4.10.1

v* is the least element of $\mathcal{L}_F$.

Proof.

Any $v \in \mathcal{L}_F$ is a feasible solution. Hence, by Theorem 4.6.3, $v^* \leqq v$. Now $v^* \in \mathcal{L}_F$ since v* is feasible and v* is determined by some A_J', $J \in M$.

Q.E.D.

Motivated by Theorem 4.10.1, we prove Theorem 2.10.1.

Theorem 2.10.1

Suppose a given Leontief Substitution System has a bounded optimal solution. Let v* be the optimal solution vector to the dual problem. If $v^o \leqq v^*$, then

$$\lim_{n \to \infty} \mathcal{L}(\mathcal{L}^n(v^o)) \to v^*.$$

Proof.

Since $\mathcal{L}(\cdot)$ is isotone and $v^* \in \mathcal{L}_F$, we have

$$\mathcal{L}(v^o) \leqq \mathcal{L}(v^*) = v^*.$$

Suppose $J^* \in M$ maximizes the primal problem. Then

$$\mathcal{L}(v^o) = P_J v^o + r_J \geqq P_{J^*} v^o + r_{J^*} \quad \text{for some } J \in N.$$

By induction,

$$\mathcal{L}^n(v^o) \geqq P_{J^*}^n v^o + \sum_{\ell=0}^{n-1} P_{J^*}^{n-1-\ell} r_{J^*} \text{ for } n = 1, 2, \ldots .$$

Since $J^* \in M$, $\rho(P_{J^*}) < 1$ and we have

$$\lim_{n \to \infty} \mathcal{L}^n(v^o) \geqq \sum_{\ell=0}^{\infty} P_{J*}^{\ell} \, r_{J*} = v*.$$

Thus $\mathcal{L}^n(v^o)$ is bounded above by v* and converges from below to v*.

Q.E.D.

4.11 Some Leontief Substitution Systems

As in Section 2.9, Section 2.11 was self-contained and, hence, we offer no further discussion concerning Leontief Substitution Systems.

4.12 Illustration of the Composite Algorithm

As in Section 2.11, Section 2.12 was self-contained and, hence, we offer no further discussion concerning the Composite Algorithm.

CHAPTER 5

Extended Discussion of Leontief Systems II

As in Chapter 4, we present proof in Chapter 5 for results not proved in earlier sections. Specifically, we prove results presented in Chapter 3.

5.1 Hidden Leontief Substitution Systems

A property of Leontief matrices is given in the following. We note here that many of the results of this section are due to Saigal [109].

Theorem 3.1.1

If A is Leontief, then there is a partition $A = (A_1, A_2, \ldots, A_m)$ such that if A^i is the submatrix of A formed by dropping all columns in A_i, $A^i x > 0$, $x \geqq 0$ has no solution for each $i = 1, 2, \ldots, m$.

Proof.

Let A_i be the submatrix of A containing all columns of A having a positive element in row i. Then A^i has no positive elements in row i.

Q.E.D.

The following is used throughout.

Lemma 5.1.1

$A \in L(C)$ if and only if $A \in L(\text{conv}C)$ where convC is the convex hull of C [109].

Proof.

($\Leftarrow$) If $A \in L(\text{conv}C)$, then, since $C \subseteq \text{conv}C$ then $A \in L(C)$.

($\Rightarrow$) Assume $A \in L(C)$. If B is a basis of A where $\text{cone}B \cap \text{int}C \neq \emptyset$, then, by assumption and the definition of L(C), $C \subseteq$ coneB and, since coneB is a convex cone, convC $\subseteq$ coneB. We have only to rule out the possibility that some basis $\overline{B}$ of A satisfying

$$\text{cone}\overline{B} \cap \text{int}C = \emptyset$$

does not satisfy

$$\text{cone}\overline{B} \cap \text{int(convC)} \neq \emptyset.$$

Suppose there is such a basis $\overline{B}$. Then there is a column of $\overline{B}$, $\overline{a}$, such that $\overline{a} \in$ intC. Let B be a basis such that $C \subseteq$ coneB (and, hence, convC $\subseteq$ coneB). Then $\overline{a} \in$ int(coneB). Define for all i = 1, ...,m, B^i as the submatrix obtained from B by dropping the ith column of B. Then the matrix $(\overline{a}, B^i)$ is a basis since $\overline{a} \in$ int(coneB). Also

$$\bigcup_{i=1}^{m} \text{cone}(\overline{a}, B^i) = \text{coneB}.$$

Then, since $C \subseteq$ coneB, intC $\cap$ cone$(\overline{a}, B^k) \neq 0$ for some k. Thus conv(C) $\subseteq$ cone$(\overline{a},B^k)$. Hence $\overline{a} \notin$ int(convC) which is a contradiction.

Q.E.D.

Lemma 5.1.2

Let A be an m by n matrix with full row rank and $C \subseteq R^m$ with cone(A) $\cap$ int(C) $\neq \emptyset$. Then the following are equivalent [109]:

1. If D is an m by m-1 submatrix of A with full rank

$$\text{cone(D)} \cap \text{int(C)} = \emptyset.$$

2. A $\in$ L(C).

Proof.

(1)$\Rightarrow$(2)

From Lemma 5.1.1 we can assume, without loss of generality, that C in convex.

Let B be an arbitrary basis of A where cone(B) $\cap$ int(C) $\neq \emptyset$. For each i = 1, ..., m define B^i as an m by m-1 submatrix of B where the ith column of B, a_i, is excluded.

By assumption cone$(B^i) \cap$ int(C) = $\emptyset$ for i = 1, ..., m. Now cone(B^i) and C are convex, hence there exists, for each i, a vector c^i such that $(c^i)'B^i \leqq 0$ and $(c^i)'x > 0$ for all $x \in int(C)$ [107]. Let $\bar{C}$ be a m by m matrix whose i^{th} row is $(c^i)'$ for each i, i =1, ..., m. Let $T = \{x: \bar{C}x \geqq 0\}$. Then $int(C) \subseteq T$. Now since $cone(B) \cap int(C) \neq \emptyset$, $(c^i)'a_i > 0$ for each i = 1, ..., m. Thus $\bar{C}$ is non-singular and $\bar{C}B \in Z$.

Since $cone(B) \cap int(C) \neq \emptyset$, there is a $b \in intC$ and $y \geqq 0$ such that $By = b$. Thus $\bar{C}By = \bar{C}b > 0$ and, hence by Theorem 2.3.4, $\bar{C}B \in K$ and $B^{-1}\bar{C}^{-1} \geqq 0$.

Now let $x \in T$, then $\bar{C}x \geqq 0$ and $(\bar{C}B)^{-1}\bar{C}x \geqq 0$. Thus $B(\bar{C}B)^{-1}\bar{C}x \in cone(B)$ or $x \in cone(B)$. Thus $T \subseteq cone(B)$ and, hence, $C \subseteq cone(B)$.

(2)⟹(1)

We show that the contrapositive is true.

Assume D is an m by m-1 submatrix of A with full rank where

$$cone(D) \cap int(C) \neq \emptyset.$$

Let the subspace spanned by the columns of D be represented by the hyperplane $H(D) = \{x: d'x = 0\}$. $d'A \neq 0$ since A has full row rank. Suppose column a_j of A gives $d'a_j > 0$. (Note that we can always find an a_j as desired.) Note also that $a_j \notin N(D)$ hence (D, a_j) is a basis of A. Thus we have

$$d'(D, a_j) \geq 0.$$

Now $cone(D) \cap int(C) \neq \emptyset$ implies $\exists\, b \in C$ such that $d'b < 0$. Hence, using Farkas lemma (see [88] for example), we have that

$$(D, a_j)x = b$$

$$x \geqq 0$$

has no solution. Thus $C \not\subseteq cone(D, a_j)$ and (2) does not hold.

Q.E.D.

The following result strengthens Lemma 5.1.1.

<u>Lemma 5.1.3</u>

Let $A \in L(C)$ and C be convex. Then there exists a polyhedral cone T such that $A \in L(T)$ and $C \subseteq T$ [109].

Proof.

Let $D_1, D_2, \ldots, D_k$, $k \leqq \binom{n}{m-1}$ be the enumeration of all m by m-1 full rank submatrices of A. By Theorem 5.1.2 $\text{cone}(D_i) \cap \text{int}(C) = \emptyset$ for all $i = 1, \ldots, k$ and there exists a c^i for each i such that $(c^i)'x \geqq 0$, $x \varepsilon C$ and $(c^i)'D_i \leqq 0$. Let D be the matrix whose i^{th} row is c^i $i = 1, \ldots, k$ and $T = \{x: Dx \geqq 0\}$. Then $C \subseteq T$ and T is a polyhedral cone. Using Theorem 5.1.2, $A \varepsilon L(T)$.

Q.E.D.

Saigal [109] gave a partial characterization of hidden Leontief matrices.

Theorem 5.1.4

Let A be an m by n full row rank matrix and C a convex subset of R^m with non-empty interior. In the following (1) implies (2) implies (3):

1. There exists a partition $A = (A_1, A_2, \ldots, A_m)$ and a simplicial cone T such that $C \subseteq T$. Also, if A^i is the submatrix obtained by dropping the columns A_i from A
   (i) for each $i = 1, \ldots, m$, $\text{cone}(A_i) \cap \text{int}(T) = \emptyset$;
   (ii) if B_i is any column of A_i, for each $i = 1, \ldots, m$ $\text{cone}(B_i, A^i) \cap \text{int}(T) \neq \emptyset$.

2. $A \varepsilon L(C)$ and is hidden Leontief.

3. There exists a simplicial cone $T = \{x: Dx \geqq 0\}$ such that $A \varepsilon L(T)$, DA is Leontief and $C \subseteq T$.

Proof.

(1)$\Rightarrow$(2)

(i) implies that there exists a vector c^i such that $(c^i)'A^i \leqq 0$ for each i and $(c^i)'x > 0$ for all $x \varepsilon \text{int}(T)$ [109]. Let D be the matrix having $(c^i)'$ as its ith row for $i = 1, \ldots, m$. Let $\overline{T} = \{x: Dx \geqq 0\}$. $T \subseteq \overline{T}$ implies D is non-singular. Furthermore DA has one positive element per column since, if it didn't, $(c^i)'B_i \leqq 0$ for some B_i in A_i. Let $b \varepsilon \text{int}(T)$, then $(c^i)'b > 0$. Also, $(c^i)'(B_i, A^i) \leqq 0$. Thus, using Farkas' lemma, $(B_i, A^i)x = b$, $x \geqq 0$ would have no solution. This contradicts (ii).

Since $\text{cone}(A) \cap \text{int}(T) \neq \emptyset$, there exists a $b \varepsilon \text{int}(T)$ such that $Ax = b$, $x \geqq 0$ has a solution, or $DAx = Db$, $x \geqq 0$ has a solution.

Since $b \in int(T)$, $Db > 0$ and, hence, DA is Leontief.

(2)⟹(3)

There exists a nonsingular matrix D such that DA is Leontief and $Db \geqq 0$ for all $b \in C$. If B is a basis of A, then DB is a basis of DA. If there exists an $x \geqq 0$ such that $DBx > 0$, then for all $y \geqq 0$, there is an $x \geqq 0$ such that $DBx = y$ or $Bx = D^{-1}y$ and, thus, $D^{-1}y \in cone(B)$ for each $y \geqq 0$. Let $T = cone(D^{-1})$. Then $T \subseteq cone(B)$. But $cone(D^{-1}) = \{D^{-1}x, x \geqq 0\} = \{x: Dx \geqq 0\}$. Also $C \subseteq T$ and the result follows.

Q.E.D.

A more complete characterization of hidden Leontief matrices was given in [72].

Theorem 3.1.3

Let A be an m by n full row rank matrix with $A = (\overline{A}, \overline{\overline{A}})$ where $\overline{\overline{A}}$ may be vacuous and $\overline{A}$ has full row rank. Let C be a convex subset of R^m with non-empty interior. Then the following are equivalent:

1. $\overline{A} \in L(C)$ and is hidden Leontief and every extreme point of $X(b)$, $b \in C$, has zero components associated with the columns of $\overline{\overline{A}}$.
2. There exists a simplicial cone $T = \{x: Dx \geqq 0\}$ such that $\overline{A} \in L(T)$, $D\overline{A}$ is Leontief, $C \subseteq T$, and no feasible basis of $X(b)$, $b \in int(C)$, contains a column of $\overline{\overline{A}}$.
3. There exists a partition $A = (A_1, A_2, \ldots, A_m)$ and a simplicial cone T such that $C \subseteq T$. Also if A^i is the submatrix formed by dropping the columns A_i from A:
   (i) for each $i = 1, \ldots, m$, $cone(A^i) \cap int(T) = \emptyset$;
   (ii) there is at least one column of A_i, call if B_i, for each $i = 1, \ldots, m$ where $cone(B_i, A^i) \cap int(T) \neq \emptyset$.

Proof.

(1)⟹(2)

Let B be an m by m full rank submatrix of A with at least one column from $\overline{\overline{A}}$. If B is a feasible basis of $X(b)$ for some $b \in int(C)$, then, denoting B as $B = (\overline{B}, \overline{\overline{B}})$ where $\overline{B}$ and $\overline{\overline{B}}$ are submatrices of $\overline{A}$ and $\overline{\overline{A}}$ respectively, we have $cone(\overline{B}) \cap C \neq 0$ which together with (1), contradicts Lemma 5.1.2. Thus no feasible basis of $X(b)$ contains columns of $\bar{\bar{A}}$. The remainder of the implication follows from Lemma 5.1.3 and Theorem 5.1.4.

(2)$\Rightarrow$(3)

Since $D\bar{A}$ is Leontief there exists a partition $\bar{A} = (\bar{A}_1, \bar{A}_2, \ldots, \bar{A}_m)$ such that the columns of $D\bar{A}_i$ have their i^{th} element positive. Distribute the columns of $\bar{\bar{A}}$ arbitrarily in the above partitioning. We now have $A = (A_1, A_2, \ldots, A_m)$. Let $b > 0$. Then $DA^i x = b$, $x \geqq 0$ has no solution if A^i contains no columns of $\bar{\bar{A}}$ since then the ith row is non-positive. The system also has no solution if A^i contains columns of $\bar{\bar{A}}$ for if it did we could construct a feasible basis having a column of $\bar{\bar{A}}$. Thus $A^i x = D^{-1}b$, $x \geqq 0$ has no solution for all $b > 0$. Define $T = \{x\colon Dx \geqq 0\}$. Thus $\text{cone}(A^i) \cap \text{int}(T) = \emptyset$ for each $i = 1, \ldots, m$. Since $D\bar{A}$ is Leontief there is at least one basis, DB, where $DB \in K$. Let DB_i be the column of $D\bar{B}$ having a positive entry in row i. Then $D(B_i, A^i) \cap \text{int}(T) \neq \emptyset$.

(3)$\Rightarrow$(1)

(i) implies there exists a c^1 such that $(c^1)'A^1 \leqq 0$ and $(c^1)'x > 0$ for all $x \in \text{int}(T)$ [107]. At least one column of A_1, call it B_1, satisfies $(c^1)'B_1 > 0$ or else $(c^1)'(B_1, A') \leqq 0$ and $(c^1)'b > 0$ for $b \in \text{int}(T)$ which, using Farkas' lemma, gives that $(B_1, A^1)x = b$, $x \geqq 0$ has no solution which contradicts (ii). Take all columns B_j of A_1 that give $(c^1)'B_j \leqq 0$ and repartition A so that A_2 contains these columns. We now have a new partition of A in which (i) and (ii) still apply.

Repeat the above procedure on $A_2, \ldots, A_m$ with the exception that columns of A_m giving $(c^m)'B_j \leqq 0$ are used to form $\bar{\bar{A}}$. Let $\bar{A} = (A_1, A_2, \ldots, A_m)$ after all repartitioning takes place.

Let D be the matrix whose i^{th} row is $(c^i)'$. Let $\bar{T} = \{x\colon Dx \geqq 0\}$. $T \subseteq \bar{T}$ implies D is nonsingular. By construction we have that $D\bar{A}$ has one positive element per column and at least one positive element per row. Furthermore, $D\bar{\bar{A}} \leqq 0$ and $\text{cone}(\bar{A}) \cap \text{int}(T) \neq \emptyset$ which implies $\bar{A}x = b$, $x \geqq 0$ has a solution for $b \in \text{int}(T)$. Thus $D\bar{A}x = Db$, $x \geqq 0$ has a solution and $Db > 0$ for $b \in \text{int}(T)$. Hence $D\bar{A}$ is Leontief. Finally, by direct application of Theorem 2.5.2, $D(\bar{A}, \bar{\bar{A}})$ is pre-Leontief and any extreme point of

$$\left\{ \begin{bmatrix} x_1 \\ x_2 \end{bmatrix} : D(\bar{A}, \bar{\bar{A}}) \begin{bmatrix} x_1 \\ x_2 \end{bmatrix} = Db,\ x_1, x_2 \geqq 0 \right\}$$

for $b \in T$ implies $x_2 = 0$.

Q.E.D.

5.2 An Application Exploiting Hidden Leontief Properties

Let $\overline{N}_i = \{j: (B_1)_{ij} > 0\}$ and $\overline{N} = \overset{m-1}{\underset{i=1}{\mathrm{x}}} \overline{N}_i$. Then any $B_{1\overline{J}}$ for $\overline{J} \varepsilon \overline{N}$ is of the form:

$$B_{1\overline{J}} = I - P'_{\overline{J}}$$

where $P'_{\overline{J}}$ was originally a square submatrix of P'_J for $J \varepsilon M$. That is,

$$P'_J = \begin{bmatrix} P'_{\overline{J}} & a \\ b' & c \end{bmatrix}.$$

Theorem 3.2.1

B_1, as given in Equation 3.2.5, is totally Leontief.

Proof.

Since P'_J was assumed to be irreducible there does not exist a permutation matrix P such that

$$PP'_JP' = \begin{bmatrix} P_1 & P_2 \\ 0 & P_3 \end{bmatrix}.$$

If $P_{\overline{J}}\, e = e$, then we have that $b = 0$ and that P'_J is not irreducible, a contradiction. Hence $P_{\overline{J}}\, e \leq e$ and, by Corollary 4.3.2.1, $\rho(P'_{\overline{J}}) < 1$. Thus $B_{1\overline{J}} \varepsilon K$ for all $\overline{J} \varepsilon \overline{N}$. Thus, by Theorem 2.5.4, B_1 is totally Leontief.

Q.E.D.

We now turn our attention to Equation (3.2.7). Let $\overline{N}_m = M_m$. Then define $N = \overline{N} \times \overline{N}_m$. A submatrix A_J, $J \varepsilon N$ looks like

$$\begin{bmatrix} e_1' - y'B_{1\bar{J}} & 1 - y'B_{2i} \\ B_{1\bar{J}} & B_{2i} \end{bmatrix} .$$

Since $B_{1\bar{J}} \varepsilon K$, we know from Theorem 2.3.4 that

$$\det(B_{1\bar{J}}) > 0.$$

Theorem 3.2.2

The matrix A, as given in Equation (3.2.7), is totally Leontief.

Proof.

Consider A_J for $J \varepsilon N$. We have

$$\det(A_J) = \det\begin{bmatrix} 1 & -y' \\ 0 & I \end{bmatrix} \det\begin{bmatrix} e_1' & 1 \\ B_{1\bar{J}} & B_{2i} \end{bmatrix} = \det\begin{bmatrix} e_1' & 1 \\ B_{1\bar{J}} & B_{2i} \end{bmatrix} .$$

After appropriate permutations (which preserve the sign of the determinant) we have:

$$\det(A_J) = \det(B_{1\bar{J}}) \det(1 - e_1' B_{1\bar{J}}^{-1} B_{2i}).$$

Since $\det(B_{1\bar{J}}) > 0$, $B_{1\bar{J}}^{-1} \geqq 0$, and $B_{2i} \leqq 0$, we get $\det(A_J) > 0$. Hence by Theorem 2.3.4, $A_J \varepsilon K$. Again, using Theorem 2.5.4, A is totally Leontief.

Q.E.D.

5.3 Integral Leontief Substitution Systems

In this section we provide the proof given by Veinott and Dantzig [127] to a theorem generalizing a result due to Hoffman and Kruskal [60].

Theorem 3.3.1

If A is an integral matrix having linearly independent rows, the following are equivalent:

(1) Every basis is unimodular.

(2) The extreme points of X(A, b) are integral for all integral b.

(3) Every basis has an integral inverse.

Proof.

(1)⟹(2)

Let b be integral and A_J be unimodular for every basis J (here J is a set of column identifications defining a basis). Then for

$$x_J = A_J^{-1} b$$

$$x_{\bar{J}} = 0$$

and using Cramer's Rule [96] with $\det(A_J) = \pm 1$, x_J is integral. Hence any extreme point of X(A, b) is integral for b integral.

(2)⟹(3)

Let y be chosen integral so that

$$z = y + A_J^{-1} e_i \geqq 0$$

where A_J is some full rank basis of A. Then $A_J z = A_J y + e_i$ implies that z consists of the nonvanishing portion of an extreme point associated with basis A_J and $b = A_J y + e_i$. By (2), z is integral. Thus $z - y = A_J^{-1} e_i$ is integral and, hence, the ith column of A_J^{-1} is integral.

(3)⟹(1)

Given that A_J and A_J^{-1} are integral and

$$\det(A_J)\det(A_J^{-1}) = 1,$$

we must have $\det(A_J)$ and $\det(A_J^{-1})$ integral and satisfying

$$\det(A_J) = \det(A_J^{-1}) = \pm 1.$$

Q.E.D.

5.4 Some Integral Leontief Problems

Suppose we are given a problem of the form

5.4.1 $$\text{Max } c'x$$

subject to

$$Ax = b \geqq 0$$

$$0 \leqq \ell \leqq x \leqq u$$

$$x \text{ integral}$$

where A, b, ℓ, and u are integral and A is lower recursive Leontief with diagonal blocks consisting of a row of ones. In the following we attempt to solve 5.4.1 by solving (successive) problems of the form

5.4.2 $$\text{Max } c'x$$

subject to

$$Ax = b$$

$$x \geqq \ell \geqq 0$$

If we solve 5.4.2 by Equations (3.4.3) and (3.4.4) after performing a change of variables $z = (x - \ell)$

$$Az = b - A\ell$$

$$z \geqq 0$$

(we may have $b - A\ell \not\geqq 0$), then we may end up with some upper bound violated (or a lower bound violated). Now, if an upper bound is violated on some variable $x_{i_k^*}$ for $i_k^* \in M_i$, then removing i_k^* from M_i and resolving 3.4.3-3.4.4, if possible, gives dual values that satisfy complementary slackness conditions between the primal and dual problem, with the additional constraint $x_{i_k^*} = u_{i_k^*}$. The resulting primal solution will still be integral but may remain primal infeasible. We continue this process with slight modifications until one of two conditions are encountered. They are:

1. either the optimal solution to 5.4.1 is determined or
2. one of two types of primal infeasibilities are detected.

The algorithm is now described [75]:

INITIALIZATION

Let $B_i = \emptyset \quad i = 1, \ldots, m$

$T_i = M_i \quad i = 1, \ldots, m$

$h = 1$

$b^* = \bar{b} = b - A\ell$

$\bar{u} = u - \ell.$

Solve Equation (3.4.3) with T_i replacing M_i. Let $J^* = (1_{k^*}, 2_{k^*}, \ldots, m_{k^*})$. Note J_k^* is the kth element of J^*.

Step 1

Solve 3.4.4 for each $x_{J_k^*}$, $k = 1, \ldots, m$ until the first k is encountered where either

$x_{J_k^*} < 0$ (if so stop with primal infeasibility type 1)

$x_{J_k^*} > u_{J_k^*}$ (if so go to step 2).

If no such conditions are encountered stop with an optimal solution to 5.4.1 by setting

$$x^* = x + \ell.$$

Step 2

If $k > h$ go to Step 3, otherwise set

$$x_{J_k^*} = \bar{u}_{J_k^*}$$

$$\bar{b} \text{ to } \bar{b} - a_{J_k^*} x_{J_k^*}$$

$$B_k \text{ to } B_k \cup \{J_k^*\}$$

$$T_k \text{ to } M_k - B_k.$$

If $T_k = \emptyset$ stop with primal infeasibility type 2. Otherwise go to Step 4.

Step 3

Let h = k and set

$\bar{b}$ to b*

$T_i = M_i \qquad i = 1, \ldots, h-1 \qquad \text{if } h > 1$

$B_i = \emptyset \qquad i = 1, \ldots, h-1 \qquad \text{if } h > 1$

$x_{i_k} = 0 \qquad i_k \in M_i \qquad i = 1, \ldots, h-1 \qquad \text{if } h > 1$

Go to Step 2.

Step 4

Set $x_{J_k^*} = 0$ for all $J_k^* \notin \bigcup_{i=1}^{m} B_i$. Solve Equation 3.4.3 with T_i replacing M_i for π_i, i = 1, ..., k. Go to Step 1.

For example consider the problem:

$$\text{Max } 2x_1 + x_2 + x_3 + x_4 + 3x_5 + 2x_6$$

subject to

$$\begin{bmatrix} 1 & 1 & 0 & 0 & 0 & 0 \\ -2 & -2 & 1 & 1 & 0 & 0 \\ -1 & -2 & -3 & -2 & 1 & 1 \end{bmatrix} \begin{bmatrix} x_1 \\ x_2 \\ \vdots \\ x_6 \end{bmatrix} = \begin{bmatrix} 2 \\ 1 \\ 1 \end{bmatrix}$$

$$u' = (1 \quad 1 \quad 4 \quad 4 \quad 16 \quad 16)$$

$$\ell' = (1 \quad 0 \quad 2 \quad 0 \quad 8 \quad 0)$$

$$u \geqq x \geqq \ell \geqq 0$$

$$x \text{ integral.}$$

The steps of the algorithm are:

INITIALIZATION

$T_1 = M_1 = \{1,2\}$

$T_2 = M_2 = \{3,4\}$

$T_3 = M_3 = \{5,6\}$

$B_1 = B_2 = B_3 = \emptyset$

$h = 1$

$\bar{b} = b^* = b - A\ell = \begin{bmatrix} 1 \\ 1 \\ 0 \end{bmatrix}$

$u' = (0,2,3,4,8,16)$

$\pi_3 = 3$

$\pi_2 = 10$

$\pi_1 = 27$

$J^* = (2,3,5)$.

Step 1

$k = 1 \quad x_{J_1^*} = x_2 = 1$

$k = 2 \quad x_{J_2^*} = x_3 = 3 > \bar{u}_3 = 2.$ Go to Step 2.

Step 2

$k = 2 > h = 1.$ Go to Step 3.

Step 3

$h = 2$

$\bar{b} = \begin{bmatrix} 1 \\ 1 \\ 0 \end{bmatrix}$

$T_1 = \{1,2\}$

$B_1 = \emptyset$

$x_1 = x_2 = 0.$

Go to Step 2.

Step 2

$x_3 = 2$

$\bar{b} = \begin{bmatrix} 1 \\ 1 \\ 0 \end{bmatrix} - 2 \begin{bmatrix} 0 \\ 1 \\ -3 \end{bmatrix} = \begin{bmatrix} 1 \\ -1 \\ 6 \end{bmatrix}$

$B_2 = \{3\}$

$T_2 = \{4\}.$

Go to Step 4.

Step 4

$\pi_2 = 7$

$\pi_1 = 21$

$J^* = (2,4,5).$

Go to Step 1.

Step 1

$k = 1 \qquad x_2 = 1$

$k = 2 \qquad x_4 = 1$

$k = 3 \qquad x_5 = 10 > \bar{u}_5.$ Go to Step 2.

Step 2

Since $k > h$ go to Step 3.

Step 3

$h = 3$

$$\bar{b} = \begin{bmatrix} 1 \\ 1 \\ 0 \end{bmatrix}$$

$T_1 = M_1 \qquad T_2 = M_2$

$B_1 = B_2 = \emptyset$

$x_1 = x_2 = x_3 = x_4 = 0.$

Go to Step 2.

Step 2

$x_5 = 8$

$$\bar{b} = \begin{bmatrix} 1 \\ 1 \\ 0 \end{bmatrix} - 8\begin{bmatrix} 0 \\ 0 \\ 1 \end{bmatrix} = \begin{bmatrix} 1 \\ 1 \\ -8 \end{bmatrix}$$

$B_3 = \{5\}$

$T_3 = \{6\}$.

Go to Step 4.

<u>Step 4</u>

$\pi_3 = 2$

$\pi_2 = 7$

$\pi_1 = 19$

$J^* = (2,3,6)$. Go to Step 1.

<u>Step 1</u>

$k = 1 \qquad x_2 = 1$

$k = 2 \qquad x_3 = 3 > \bar{u}_3.$ Go to Step 2.

<u>Step 2</u>

$x_3 = 2$

$$\bar{b} = \begin{bmatrix} 1 \\ 1 \\ -8 \end{bmatrix} - 2 \begin{bmatrix} 0 \\ 1 \\ -3 \end{bmatrix} = \begin{bmatrix} 1 \\ -1 \\ -2 \end{bmatrix}$$

$B_2 = \{3\}$

$T_2 = \{4\}$.

Go to Step 4.

<u>Step 4</u>

$\pi_2 = 5$

$\pi_1 = 15$

$J^* = (2,4,6)$.

<u>Step 1</u>

$k = 1 \qquad x_2 = 1$

$k = 2 \qquad x_4 = 1$

$k = 3 \qquad x_6 = 2.$

$$x^* = \begin{bmatrix} 0 \\ 1 \\ 2 \\ 1 \\ 8 \\ 2 \end{bmatrix} + \begin{bmatrix} 1 \\ 0 \\ 2 \\ 0 \\ 8 \\ 0 \end{bmatrix} = \begin{bmatrix} 1 \\ 1 \\ 4 \\ 1 \\ 16 \\ 2 \end{bmatrix}.$$

Stop.

Theorem 5.4.1

When the above algorithm terminates at Step 1 with a primal feasible solution, the solution is optimal to 5.4.1.

Proof.

The dual problem to the linear programming relaxation of 5.4.1 is

$$\text{Min } b'\pi + u'\lambda - \ell'\gamma$$

subject to

$$A'\pi + \lambda - \gamma = c$$

$$\lambda,\ \gamma \geqq 0$$

We note that by defining

$$\lambda_j = \text{Max } (0, (c - A'\pi^*)_j) \qquad j = 1, \ldots, m$$

$$\gamma_j = \text{Max } (0, (A'\pi^* - c)_j) \qquad j = 1, \ldots, m$$

that $(\pi^*, \gamma, \lambda, x^*)$ satisfy all complementary slackness conditions. Hence x^* is a linear program optimal. Since x^* is necessarily integral, x^* is optimal to 5.4.1.

Q.E.D.

Note that under the conditions of Theorem 5.4.1, Equation 5.4.1 is just a linear program. If the algorithm terminates at Step 1 with a primal infeasibility and $k = 1$ there is no feasible solution to 5.4.1.

In [75] branch and bound procedures are given to handle primal infeasibilities type 1 and 2.

5.5 Concave Minimization over Leontief Substitution Systems

We present proofs (given in [124]) for the theorems of Section 3.5. We will use the same notation developed in that section.

Theorem 3.5.1

If $S \in V'$, the following are equivalent:

(i) x is an extreme point of $\text{conv}(X(b) \cap S)$.

(ii) $x \in S$ and x is an extreme point of $X(b)$.

Proof.

(not ii)$\Rightarrow$(not i)

Suppose $x \in X(b) \cap S$ and x is not an extreme point of $X(b)$. Then there are two points $x^1, x^2 \in X(b)$ where $x^1 \neq x^2$ and

$$x = \frac{1}{2} x^1 + \frac{1}{2} x^2.$$

Let

$$y^1 = \frac{1}{2} x^1 + \frac{1}{2} x$$

$$y^2 = \frac{1}{2} x^2 + \frac{1}{2} x.$$

A component of x is positive or zero if and only if the corresponding component of y^1 and y^2 is positive or zero, respectively. Thus $y^1, y^2 \in S$. Since y^1 and y^2 are convex combinations of $x, x^1, x^2 \in X(b)$ and $X(b)$ is convex, then $y^1, y^2 \in X(b)$. Thus

$$x = \frac{1}{2} y^1 + \frac{1}{2} y^2$$

is not an extreme point of $X(b) \cap S$.

(ii)$\Rightarrow$(i) obvious.

Q.E.D.

Since, if x is an extreme point of $\text{conv}(X(b) \cap S)$ then x is an extreme point of $X(b)$, then each extreme point of $\text{conv}(X(b) \cap S)$ is determined by a class K matrix (see Theorem 2.5.3).

Theorem 3.5.2

If A is Leontief, $b \geqq 0$, $S \in V'$, and $X(b) \cap S \cap T$ is bounded, then the following are equivalent:

(i) x is an extreme point of $\mathrm{conv}(X(b) \cap S)$.

(ii) $x \in X(b) \cap S \cap T$.

Proof.

(i)$\Rightarrow$(ii)

If x is an extreme point of $\mathrm{conv}(X(b) \cap S)$ then, by Theorem 3.5.1, x is an extreme point of $X(b)$ and $x \in S$. If x is an extreme point of $X(b)$, by the nature of extreme points of $X(b)$ (see Theorem 2.5.3) $x \in T$.

(ii)$\Rightarrow$(i)

If $x = 0$ the result holds trivially.

Suppose $x \neq 0$. Since $x \in T$ we can associate with x at least one $J \in N$ containing those columns associated with positive x_i. Since $X(b) \cap S \cap T$ is bounded, $\{y: A_J y = 0,\ y \geqq 0\}$ is bounded. Hence A_J is nonsingular and, thus, x is an extreme point of $X(b)$. Since $x \in S$, the rest follows by Theorem 3.5.1.

Q.E.D.

The following interesting result was given by Veinott [124].

Theorem 5.5.1

Suppose A is Leontief, $S \in V$, and $c(\cdot,\ \cdot)$ is concave on the convex polyhedral cone $C = \{(x,b): Ax \geqq 0,\ x \geqq 0,\ b \geqq 0\}$. Let

$$f(b) = \inf_{x \in X(b) \cap S} c(x,b), \qquad b \geqq 0.$$

If the infimum is attained for all $b \geqq 0$, then $f(\cdot)$ is concave on the non-negative orthant.

Proof.

Let $x(b,\ J)$ be a basic solution determined by $J \in M$. Let $M(b,\ S) = \{J: J \in M,\ x(b,\ J) \in S\}$.

From Theorem 3.5.3, $f(\cdot)$ can be written as

$$f(b) = \min_{J \in M(b,S)} c(x(b,J),\ b), \qquad b \geqq 0.$$

Choose b^1, $b^2 \geqq 0$ and $b^0 = \lambda b^1 + (1-\lambda)b^2$ for some $0 \leqq \lambda \leqq 1$. Since $x(b, J)$ is linear in b for $b \geqq 0$

$$x(b^0,J) = \lambda x(b^1,J) + (1-\lambda)x(b^2,J).$$

Now, if $x_i(b^0,J) = 0$, then $x_i(b^1,J) = x_i(b^2,J) = 0$. Thus

$$M(b^0,J) \subseteq M(b^1,J)$$

$$M(b^0,J) \subseteq M(b^2,J).$$

Thus, with the above and the fact that a concave function of a linear function is concave and that the minimum of finitely many concave functions is concave, we have

$$f(b^0) = \lambda \min_{J \epsilon M(b^1,J)} c\,(x(b^1,J),\, b^1) + (1-\lambda) \min_{J \epsilon M(b^2,J)} c\,(x(b^2,J),\, b^2) \geqq$$

$$\lambda f(b^1) + (1-\lambda)f(b^2).$$

Q.E.D.

5.6 Some Concave Minimization Problems

We reproduce below the inner-outer problem given in Equation (3.6.2) which pertains to a fixed cost minimization over a totally Leontief Substitution System:

$$\underset{y \in Y}{\text{Min}}\ d'y + \left[\begin{array}{l}\text{Min } c'x \\ \text{subject to} \\ \quad Ax = b > 0 \\ \quad x \leqq \ell y \\ \quad x \geqq 0\end{array}\right].$$

Taking the dual of the inner problem--strong duality allows this--we arrive at:

$$\underset{y \in Y}{\text{Min}}\ d'y + \left[\begin{array}{l}\text{Max } b'\pi_1 + \ell y'\pi_2 \\ \text{subject to} \\ \quad A'\pi_1 + \pi_2 \leqq c \\ \quad \pi_2 \leqq 0\end{array}\right].$$

Since $b > 0$ and $y \geqq 0$, the optimum to the inner problem is found by first solving

$$\begin{array}{l}\text{Max } b'\pi_1 \\ \text{subject to} \\ \quad A'\pi_1 \leqq c\end{array}$$

(which is the dual of a totally Leontief problem). Let π_1^* represent the optimum to the above. Then let

5.6.1 $$\pi_2^* = \left[c - A'\pi_1^*\right]^-$$

where $[z]^-$ is a vector of $[z_i]^-$ and

$$[z_i]^- = \begin{cases} 0 & \text{if } y_i = 1 \text{ or } z_i > 0 \\ z_i & \text{otherwise.} \end{cases}$$

To show optimality we first assume that ℓ is large enough so that

$$b'(A_J')^{-1}e_i < \ell e_i \qquad J \varepsilon M \tag{5.6.2}$$

which is equivalent to assuming $\ell > x_i$ for any component i of $x \varepsilon X(b)$. With this being the case

$$b'\pi_1^* \geqq b'\pi_1 \qquad \pi_1 \varepsilon \{\pi\colon A'\pi \leqq c\}$$

and

$$\ell y' \pi_2^* = 0.$$

Then

$$\{\pi\colon A'\pi + \pi_2^* \leqq c\} = \{\pi\colon A'\pi \leqq c\}.$$

With 5.6.2 it is evident that π_2^* as given in 5.6.1 is optimal (although not necessarily unique).

REFERENCES

1. Abbott, J. C., Sets, Lattices and Boolean Algebra, Allyn and Bacon, Inc., Boston, Massachusetts, 1969.

2. Bartels, R. H., and G. H. Golub, "The Simplex Method of Linear Programming Using LU Decomposition," Communications of the Association for Computing Machinery, 12, No. 5, pp. 266-268, 1969.

3. Beale, E. M. L., "Sparseness in Linear Programming," in Large Sparse Sets of Linear Equations, Ed. J. K. Reid, Academic Press, New York, 1971.

4. Benders, J. F., "Partitioning Procedures for Solving Mixed Variables Programming Problems," Numerishe Mathematik, 4, pp. 238-252, 1962.

5. Ben-Israel, A., and A. Charnes, "Contributions to the Theory of Generalized Inverses," Journal of the Society for Industrial and Applied Mathematics, 11, No. 3, pp. 667-699, 1963.

6. Berge, C., "Balanced Matrices," Mathematical Programming, 2, pp. 19-31, 1972.

7. Birkhoff, G., Lattice Theory, Third Edition, American Mathematical Society, Providence, Rhode Island, 1967.

8. Blackwell, D., "Discounted Dynamic Programming," Annals of Mathematical Statistics, 36, pp. 226-235, 1965.

9. Blackwell, D., "Discrete Dynamic Programming," Annals of Mathematical Statistics, 33, pp. 719-726, 1962.

10. Bradley, G. H., "Equivalent Integer Programs and Canonical Problems," Management Science, 17, No. 5, pp. 354-366, 1971.

11. Brayton, R. K., F. G. Gustavson, and R. A. Willoughby, "Some Results on Sparse Matrices," Mathematics of Computation, 24, No. 112, pp. 937-954, 1970.

12. Charnes, A., and W. W. Cooper, "Generalizations of the Warehousing Model," Operational Research Quarterly, 6, pp. 131-172, 1955.

13. Collatz, L., "Aufgaben Monotoner Art," Archives of Mathematics, 3, pp. 366-376, 1953.

14. Cottle, R. W. and A. F. Veinott, Jr., "Polyhedral Sets Having a Least Element," Mathematical Programming, 3, pp. 238-249, 1972.

15. Dantzig, G. B., "Large Scale Linear Programming," in Mathematics of the Decision Sciences, Eds. G. B. Dantzig and A. F. Veinott, Jr., American Mathematical Society, Providence, Rhode Island, 1969.

16. Dantzig, G. B., "On the Status of Multistage Linear Programming Problems," Management Science, 6, pp. 53-72, 1959.

17. Dantzig, G. B., "Optimal Solution of a Dynamic Leontief Model with Substitution," Econometrica, 23, pp. 295-302, 1955.

18. Dantzig, G. B., R. W. Cottle, B. C. Eaves, F. S. Hillier, and A. S. Manne, "On the Need for a Systems Optimization Laboratory," in Mathematical Programming, Eds. T. C. Hu and S. M. Robinson, Academic Press, New York, 1973.

19. Dantzig, G. B. and W. Orchard-Hays, "Alternative Algorithm for the Revised Simplex Method Using Product Form for the Inverse," The Rand Corporation, RM-1268, 1953.

20. Dantzig, G. B. and R. M. Van Slyke, "Generalized Upper Bounding Techniques," Journal of Computer System Science, 1, pp. 213-226, 1967.

21. Debreu, G. and J. N. Herstein, "Nonnegative Square Matrices," Econometrica, 21, pp. 597-607, 1953.

22. Denardo, E. V., "A Markov Decision Problem," Mathematical Programming, Eds. T. C. Hu and S. M. Robinson, Academic Press, New York, 1973.

23. Denardo, E. V., "Computing a Bias-Optimal Policy in a Discrete-Time Markov Decision Problem," Operations Research, 18, pp. 279-289, 1970.

24. Denardo, E. V., "Contraction Mapping in the Theory Underlying Dynamic Programming," SIAM Review, 9, No. 2, pp. 165-177, 1967.

25. D'Epenoux, "A Probabilistic Production and Inventory Problem," Management Science, 10, No. 1, pp. 98-108, 1963.

26. Derman, C., Finite State Markovian Decision Processes, Academic Press, New York, 1970.

27. Derman, C., "Markovian Sequential Control Processes - Denumerable State Space," Journal of Mathematical Analysis and Applications, 10, pp. 295-302, 1965.

28. Dreyfus, S. E., "An Appraisal of Some Shortest-Path Algorithms," Operations Research, 17, pp. 395-412, 1969.

29. Dorfman, R., P. A. Samuelson, and R. M. Solow, Linear Programming and Economic Analysis, Rand Corporation, McGraw-Hill Book Company, New York, 1958.

30. Easterfield, R. E., "Matrix Norms and Vector Measures," Duke Mathematical Journal, 24, pp. 663-669, 1957.

31. Faaland, B., "Generalized Equivalent Integer Programs and Canonical Problems," Management Science, 20, No. 12, pp. 1554-1560, 1974.

32. Fiedler, M. and V. Ptak, "On Matrices with Non-Positive Off-Diagonal Elements and Positive Principal Minors," Czech Mathematics Journal, 12, pp. 382-400, 1962.

33. Fiedler, M. and V. Ptak, "Some Results on Matrices of Class K and Their Application to the Convergence Rate of Iteration Procedures," Czech Mathematics Journal, 16, pp. 260-273, 1966.

34. Florian, M. and M. Klein, "Deterministic Production Planning with Concave Costs and Capacity Constraints," Management Science, 18, No. 1, pp. 12-20, 1971.

35. Florian, M. and M. Klein, "Erratum: Deterministic Production Planning with Concave Costs and Capacity Constraints," Management Science, 18, No. 11, p. 721, 1972.

36. Florian, M. and P. Robillard, "An Implicit Enumeration Algorithm for the Concave Cost Network Flow Problem," Management Science, 18, No. 3, pp. 184-193, 1971.

37. Forrest, J. J. H. and J. A. Tomlin, "Updated Triangular Factors of the Basis to Maintain Sparsity in the Inner Product Form Simplex Method," Mathematical Programming, 2, pp. 263-278, 1972.

38. Fox, B., "Discretizing Dynamic Programs," Journal of Optimization Theory and Applications, 11, pp. 228-234, 1973.

39. Fox, B., "Finite-State Approximation to Denumerable-State Dynamic Programs," Journal of Mathematical Analysis and Applications, 34, pp. 665-670, 1971.

40. Fox, B. L. and D. M. Landi, "An Algorithm for Identifying the Ergodic Subchains and Transient States of a Stochastic Matrix," The Rand Corporation, RM-5269-PR, 1967.

41. Frobenius, G., "Über Matrizen aus nicht Negativen Elementen," S.-B., Preuss. Akad. Wiss., Berlin, pp. 456-477, 1912.

42. Gale, D., The Theory of Linear Economic Models, McGraw-Hill Book Company, New York, 1960.

43. Garfinkel, R. S. and G. L. Nemhauser, "Optimal Set Covering: A Survey," in Perspectives on Optimization: A Collection of Expository Articles, Ed. A. M. Geoffrion, Addison-Wesley Publishing Company, Reading, Massachusetts, pp. 164-183, 1972.

44. Gass, S. I., Linear Programming, McGraw-Hill Book Company, New York, 1969.

45. Geoffrion, A. M., "Elements of Large-Scale Mathematical Programming. Part I: Concepts," Management Science, 16, No. 11, pp. 652-675, 1970.

46. Geoffrion, A. M., "Elements of Large-Scale Mathematical Programming. Part II: Synthesis of Algorithms and Bibliography," Management Science, 16, No. 11, pp. 676-691, 1970.

47. Glover, F., D. Karney, and D. Klingman, "Implementation and Computational Comparisons of Primal, Dual, and Primal-Dual Computer Codes for Minimum Cost Network Flow Problems," Networks, 4, pp. 191-212, 1974.

48. Greenberg, H. J., "On the Minimum Number of Spikes in a Matrix," Technical Report No. CP 73004, Computer Science/Operations Research Center, Southern Methodist University, February, 1973.

49. Greenberg, H. J., "Permanent Bounds for the Number of Spikes in a Matrix," Technical Report No. CP 73001, Computer Science/Operations Research Center, Southern Methodist University, January, 1973.

50. Greenberg, H. J. and W. P. Pierskalla, "A Review of Quasi-Convex Functions," Operations Research, 19, pp. 1553-1570, 1971.

51. Grinold, R. C., "A Generalized Discrete Dynamic Programming Model," Management Science, 20, No. 7, pp. 1092-1103, 1974.

52. Hadley, G., Linear Algebra, Addison-Wesley Publishing Company, Reading, Massachusetts, 1961.

53. Hadley, G., Linear Programming, Addison-Wesley Publishing Company, Reading, Massachusetts, 1962.

54. Harary, F., "Sparse Matrices and Graph Theory," Large Sparse Sets of Linear Equations, Ed. J. K. Reid, Academic Press, New York, 1971.

55. Harvey, R. P., G. B. Dantzig, R. D. McKnight, and S. S. Smith, "Sparse Matrix Techniques in Two Mathematical Programming Codes," in Proceedings of the Symposium on Sparse Matrices and Their Applications, Ed. R. A. Willoughby, IBM Corporation, Yorktown Heights, New York, 1969.

56. Hastings, N. A. J. and J. M. C. Mello, "Tests For Suboptimal Actions in Discounted Markov Programming," Management Science, 19, No. 9, pp. 1019-1022, 1973.

57. Hastings, N. A. J. and J. M. C. Mello, "Erratum: Tests For Suboptimal Actions in Discounted Markov Programming," Management Science, 20, No. 17, p. 1143, 1974.

58. Hellerman, E. and D. Rarick, "Reinversion with the Preassigned Pivot Procedure," Mathematical Programming, 1, pp. 195-216, 1971.

59. Hellerman, E. and D. C. Rarick, "The Partitioned Pre-assigned Pivot Procedure (P^4)," in Sparce Matrices and Their Applications, Eds. D. J. Rose and R. A. Willoughby, Plenum Press, New York, 1972.

60. Hoffman, A. J. and J. B. Kruskal, "Integral Boundary Points of Convex Polyhedra," in Linear Inequalities and Related Systems, Eds. H. W. Kuhn and A. W. Tucker, Princeton University Press, Princeton, New Jersey, 1956.

61. Howard, R. A., Dynamic Programming and Markov Processes, MIT Press, Cambridge, Massachusetts, 1960.

62. Howard, R. A., Dynamic Probabilistic Systems, Volumes I and II, John Wiley and Sons, Inc., New York, 1971.

63. Jeroslow, R. G., "An Algorithm for Discrete Dynamic Programming with Interest Rates Near Zero," Management Science Research Report No. 300, Carnegie-Mellon University, November, 1972.

64. Jeroslow, R. G., "Asymptotic Linear Programming," Operations Research, 21, No. 5, pp. 1128-1141, 1973.

65. Jewell, W. S., "Markov-Renewal Programming. I. Formulation, Finite Return Models," Operations Research, 11, pp. 938-948, 1963.

66. Jewell, W. S., "Markov-Renewal Programming. II. Infinite Return Models Example," Operations Research, 11, pp. 949-971, 1963.

67. Kalan, J. E., "Aspects of Large-Scale, In-Core Linear Programming," Proceedings of ACM Annual Conference, Chicago, Illinois, August 3-5, 1971.

68. Kalymon, B. A., "A Decomposition Algorithm for Arborescence Inventory Systems," Operations Research, 20, pp. 860-874, 1972.

69. Kappauf, C. H., "A Note On 'The Equivalence of Integer Programs to Constrained Recursive Systems'," Management Science, forthcoming, 1975.

70. Karlin, S., "The Structure of Dynamic Programming Models," Naval Research Logistics Quarterly, 2, pp. 285-295, 1955.

71. Kemeny, J. G. and J. L. Snell, Finite Markov Chains, D. Van Nostrand Company, Inc., Princeton, New Jersey, 1960.

72. Koehler, G. J., "A Generalization of Leontief Substitution Systems and Their Solution By Recursive Procedures," submitted for publication, January, 1975.

73. Koehler, G. J., A. B. Whinston, and G. P. Wright, "An Iterative Procedure for Non-Discounted Discrete-Time Markov Decisions," Naval Research Logistics Quarterly, 21, No. 4, pp. 719-723, 1974.

74. Koehler, G. J., A. B. Whinston, and G. P. Wright, "Fixed Cost Minimization over a Leontief Substitution System," Revue Française d'Automatique Informatique, et Recherche Operationnelle, 2, pp. 119-124, 1974.

75. Koehler, G. J., A. B. Whinston, and G. P. Wright, "The Solution of Constrained Recursive Integer Programs," presented at ORSA/TIMS Conference, San Juan, October, 1974.

76. Koehler, G. J., A. B. Whinston, and G. P. Wright, "The Solution of Leontief Substitution Systems Using Matrix Iterative Techniques," Management Science, forthcoming, 1975.

77. Koopmans, T. C. (ed.), "Activity Analysis of Production and Allocation," Cowles Commission Monograph 13, John Wiley and Sons, Inc., New York, 1951.

78. Kushner, H., Introduction to Stochastic Control, Holt, Rinehart and Winston, Inc., New York, 1971.

79. Lasdon, L. S., Optimization Theory for Large Systems, MacMillan Company, New York, 1970.

80. Leontief, W. W., Structure of the American Economy, 1919-1939, Second Edition, Oxford University Press, New York, 1951.

81. Lippman, S. A., "Economic Order Quantities and Multiple Set-Up Costs," Management Science, 18, No. 1, pp. 39-47, 1971.

82. Lippman, S. A., "On the Set of Optimal Policies in Discrete Dynamic Programming," Journal of Mathematical Analysis and Applications, 24, pp. 440-445, 1968.

83. Lippman, S. A., "Optimal Inventory Policy with Multiple Set-Up Costs," Management Science, 16, No. 1, pp. 118-138, 1969.

84. Love, S. F., "A Facilities in Series Inventory Model with Nested Schedules," Management Science, 18, No. 5, Part 1, pp. 327-338, 1972.

85. MacLane, S., and G. Birkhoff, Algebra, MacMillan Company, New York, 1967.

86. MacQueen, J., "A Modified Dynamic Programming Method for Markovian Decision Problems," Journal of Mathematical Analysis and Applications, 14, pp. 38-43, 1966.

87. MacQueen, J., "A Test for Suboptimal Actions in Markovian Decision Problems," Operations Research, 15, pp. 559-561, 1967.

88. Mangasarian, O. L., Nonlinear Programming, McGraw Hill Book Company, New York, 1969.

89. Manne, A. S., "Linear Programming and Sequential Decisions," Management Science, 6, pp. 259-267, 1960.

90. Manne, A. S., "Optimal Dividend and Investment Policies for a Self-Financing Business Enterprise," Management Science, 15, No. 3, pp. 119-129, 1968.

91. Manne, A. S. and A. F. Veinott, Jr., "Optimal Plant Size with Arbitrary Increasing Time Paths of Demand," in Investments for Capacity Expansion: Size, Location, and Time Phasing, Ed. A. Manne, MIT Press, Cambridge, Massachusetts, 1967.

92. Markowitz, H. M., "The Elimination Form of the Inverse and Its Application to Linear Programming," Management Science, 3, pp. 255-269, 1957.

93. Miller, B. L. and A. F. Veinott, Jr., Discrete Dynamic Programming with a Small Interest Rate," Annals of Mathematical Statistics, 40, No. 2, pp. 366-370, 1969.

94. Morgenstern, D. (Ed.), Economic Activity Analysis, John Wiley and Sons, Inc., New York, 1954.

95. Nanda, P. S., "The Equivalence of Integer Programs to Constrained Recursive Systems," Management Science, 19, No. 7, pp. 809-824, 1973.

96. Nering, E. D., Linear Algebra and Matrix Theory, Second Edition, John Wiley and Sons, Inc., New York, 1970.

97. Oldenburger, R., "Infinite Powers of Matrices and Characteristic Roots," Duke Mathematical Journal, 6, pp. 357-361, 1940.

98. Padberg, M. W., "Perfect Zero-One Matrices," Mathematical Programming, 6, pp. 180-196, 1974.

99. Perron, O., "Zur Theorie der Matrices," Mathematische Annalen, 64, pp. 248-263, 1907.

100. Ponstein, J., "Seven Kinds of Convexity," SIAM Review, 9, pp. 115-119, 1967.

101. Porteus, E. L., "Bounds and Transformations for Finite Markov Decision Chains," Working Paper No. 203, Graduate School of Business, Stanford University, 1974.

102. Porteus, E. L., "Bounds and Transformations in the Computational Theory for Finite State and Action Markov Decisions," Research Paper No. 97, Graduate School of Business, Stanford University, August 1973.

103. Porteus, E. L., "Some Bounds for Discounted Sequential Decision Processes," Management Science, 18, No. 1, pp. 7-11, 1971.

104. Pullman, N. J., "A Geometric Approach to the Theory of Non-Negative Matrices," Linear Algebra and Its Applications, 4, pp. 297-312, 1971.

105. Rebman, K. R., "Total Unimodularity and the Transportation Problem: A Generalization," Linear Algebra and Its Applications, 8, pp. 11-24, 1974.

106. Rheinboldt, W. C., "On M-Functions and Their Application to Nonlinear Gauss-Seidel Iterations and to Network Flows," Journal of Mathematical Analysis and Applications, 32, pp. 274-307, 1970.

107. Rockafellar, R. T., Convex Analysis, Princeton University Press, Princeton, New Jersey, 1970.

108. Ross, S. M., Applied Probability Models with Optimization Applications, Holden-Day, Cambridge, Massachusetts, 1970.

109. Saigal, R., "On a Generalizaton of Leontief Substitution Systems," Working Paper No. CP-325, Center for Research in Management Science, University of California Berkeley, January 1971.

110. Seelenfreund, A., "Optimal Allocation for a Class of Finite Horizon Processes," Management Science, 15, No. 11, pp. 728-738, 1969.

111. Shapiro, J. F., "Turnpike Planning Horizons for a Markovian Decision Model," Management Science, 14, pp. 292-300, 1968.

112. Shapley, L. S., "Stochastic Games," Proceedings of the National Academy of Science, U.S., 39, 1953.

113. Tamir, A., "Minimality and Complementarity Properties Associated with Z-Functions and M-Functions," Mathematical Programming, 7, pp. 17-31, 1974.

114. Tarski, A., "A Lattice-Theoretical Theorem and Its Applications," Pacific Journal of Mathematics, 5, pp. 285-309, 1955.

115. Tewarson, R. P., Sparse Matrices, Academic Press, New York, 1973.

116. Thompson, Jr., W. A. and D. W. Parke, "Some Properties of Generalized Concave Functions," Operations Research, 21, No. 1, pp. 305-313, 1973.

117. Tinney, W. F. and E. D. Ogbuobiri, "Sparsity Techniques: Theory and Practice," Bonneville Power Administration, Portland, Oregon, 1970.

118. Tomlin, J. A., "Maintaining a Sparse Inverse in the Simplex Method," IBM Journal of Research and Development, 16, No. 4, pp. 415-423, 1972.

119. Tomlin, J. A., "Modifying Triangular Factors of the Basis in the Simplex Method," in Sparse Matrices and Their Applications, Eds. D. J. Rose and R. A. Willoughby, Plenum Press, New York, 1972.

120. Tomlin, J. A., "Survey of Computational Methods for Solving Large Scale Systems," Operations Reserach House, Technical Report 72-25, Stanford University, October, 1972.

121. Totten, J., "Computational Methods for Finite State Finite Valued Markovian Decision Problems," ORC 71-9, Operations Research Center, University of California, Berkeley, 1971.

122. Varga, R. S., Matrix Iterative Analysis, Prentice-Hall, Inc., Englewood, Cliffs, New Jersey, 1962.

123. Veinott, Jr., A. F., "Discrete Dynamic Programming with Sensitive Discount Optimality Criteria," Annals of Mathematical Statistics, 40, pp. 1635-1660, 1969.

124. Veinott, Jr., A. F., "Extreme Points of Leontief Substitution Systems," Linear Algebra and Its Applications, 1, pp. 181-194, 1968.

125. Veinott, Jr., A. F., "Minimum Concave-Cost Solution of Leontief Substitution Models of Multi-Facility Inventory Systems," Operations Research, 17, No. 2, pp. 262-291, 1969.

126. Veinott, Jr., A. F., "On Finding Optimal Policies in Discrete Dynamic Programming with No Discounting," Annals of Mathematical Statistics, 37, pp. 371-372, 1966.

127. Veinott, Jr., A. F. and G. B. Dantzig, "Integral Extreme Points," SIAM Review, 10, No. 1, pp. 98-108, 1971.

128. Veinott, Jr., A. F. and H. M. Wagner, "Optimal Capacity Scheduling - I and II," Operations Research, 10, pp. 518-546, 1962.

129, Wagner, H. M., "A Linear Programming Solution to Dynamic Leontief Type Models," Management Science, 3, No. 3, pp. 234-254, 1957.

130. Wagner, H. M. and T. M. Whitin, "Dynamic Problems in the Theory of the Firm," Naval Research Logistics Quarterly, 5, pp. 53-74, 1958.

131. Weil, R. L. and P. C. Kettler, "Rearranging Matrices to Block Angular Form for Decomposition (and other) Algorithms," Management Science, 18, No. 1, pp. 98-108, 1971.

132. Young, D. M., Iterative Solutions of Large Linear Systems, Academic Press, New York, 1971.

133. Zaldivar, M. and T. Hodgson, "Rapid Convergence Techniques for Markov Decision Processes," Decision Sciences, forthcoming January, 1975.

134. Zangwill, W. I., "A Backlogging Model and a Multi-Echelon Model of a Dynamic Economic Lot Size Production System - A Network Approach," Management Science, 15, No. 9, pp. 506-527, 1969.

135. Zangwill, W. I., "A Deterministic Multi-Product Multi-Facility Production and Inventory Model," Operations Research, 14, pp. 486-507, 1966.

136. Zangwill, W., "The Piecewise Concave Function," Management Science, 13, pp. 900-912, 1967.

SUBJECT INDEX

absorbing, 138-139
action, 99
aperiodic, 99
arborescence multi-echlon model, 75
asymptotic convergence, 40, 47
asymptotic isotone contraction, 27-28, 171-172, 185
asymptotic isotone split, 44, 158

backlogging, 75, 80, 84, 116
balance equations, 74, 76, 82, 84, 115
balanced, 106
basis, 66, 175, 188, 191-192, 195
basis elimination, 59, 67
basis inverse, 55
batch queueing, 81
Bender's partitioning procedure, 123
bias, 100
bias optimal problem, 104-105
binary variable, 122
block diagonal matrix, 75
block pivot, 57
block triangular, 73, 162
block upper triangular, 68, 75
Boolean representation, 138, 140
boundary conditions, 17
bounded, 35-36, 66, 78, 110-112, 119, 161-162, 165-166, 172, 186, 205
branch and bound, 114, 203
Brouwer fixed point theorem, 142

chain, 52-53, 179-180
characteristic equation, 128
cheap iteration, 56, 66
class K, 14, 19-21, 26-27, 34, 77, 102, 115, 117, 153, 161, 165
class Z, 14, 17, 27, 34, 77, 141, 148, 151, 161
class P, 148
column elimination, 59, 61
combinatorial problems, 4
communicating state, 138
complement, 130, 150, 163
complementary slackness, 176, 197, 203
composite algorithm, 66
computational effort, 28
computer storage, 28
concave function, 115, 119, 205-206
concave minimization, 121, 184, 204
condensation, 2
cone, 96, 119, 187-191, 205
constraint matrix, 54, 75, 77, 179
consumption matrix, 15
convergence, 6, 10, 12, 47, 55, 78, 93, 134-135, 173, 186
convex hull, 117, 119, 187
convex subset, 96, 189, 191
Cornfield-Leontief Multiplier Process, 25
Cramer's rule, 107, 195

density, 2
diagonal matrix, 19, 22, 55, 149, 153-154, 181, 197
direct sum vector, 183
discount factor, 16, 48
discounted profit, 16, 26
dominant positive principal diagonal, 19, 146, 153-154
dual bases, 37, 185
dual problem, 37-39, 69, 78, 102, 167, 182, 197, 203, 207
dual theorem, 165-166, 176-177
dynamic Leontief, 70-71, 121, 184
dynamic programming, 170

economic-lot-size model, 74, 80, 84, 115, 121
efficiency, 85, 124
eigenvalue, 18, 21, 38, 128-129, 131, 133, 141-145, 149-152, 155
eigenvector, 132-134, 141-142, 146, 150, 156-157
elementary matrix, 2
elementary operations, 83
ergodic, 15, 99, 139, 141
error, 9-10
Euclidean space, 116
extreme points, 30-33, 57, 106-107, 114-115, 117-119, 121, 161, 163-165, 192, 195, 204-205

Farkas' lemma, 189-190, 192
feasible bases, 40
feasible solution, 33, 182
fixed cost, 121-122
fixed point, 38-39, 171-172, 185

gain optimal decision, 100
gain rate, 100
Gaussian elimination, 166
Gauss-Seidel split, 23-24, 28-29, 42, 44, 58, 93
generalized inverse, 175
generalized Leontief, 96
generalized upper bounding, 3
good, 94
graph, 52, 54, 180
hidden Leontief, 83, 96-97, 102, 105, 190-191
homogeneous system, 129
Howard's taxicab problem, 40
hyperplane, 189

identity matrix, 5-6
infinite horizon, 26
infinite power, 10
input-output problem, 14, 25, 31, 33, 94
integer extreme points, 108, 110-111
integer linear program, 110-112
integrality constraints, 94, 106
interior, 96-97, 187-189, 191-192
inventory problems, 5, 80, 82
inventory shrinkage, 75, 84
inverse, 10
inversion, 2, 3
irreducible, 15, 136-137, 139, 141-145, 156-157, 193
iterations, 28
iterative matrix, 8-9
iterative methods, 8, 12, 25, 78, 85
iterative programming, 3

Jacobi split, 23-24, 28-29, 42
Jordan form, 131, 134, 173

labeled state, 139
large scale problems, 2
lattice, 185
Leontief basis, 34
Leontief constraint set, 5, 14
Leontief economy, 51
Leontief matrix, 30-32, 34, 52, 77, 80, 84, 94, 107, 160, 163-164, 205
Leontief Substitution Systems, 4, 30-31, 33, 48, 78-79, 95, 105, 115, 161
linear independence, 161, 164, 195
linear programming, 5, 8, 14, 49, 114, 165, 203
lower bound, 197
lower triangular matrix, 20, 22, 111, 147-148, 153, 156

M-functions, 167
Markov chain, 15-16, 138
Markov decision problems, 5, 48, 50, 77
Markov process, 26
matrix techniques, 5, 8, 13, 21, 37
mesh point, 17
modulus, 128
multidivisional problems, 4
multi-facility, 74, 83
multiplicity, 131, 144

net production matrix, 15
network problems, 5, 54
Neumann Series, 10, 152
node, 51-53, 179-180
non-linear objective, 94
non-producible activities, 33
non-producible goods, 33
non-singular matrix, 8, 13, 19-21, 26-27, 94, 96, 102-103, 108, 134, 149, 152-154, 156-157, 161, 177, 189-192, 205
non-substitutability, 14
norm, 5, 127
null space, 5, 160

one-hoss shay, 72
optimal basis, 39, 49
optimality criterion, 176
outcome, 48

partition, 32
perfect, 106
permutation matrix, 20, 136, 144, 153, 193
Perron-Frobenius Theorem, 141, 144
point input-output stream output, 71
policy, 174
pre-Leontief matrix, 30-32, 36, 52, 84, 102, 159, 162, 164
pre-Leontief Substitution System, 30-31, 161
preserving dimensionality, 60
primal infeasibility, 198, 203
primal problem, 185, 197
primary storage, 2
principal minors, 149, 153
producible goods, 33
product assortment, 81
product form, 2
production problems, 5
productive activities, 33
productive matrix, 20

quasi-concave, 119, 122-123

range space, 5, 129
rank, 155, 177, 188, 190-191, 195
re-inversion, 2, 55
rectangular matrices, 14, 30
recursive methods, 8, 97
recursive Leontief, 70, 76, 110-111, 197
reducible, 67, 70, 136-137, 139, 142, 144
redundant, 101
relaxation programming, 3
reservoir control, 81
retail facility, 76
Revised Simplex, 2, 55
rounding errors, 2

Semi-Markov Decision Process, 49
set packing problem, 106
shortest path problem, 51
simplex, 142
Simplex method, 5, 56-57
Simplicial cone, 96-97, 190-191
sink, 179
spanning set, 130
sparsity, 2, 8, 28
spectral radius, 5, 9-10, 13, 47, 128, 134, 141, 143-144
spectrum, 5, 128
split, 8, 11-13, 21, 23, 25-28, 93
Split Comparison Theorem, 29, 134
stages, 70, 99
starting vector, 56
states, 15, 48, 99, 138-139
stationarity, 14, 48
steady-state probabilities, 16
stochastic matrix, 20
stochastic problems, 4, 48
sub-Leontief matrix, 31-32, 160, 162, 179
sub-optimal basis, 60, 88-89, 92-93
submatrix, 6-7, 32, 94, 96, 106, 108, 130, 136, 139, 144, 164-165, 187-188, 190-191
subspace, 129, 189
superscript, 6, 9
supersparsity, 3
symmetric matrix, 129
System Optimization Laboratory, 1

tolerance, 39, 56
totally Leontief linear program, 49-50, 61, 68, 103
totally Leontief matrix, 35-36, 39, 48, 53-54, 84, 86, 102, 107, 165, 180-181, 193-194
totally Leontief Substitution System, 59, 122, 207
totally productive system, 51
transient, 50, 77, 138-139
transition matrix, 15, 50
transshipment matrix, 51, 54, 109-110, 180
triangular factored basis, 2
triangular matrix, 55
trivial row (column), 159-161
turnpike theorem, 55

unimodular, 106-107, 109-110, 195
unlabeled row, 139, 141
upper bound, 197
upper triangular matrix, 20, 22, 147-148, 153, 156

warehouse model, 82-83
wholesale facility, 76

AUTHOR INDEX

Abbott, J.C., 185

Bartels, R.H., 28
Beale, E.M.L., 1-2, 28
Benders, J.F., 123
Ben-Israel, A., 175
Berge, C., 106
Birkhoff, G., 185, 131, 144
Blackwell, D., 48, 104, 167
Bradley, G.H., 110-111
Brayton, R.K., 28

Charnes, A., 82, 175
Collatz, L., 131
Cooper, W.W., 82
Cottle, R.W., 174

Dantzig, G.B., 1-2, 3, 28, 67-68, 106, 182, 195
Debreu, G., 141
Denardo, E.V., 56, 51, 100, 104, 167, 170
D'Epenoux, 49
Derman, C., 48, 100-101
Dorfman, R., 14, 25
Dreyfus, S.E., 54

Easterfield, R.E., 127
Eaves, B.C., 1

Faaland, B., 110
Fiedler, M., 14, 21, 37, 130, 146, 150
Florian, M., 121
Forrest, J.J.H., 2
Fox, B., 61, 138
Frobenius, G., 141

Gale, D., 14, 20, 31, 33
Garfinkel, R.S., 106
Gass, S.I., 164
Geoffrion, A.M., 1, 2, 4
Glover, F., 54
Golub, G.H., 28
Greenberg, H.J., 28, 119
Grinold, R.C., 55
Gustavson, F.G., 28

Hadley, G., 129, 165
Harary, F., 28
Harvey, R.P., 28
Hastings, N.A.J., 59
Hays, W.O., 2, 28
Hellerman, E., 2, 28
Herstein, J.N., 141
Hillier, F.S., 1
Hodgson, T., 67
Hoffman, A.J., 106, 109, 195
Howard, R.A., 15, 40, 48, 49, 99

Jeroslow, R.G., 104
Jewell, W.S., 49

Kalan, J.E., 2, 3, 28
Kalymon, B.A., 121
Kappauf, C.H., 110, 112, 114
Karlin, S., 48
Karney, D., 54
Kemeny, J.G., 15, 99
Kettler, P.C., 67
Klein, M., 121
Klingman, D., 54
Koehler, G.J., 100, 112, 114, 122, 185, 191, 197, 203
Koopmans, T.C., 14
Kruskal, J.B., 106, 109, 195
Kushner, H., 43

Landi, D.M., 138
Lasdon, L.S., 80
Leontief, W.W., 14
Lippman, S.A., 104, 121
Love, S.F., 121

MacLane, S., 131, 144
MacQueen, J., 59, 64
McKnighty, R.D., 28
Mangasarian, O.L., 115, 189
Manne, A.S., 1, 71, 74, 100, 121
Markowitz, H.M., 2, 28
Mello, J.M.C., 59
Miller, B.L., 104
Morgenstern, D., 14

Nanda, P.S., 110-111
Nemhauser, G.L., 106
Nering, E.D., 107, 195

Ogbuobiri, E.D., 28
Oldenburger, R., 134

Padberg, M.W., 106
Parke, D.W., 119
Perron, O., 141
Pierskalla, W.P., 119
Ponstein, J., 119
Porteus, E.L., 47, 56, 60-62, 64, 66-67, 158
Ptak, V., 14, 21, 37, 130, 146, 150
Pullman, N.J., 141

Rarick, D., 2, 28
Rebman, K.R., 109
Rheinboldt, W.C., 167
Robillard, P., 121
Rockafellar, R.T., 189, 192
Ross, S.M., 48-50

Saigal, R., 94, 96, 187-188, 190
Samuelson, P.A., 14, 25
Seelenfreund, A., 121
Shapiro, J.F., 55
Shapley, L.S., 167, 170
Smith, S.S., 28
Snell, J.L., 15, 99
Solow, R.M., 14, 25

Tamir, A., 167
Tarski, A., 185
Tewarson, R.P., 8, 28
Thompson, Jr., W.A., 119
Tinney, W.F., 28
Tomlin, J.A., 1, 2, 28
Totten, J., 26, 158

Van Slyke, R.M., 3
Varga, R.S., 16-17, 19, 23, 28-29, 141, 156-158
Veinott, Jr., A.F., 30, 47, 50, 52, 54, 71, 74-76, 80-83, 104, 106, 107, 116-119, 121, 159, 167, 170, 172-174, 184, 195, 204-205

Wagner, H.M., 80-, 81-82, 121
Weil, R.L., 67
Whinston, A.B., 100, 112, 114, 197, 203
Whitin, T.M., 121
Willoughby, R.A., 28
Wright, G.P., 100, 112, 114, 197, 203

Young, D.M., 158

Zaldivar, M., 67
Zangwill, W.I., 74, 119, 121